CONDUCT
AND CHARACTER
Readings in Moral Theory

Mark Timmons
Memphis State University

WADSWORTH PUBLISHING COMPANY
A Division of Wadsworth, Inc.
Belmont, California

Philosophy Editor: Kenneth King
Editorial Assistant: Michelle Palacio
Production Editor: Rosaleen Bertolino, Bookman Productions
Print Buyer: Randy Hurst
Compositor: Kachina Typesetting, Inc.
Signing Representative: Harriet McQuarie
Cover Design: Hal Lockwood and Renee Deprey, Bookman Productions
Cover Painting: Giorgio de Chirico, "The Song of Love" (1914). Oil on canvas, 28¾ × 23⅜". Collection, The Museum of Modern Art, New York. Nelson A. Rockefeller Bequest. Photograph © 1989 The Museum of Modern Art, New York.

Printed in the United States of America

1 2 3 4 5 6 7 8 9 10—94 93 92 91 90

Library of Congress Cataloging-in-Publication Data
Timmons, Mark, 1951–
    Conduct and character: readings in moral theory/Mark Timmons.
        p.   cm.
    ISBN 0-534-12126-8
    1. Ethics.   I. Title.
BJ1012.T55   1990   89-14607
170—dc20   CIP

ISBN 0-534-12126-8

for Emily Renee and Elizabeth Anne

Contents

Preface

This collection includes a balance of classical and contemporary writings on moral theory designed to introduce students to the study of ethics. The book is organized by types of moral theory, one chapter devoted to each type. In order to provide students with the needed conceptual framework for studying moral theory, the collection of readings is preceded by an introduction to moral theory.

This collection is suitable for ethics courses that focus on theory, and it can serve as a supplementary text for "applied" ethics courses. It also supplies readings for an ethics component of an introduction to philosophy course.

The order of the chapters reflects how I like to proceed in presenting the various moral theories. It has been my experience that beginning ethics students often ask such questions as these: "Why not just do whatever you think will benefit yourself?" "Isn't morality just a matter of what some authority says, like society or perhaps God?" I find it useful to deal with these questions first, and so the collection begins with chapters on egoism, relativism, and the divine command theory. Given problems with egoism and with attempting to base morality on some authority, it is natural to go on and ask whether morality is somehow based on human nature. The natural law theory and Kant's moral theory attempt to carry out just such a project. The placement of the chapter on utilitarianism reflects the fact that this theory was developed in response to the approaches of natural law and Kant. Finally, since virtue-based theories represent an apparent shift in focus from questions of conduct to questions of character, the chapter on this type of theory follows the rest. Obviously, other orderings are equally suitable for teaching ethics.

In editing this book, I have received encouragement and good advice from many people. I would like to thank the following reviewers for their most helpful suggestions and comments: Burton Hurdle, Virginia State University; Philip Jung, Grand Rapids Junior College; H. M. Ducharme, University of Akron; Louis P. Pojman, University of Mississippi, and S. D. Cook, San Jose State University.

I also wish to thank Harriet McQuarie for encouraging me to go ahead with the project, and my editor, Kenneth King, whose advice and assistance proved invaluable. Judith McKibben, Kevin Possin, and Michael Gorr made useful comments on the introductory chapter. Finally, I wish to thank Iris Baird and especially Katheryn D. Skates for their expert administrative help with this project.

CHAPTER 1

Introduction to Moral Theory

THE AIMS, STRUCTURE, AND EVALUATION OF MORAL THEORIES

The two main concepts of ethics are those of the right and the good; . . . The structure of an ethical theory is, then, largely determined by how it defines and connects these two basic notions.

—John Rawls

The area of philosophical inquiry called ethics is primarily concerned with moral theory. But what is moral theory? And why is it important? This introduction addresses these questions, which are likely to occur to individuals unfamiliar with the philosophical study of ethics. As we shall see, a moral theory is a construction intended to answer questions about right and wrong action, about what goals are worth pursuing in life, and about what sorts of things are valuable or good. In short, moral theory purports to answer very general questions about what to *do* and how to *be*.

In order to clarify the nature of moral theorizing—to explain what it is and why it is important—we must do three things. First, we must specify the main *aims* of moral theory, in order to establish what moral theorizing is intended to accomplish. Second, since the notions of the right and the good are central in moral theory, we must clarify these and related notions. Clarifying and explaining connections among such notions involve inquiring into what philosophers call the *structure* of a moral theory. Finally, since philosophers have developed a number of compet-

1

ing moral theories, we must consider the issue of how to *evaluate* their relative merits and deficiencies.

So let us begin our study of moral theory by clarifying its central aims. We can best focus our attention on this matter if we pause to consider the sorts of situations that might lead someone to ask questions that are of interest to the moral theorist.

I.   The Aims of Moral Theory

People normally take an interest in what to do and how to be, and they think that on occasion their decisions and actions have great significance for their own lives and for the lives of others. One source of this interest is people's recognition of certain demands that prescribe how they *should* decide and act. Such demands may have various sources: the laws enforced in society, the rules governing membership in a club, the table manners parents teach children. In addition, certain felt demands, often formulated as rules, make up what we ordinarily refer to as *moral demands*. In fact, the moral demands that a person acknowledges often strike the person as being more demanding than rules of etiquette or rules governing club membership, and perhaps even more demanding than any of society's legal rules. This is frequently the view asserted by people who engage in civil disobedience: they publicly break some law on the grounds that doing so is required by morality.

Because we take moral demands seriously, and because we often face personal decisions in which moral considerations come into play, it is particularly distressing that we should encounter so much conflict and uncertainty about what we should do and about what sort of person we should be. Consider the following cases.[1]

A.   John and Linda, both in their early 40s, have been happily married for ten years and have two children, Eric, who is 8 and Amanda, who is 5. For a number of years now Linda has looked forward to resuming her career as a nutritionist, which she put on hold after she and John agreed that she would be a full-time mother until their younger child began school. In order to prevent any further pregnancies, Linda was fitted with an IUD, but now finds that she is two months pregnant. John is delighted at the news: he had all along wanted another child, but hadn't made his feelings known to Linda, because he knew how much she wanted to rejoin the workforce. Linda does not want another child and insists on an immediate abortion. To John, however, abortion is out of the question, even though both he and Linda agree that at the two-month stage the fetus is not a full-fledged person, but only a potential person. John insists that having an abortion, even in the early months of pregnancy, is morally wrong and that Linda, in putting her career ahead of her family, is being selfish. Linda strongly disagrees. She feels that she has every right to have an abortion since the pregnancy was unplanned, since she acted responsibly in trying to avoid getting pregnant, and since, anyway, the fetus is not a person. Moreover, she disagrees that she is being selfish; she has, after all, been a devoted mother to Eric and Amanda.

B. Mary and Pat, now seniors in college, have known each other since they were roommates their freshman year; although they are by no means best friends, they like each other and occasionally do things together. Pat, recently married, lives with her husband in a small apartment near campus. Mary, who shares an apartment with two other women, has been engaged to Tom for several months. Tom, also a senior, has a job lined up with an advertising agency, which he'll begin after graduating in May. Mary isn't sure about her career plans, but the couple has set an August date for getting married, by which time Tom will be settled into his new job. Recently, Pat found out through one of her friends that, a week or so ago, Tom had slept with this friend's sister, who was visiting for a weekend. The news greatly distresses Pat. In thinking about what, if anything, she should do, she finds herself caught in a dilemma. On the one hand, she knows that, if she were in Mary's place, she would want to be told about her fiancé's one-night stand, despite the hurt it would cause. Furthermore, she feels that it would be disloyal to withhold the information from her friend. On the other hand, she worries that revealing all to Mary might well result in the breakup of the couple, perhaps making things worse for everyone involved. Besides, many women in Mary's situation might prefer not to know, and anyway she doesn't want to be a meddlesome busybody. So maybe she shouldn't tell Mary after all.

C. Jim and Gail, both in their mid-30s, have been married for eight years, for the past five of which Gail has tried to become pregnant. The couple very much wants a child, and Gail has felt somehow inadequate as a result of not having been able to conceive. After years of frustration, the couple finally decided to go to a nearby fertility clinic, where tests revealed that Gail is infertile due to an obstruction of her fallopian tubes. The attending physician suggested that they consider an *in vitro* (literally, "in glass") fertilization, in which an ovum is taken from the woman's body, fertilized under laboratory conditions, and then implanted into the woman's uterus where the normal process of gestation can occur. Initially, Jim and Gail were quite relieved that something could be done to help them and, of course, excited about the prospect of finally being able to have children. Their initial excitement was dampened, however, shortly after finding out about *in vitro* and other means of artificial reproduction, when they saw a television special about reproductive technology in which critics voiced certain moral objections to such medical procedures. Although neither Jim nor Gail had originally thought of it this way, the critics claimed that, since such procedures break the connection between reproduction and sexual intercourse, they are unnatural and hence morally wrong. While not entirely convinced by this argument, both Jim and Gail now wonder about the morality of what they were planning to do. Furthermore, the couple does not want to be in any way reckless or negligent in making such an important decision; and in light of the moral controversy surrounding these types of medical procedures, they feel especially hesitant in going ahead with such a procedure. At this point, they aren't sure what to do.

The sorts of phenomena illustrated in these stories—*interpersonal conflict* in the first, *intrapersonal conflict* in the second, and *uncertainty* in the third—seem to be pervasive features of everyday thought and discussion about morality. From time to time, we find that our own moral beliefs conflict with one another or with the moral beliefs of other people, and often we are simply uncertain about what moral beliefs to hold. Resolving such conflicts and uncertainty in a rational manner often requires an investigation into both *factual* and *conceptual* matters. Would Mary want to know about her fiance's sexual encounter? This is a factual issue. What does it mean to say that an action is "unnatural"? This is a conceptual issue about the meaning of a word. But most important, reflecting on these situations naturally leads a person to ask: "What makes an action morally right or morally wrong?" "What sorts of things are worth pursuing in life?" "What sort of person should I strive to become?" Such questions are obviously relevant because, if we could determine what particular features make actions wrong, we could use this information to help dispose of the kind of uncertainty and conflict illustrated in the preceding cases.

Take, for example, the case of John and Linda. If Linda's act of having an abortion involves the various features that make an action wrong, we could conclude that it would be wrong for her to go through with the abortion. Otherwise, we could conclude that it would not be wrong for her to do so. The same holds for the other two cases. Thus, if we could answer the general moral question, "What features of an action make it right or wrong?" we could then formulate a standard or principle that would help us evaluate the morality of actions. And, with that principle in hand, we could readily assess the sorts of cases described earlier and judge whether the actions in question were right or wrong.

PRINCIPLES OF RIGHT CONDUCT AND VALUE

Some philosophers have argued that only the *consequences* of an action determine whether it is right or wrong. Their view is that an action is wrong just in case it brings about worse consequences than would have resulted from some alternative action that could have been performed instead. Corresponding to this theory about what makes an action wrong is the following moral principle:

An action is forbidden if and only if its consequences are more undesirable than the consequences of some alternative action one could do instead.

Referring again to the case of John and Linda, imagine that we somehow determined that, of the various actions open to Linda, having an abortion would produce effects more undesirable than the effects of some alternative action. This information, together with the moral principle, would yield the result that her having the abortion would be morally wrong. The general idea, then, is that, if we could formulate moral principles that specify the conditions under which an action is right or wrong, we could use them to help settle cases of conflict and uncertainty in moral belief. And since the decisions we make and the actions we perform are guided by our thinking—by what we believe—such principles would be of great practical importance in helping us decide what to do.

Similar points can be made about moral questions having to do with how one should *be*—that is, with what sorts of character traits are worth developing. In each of the preceding cases, the people involved not only worry about what to do, they also worry about how to be a certain kind of person: unselfish, loyal, responsible, and so forth. Such worries raise general moral questions about the worth or value of certain character traits in particular, and of people in general. One aim of moral theory is to provide principles or standards for determining what is and what is not of value, in order to help resolve conflict and uncertainty about what sort of person to be.

Moral theorizing, then, aims at providing general principles: *principles of right conduct* that specify the conditions under which an action is right or wrong, and *principles of value* that specify under what conditions something is good or bad (has value or disvalue). But while we want to be able to use these principles in reaching decisions about what to do and how to be, we are aware that not just any principles will do. We want to make *reasonable* decisions, and we want to be *confident* of the principles we accept. Consequently, we want the principles that we believe to be *well supported*—principles that are not arbitrarily made up, but ones that can be shown to be reasonable.

The Central Aim.   Bringing together the points just discussed, we can as a first approximation express the *central aim* of a moral theory as follows:

CA: The central aim of moral theory is to provide well-supported principles of right conduct and value that are useful in guiding the thought and action of individuals and groups.

   Although not all philosophers would agree with this characterization, it does capture a dominant view about the aim of moral theorizing. Our formulation of the central aim mentions *well-supported* and *useful* moral principles, about which more will be said later. As we shall see, evaluating a moral theory involves determining whether (and to what extent) the principles of the theory are useful and well supported. Just what is involved in such an evaluation can only be explained after we have considered more fully some of the ingredients that go into moral theories. To this subject we now turn.

II.   The Structure of a Moral Theory

Moral theory attempts to provide moral principles for guiding and evaluating conduct and character. As we have seen, the two main sorts of moral principles are principles of right conduct, which have to do with the morality of actions, and principles of value, which are related to the morality of character. In fact, corresponding to these two sorts of principles are two main branches of moral theory: the theory of right conduct, and the theory of value.

   To deepen our understanding of moral theory, we must explore the ordering and structure that theories of right conduct and theories of value tend to exhibit. Doing so requires us to focus on the meanings and interrelations of certain moral categories—categories referred to by such terms as *right, wrong, obligation, permission, good, bad, virtuous,* and *vicious.* Since moral philosophers have typically expended most of their efforts on the theory of right conduct, let's begin there.

THE THEORY OF RIGHT CONDUCT

The central aim of any theory of right conduct can be extracted from our previous statement of the central aim of moral theory:

CA': The central aim of a theory of right conduct is to provide well-supported principles of right conduct that are useful in guiding the thought and action of individuals and groups.

In order to clarify this branch of moral theory further, we need to consider three topics: the subject matter of the theory of right conduct, namely, actions; the relationships among the various moral categories involved in an assessment of the morality of actions; and the application of moral principles of right conduct in an assessment of the morality of actions.

Actions. Sometimes, in speaking of actions, we have in mind *types* of actions: eating, running, reading, writing, studying, and so forth. An action type is something that is repeatable; both you and I can read the newspaper, and in doing so we perform actions of the same general type. However, *my* reading the newspaper at some particular time differs from *your* reading the newspaper at some particular time. Furthermore, my reading of the paper is something done by me at some particular time, and *that very act* of reading cannot be repeated by me. Of course, after I've read the Sunday *New York Times* editorial page, I can later reread that page, but this rereading is still a different reading from the first.

We can call specific, nonrepeatable doings *concrete actions*. Every concrete action—something done by a particular person at a particular time and place—is an instance of some general type. In fact, concrete actions are always instances of many different action types. Suppose that a police commissioner lies to a murder suspect in order to extract a confession. The concrete act of the police commissioner is an instance of each of the following action types: uttering words, lying, lying to a murder suspect, and breaking the law, to mention just a few.

Moral Categories of Right Action. In providing principles of right conduct, we are interested in evaluating the morality of action types and of concrete actions. But what sort of evaluation are we concerned with here? In English, the terms, *right, wrong, forbidden, obligatory, permissible, optional, ought,* and *should* are typically used in judging the morality of actions. Of course, these terms can be used for purposes other than moral evaluation, as in the statements "You took the wrong turn," and "Brown shoes should not be worn with a tuxedo." However, in moral contexts, these terms refer to particular moral categories into which an action may fall. The basic categories used in the moral evaluation of actions—both of action types and of concrete actions—are as follows:

1. The category of the *obligatory*: the category of actions that, from the point of view of morality, are mandatory; actions that one should or must do.

2. The category of the *forbidden*: the category of actions that, from the point of view of morality, it is mandatory not to do; actions that one should not or must not do.

3. The category of the *optional*: the category of actions that are neither obligatory (it is not mandatory that one do them) nor forbidden (it is not mandatory that one not do them).

Now it should be clear that some of the moral terms mentioned above refer to the same moral category as, for example, *wrong, forbidden*, and *impermissible*. Some of the terms refer to overlapping categories. For example, the category of the right or permissible overlaps the categories of the obligatory and the optional. The relationships among these categories is represented in Figure 1.

Because the three basic moral categories are of primary interest, a philosopher setting forth a theory of right conduct will typically formulate principles for determining whether an action is obligatory, optional, or forbidden. A moral principle states the conditions under which an action belongs to one of the moral categories. An example from our earlier discussion is this:

An action is forbidden if and only if its consequences are more undesirable than the consequences of some alternative action one could do instead.

FIGURE 1   Moral categories of right action.

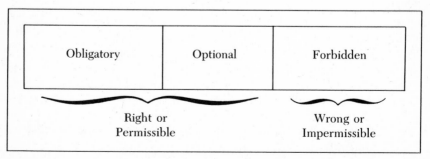

In presenting a theory of right conduct, a philosopher rarely explicitly formulates separate principles, one for each moral category. Instead, philosophers usually propose a single principle. But since the notions central to the theory of right conduct are *interdefinable,* an author need only present a single principle, after which other principles can be derived from the principle by definition.

For example, if we took as our basic notion the notion of an action that is forbidden, we could then define the notion of an obligatory action as follows:

1. An action A *is obligatory if and only if failing to perform* A *is forbidden.*

Similarly, we could define the notion of an optional action as follows:

2. An action A *is optional if and only if performing* A *is not forbidden and failing to perform* A *is not forbidden.*

Suppose that, in addition to these definitions, we have the following as a principle of right conduct:

3. An action A *is forbidden if and only if performing* A *conflicts with human nature.*

Now we can reason as follows. By definition,

1. An action A *is obligatory if and only if failing to perform* A *is forbidden.*

Therefore, from 3 and 1,

4. An action A *is obligatory if and only if failing to perform* A *would conflict with human nature.*

The same sort of reasoning could be used to formulate a principle for determining when actions are optional. The important point here is that many philosophers present their theory of right conduct in the form of a single principle, and different authors differ in their choice of the moral category to use in enunciating that principle. But given the interdefinability of the moral categories, these differences do not matter.

Applying Moral Principles.   Given that our aim in moral theorizing is to provide principles that we can then *use* to guide thought and action, it is reasonable to ask how we are supposed to use them for this purpose. Suppose that someone presents us with principles of right action—principles concerning the conditions under which actions are obligatory, optional, and forbidden. If we now want to use them, how do we proceed? From what has been said so far, the answer should be pretty obvious. We take the moral principles in question, plus any relevant factual information about the action we wish to evaluate, and derive a moral conclusion about the action. Consider, for example, how to use the following principle:

An action is forbidden if and only if it would involve treating some person merely as a means to one's own ends.

Assuming that we can determine whether or not a contemplated action involves treating a person merely as a means, we simply take the principle, plus factual information about whether or not the action would involve such treatment, and draw a conclusion about the morality of the act. The basic argument scheme, together with an example, is contained in Table 1.

Summing up, a theory of right conduct attempts to provide principles of right conduct—principles that set forth conditions under which actions (both concrete actions and action types) belong in one or another of

TABLE 1

Argument Component	Argument Scheme	Example Argument
Premise	1. Moral principle	1'. An action is forbidden if and only if it would involve treating some person merely as a means to one's own ends.
Premise	2. Relevant factual information	2'. James's act of lying to Brenda involved treating Brenda merely as a means to James's own ends.
Conclusion	3. Conclusion about the morality of an action	3'. James's act of lying to Brenda was forbidden.

the basic moral categories. Such principles, together with relevant factual information, can then be applied to specific situations in order to make judgments about the morality of actions performed in those situations.

The central notions involved in the theory of value include *good, bad, virtuous, vicious, praiseworthy, blameworthy, honest,* and *courageous.* Since moral theory[2] generally involves questions about what to do and how to be, and since (as we have seen) the theory of right conduct focuses exclusively on what to do, the theory of value focuses on questions of how to be—on questions of character. In addition, however, we also judge the value (or the goodness and badness) of physical objects, experiences, and certain states of affairs. For example, the following items are often called good: money, fast cars (physical objects); pleasure, contentment, happiness (experiences); peace on Earth, economic prosperity, health (states of affairs). We say of such things that they have nonmoral value, and we say of people (or certain features of them) that they have or fail to have moral value. Judgments of nonmoral value are important for the moral evaluation of actions and persons and so must be included in our discussion. Consequently, the theory of value divides into the theory of moral value and the theory of nonmoral value.

Nonmoral Value. Why should we bother with issues having to do with nonmoral value when our concern is with moral theory? According to some theories of right conduct, the morality of an action depends on the nonmoral value that would result if the action were performed. For example, according to a classical version of utilitarianism, whether an action is right or wrong depends solely on the balance of good versus bad that would result from the action, were it performed. Here, talk of good and bad refers to nonmoral value. Similarly, according to the natural law theory, the morality of an action depends on whether or not it would interfere with certain valuable states of affairs such as human life, procreation, and knowledge. So according to some theories of right conduct, judging the morality of an action requires us to judge the nonmoral value brought about by actions. Thus, the study of nonmoral value must be included in our investigation of the theory of value.

To understand further the theory of nonmoral value, we must distinguish between *intrinsic* and *instrumental* value. An object, experience, or state of affairs is intrinsically valuable if it is good simply because of what it is. By contrast, something is instrumentally good if it serves as a means to what is intrinsically good.

This latest distinction between two types of value is reflected in ordinary thought. Were I to ask you what things you find valuable in life, you might respond with a list that includes such items as wealth, power, playing softball, eating pizza, and so forth. If I then were to ask you why, for example, you find money valuable, you might reply by saying that it is useful for obtaining all sorts of things you want (like a big house with a swimming pool), thus indicating that you consider money to be instrumentally good. If I were to press on and ask why you value this second array of things, you might well say that having such things is part of what makes (or would make) you happy, and that your own happiness is something you find valuable *as such* and not for any other thing it might bring about. This would indicate that you value happiness intrinsically—simply because of the sort of thing it is—and that you value the other things (money, big houses, and so forth) instrumentally—as a means to happiness.

Since whatever is instrumentally good or valuable depends for its value on what is intrinsically good or valuable, the latter notion is the more important one. Therefore, in theorizing about nonmoral value, philosophers have sought to provide principles of intrinsic value—principles specifying what is intrinsically good and intrinsically bad.

Two general views about intrinsic value have been proposed. According to *hedonism*, pleasure and pleasure alone is intrinsically good; pain and pain alone is intrinsically bad. All other things have value or disvalue only as a result of being a means to what has intrinsic value or disvalue. Opposed to this view is *nonhedonism*. A nonhedonist, while perhaps agreeing that pleasure is intrinsically good (and that pain is intrinsically bad), flatly denies that *only* such things have intrinsic value. In defending this view, some philosophers have argued that such things as life, knowledge, self-expression, friendship, and creativity (to mention a few) are intrinsically good.

Moral Value.   Moral value, as has already been noted, depends on features of people such as their motives, intentions, and character traits. The primary aim of this part of the theory of value is to identify the particular features of people that have moral value and as a result of which a person can be said to be morally good. Two sorts of views are typically discussed. According to an extreme view held by the Stoic philosophers and by the German philosopher, Immanuel Kant, acting out of a sense of duty is the only thing that has moral value. A morally good person is one who is disposed to act on that sort of motive. Less exacting theories grant that other features of people have moral worth—for example, such motives as brotherly love and compassion, and such character traits as honesty and benevolence.

Summarizing, the theory of value can be divided into theories of nonmoral value and of moral value. The central aim of the theory of value generally can be put this way:

CA'': *The central aim of the theory of value is to provide well-supported principles of moral and nonmoral value that are useful in guiding the thought and action of individuals and groups.*

TYPES OF MORAL THEORY:

TELEOLOGICAL AND DEONTOLOGICAL

Moral theories are typically classified according to how the theory connects the notions of right conduct to the notions of value. According to *teleological* theories (from the Greek word *telos,* which means end or goal), the determination of whether an action is obligatory, optional, or forbidden depends entirely on whether and to what extent it produces or maintains some sort of valuable end. In such theories, value notions such as good and bad are more basic than the notions of right conduct; right and wrong action are understood in terms of their contribution to something valuable. For example, according to one sort of teleological theory, utilitarianism, the morality of an action depends on the nature of its contribution to such valuable ends as human happiness. Other teleological theories include natural law theory, egoism, and virtue-based theories.

By contrast, moral theories that are classified as *deontological* (from the Greek word *deon,* meaning duty) assess the morality of an action on the basis of features intrinsic to the action itself. Such theories typically assert notions belonging to the theory of right conduct as basic and use them to define such value notions as good and bad. Thus, moral theories like Kant's, according to which the notion of right action is basic and the notion of moral goodness is defined in terms of right (or obligatory) action, are deontological.[3]

In recent years, many philosophers have preferred to use the terms *consequentialist* and *nonconsequentialist* in classifying moral theories, although in many cases this terminology is used to mark the same distinction just discussed. A consequentialist theory is one according to which the morality of an action depends entirely on the value of its consequences; all other theories are nonconsequentialist.[4]

III.   *The Evaluation of a Moral Theory*

Since theories are constructed with certain aims in mind, it makes sense to ask how well a theory helps us accomplish those aims. The better the theory does in this regard, the better or more adequate the theory is.

The first part of this chapter presented a very general formulation of the central aim, CA, of a moral theory. Since a moral theory has two parts—a theory of right conduct and a theory of value—we made CA more precise by formulating the central aims of each part: CA' for the theory of right conduct, and CA'' for the theory of value. Now, in evaluating a moral theory, we need to examine both parts.

This section briefly explains some criteria philosophers use in trying to determine the adequacy of a moral theory in relation to its aims. Since (as was noted earlier) philosophers have devoted more attention to the theory of right conduct than to the theory of value, we will focus on criteria for evaluating it, too. In fact, however, most such criteria can easily be adapted for evaluating theories of value.

CRITERIA FOR EVALUATION

Recall the central aim of the theory of right conduct:

CA': The central aim of a theory of right conduct is to provide well-supported principles of right conduct that are useful in guiding the thought and action of individuals and groups.

Notice that, in constructing a theory of right conduct, we are not satisfied with any random set of principles; we want *well-supported* principles that will be *useful* in guiding thought and action. In judging the usefulness and support of moral principles, philosophers have employed six criteria: consistency, determinacy, livability, publicity, coherence, and external support. Let us briefly consider each of these in turn.

Consistency. The principles of a theory of right conduct are inconsistent if they classify a particular action as belonging in one moral category (obligatory, optional, forbidden, permitted) *and* they classify the very same action as belonging in an opposing moral category. For example, if a moral principle, when applied to some situation, implies that some concrete action—say, someone killing in self-defense—is both obligatory and forbidden (hence, *not* obligatory), the principle has inconsistent implications. And, of course, any theory whose principles lead to such a result is unacceptable and must either be revised or rejected.

We should be careful here. If a theory leads to the conclusion that some *concrete* action both is and is not obligatory (for example), it is guilty of inconsistency. Similarly, if a theory leads to the conclusion that some action *type* both is and is not forbidden (for example), it is again inconsistent. But it is not inconsistent for a theory to yield the result that *in general* lying (as an action type) is forbidden and at the same time to yield the result that *in some specific case* a concrete act of telling a lie is not forbidden. There need be no inconsistency here, because from the outset the claim that lying is forbidden has been limited by the implicit modifier *in general,* implying that the normal rule may, in special circumstances, have exceptions.

The rationale for consistency relates to the aim of providing useful moral principles. Quite simply, principles asserting that some action both is and is not forbidden, or both is and is not obligatory, are useless for guiding action.[5]

Determinacy.   Part of the aim of any theory of right conduct is to provide principles that can be used by individuals and groups as guides to desirable thought and action. This aim requires that the principles of a theory be *determinate*—that they can be used to draw conclusions about the morality of actions. A moral principle yields a determinate conclusion when the principle, together with relevant factual information, implies that the action belongs in one of the moral categories. A moral principle is indeterminate when, together with relevant factual information, it fails to classify the action. Imagine, for example, a theory having the following basic principle:

An action is forbidden if and only if performing that action is degrading to humanity.

The problem with this principle is that its application in a great many cases would yield no determinate conclusion about the morality of the action under scrutiny, since talk of what is *degrading to humanity* is extremely vague. Of course, as part of an overall theory of right conduct, one might attempt to specify just what is degrading to humanity; but unless that is done, the principle (and therefore the theory, too) lacks determinacy. Obviously, the determinacy of a moral principle or a set of moral principles is a matter of degree, since a principle can be more or less determinate in its implications. The criterion of *determinacy,* then, can be put this way: for any two competing moral theories, if the principles of the first are more determinate than those of the second, then the first is (in this respect) more satisfactory than the second.

Livability.   Two other criteria, *livability* and *publicity,* also relate to the usefulness of a theory. Some philosophers have complained that the principles of right conduct of some theories are not livable or, to use J. L. Mackie's term, "practicable." Acting morally involves constraining one's behavior in ways that frequently conflict with what one would otherwise like to do. But for most people conformity to the demands of a system of morality is possible. If one were to propose principles for right conduct that required so great a personal sacrifice that most people would find themselves unable to comply with them voluntarily, then those principles would not be livable or practicable. Since part of the aim of a theory of right conduct for human beings is to set forth usable (as well as useful) principles, a moral theory is inadequate if its principles cannot serve this function.

The *livability* criterion can be expressed this way: of two competing theories, if the first is more livable than the second, then the first is (with regard to livability) the more satisfactory of the two.

Publicity.   If a set of moral principles is to help guide people's behavior, it must be taught and communicated to them. Imagine that, according to some set of moral principles, it is morally forbidden to teach or publicize the very principles in question. According to ethical egoism, for example, we are each obligated to do whatever will best serve our own self-interest. If you were an ethical egoist, then—since it would not be in your self-interest to make your theory public (because other people would react negatively toward you)—you would be morally forbidden to teach or publicize the principles of your theory. Thus it would appear that ethical egoism is at odds with the aim of providing useful moral principles—since to be useful to people, they must be transmitted to them somehow. Therefore, according to the criterion of *publicity*, if the principles of a theory of right conduct forbid the teaching of those principles, then the theory is (in this regard) inadequate.

Coherence.   The final two criteria—coherence and external support—involve types of support that philosophers have marshaled in defending various principles of right conduct. Of course, considerations of consistency, determinacy, livability, and publicity are important in determining the adequacy of a set of moral principles as a guide to choice and action. But philosophers championing moral theories have also sought to produce arguments that show the correctness of some set of moral principles. One measure of correctness involves determining whether or not the principles of a theory cohere with people's "core moral beliefs." The idea behind this criterion can be explained as follows.

We all have firm moral convictions about the morality of certain actions. For instance, we believe that the concrete action of intentionally torturing another person for fun is forbidden. Furthermore, we agree that certain types of action (lying, theft, kidnapping, murder) are generally forbidden. In fact, widespread agreement exists among people about what actions are right and wrong, although this fact is obscured because we tend to focus on cases over which there is disagreement in moral belief. Let us call the set of more-or-less agreed-upon beliefs *core moral beliefs*—beliefs about the morality of actions that we all tend to share and that we hold with some high degree of conviction.

The criterion of coherence invites us to evaluate a theory by checking the implications of its principles against our set of core moral beliefs. For example, it is safe to say that, exceptional circumstances excluded, torture is forbidden. Were the principles of a theory to imply that an act of torture is not forbidden, the principles would fail to "fit" or cohere with one of our core moral beliefs. In such a situation, we would have to choose between (1) accepting the theory and revising our belief about the action in question and (2) holding onto our belief and rejecting the theory. In many cases—since most of us, upon reflection, are more certain of our core moral beliefs than we are of some moral theory—we take the lack of coherence as a mark against the correctness of the principles. The *coherence* criterion, then, can be put this way: for any two competing theories, if the principles of the first cohere better with our core moral beliefs than do those of the second, then the first theory is (in this regard) more satisfactory than the second.

Two comments about this criterion are in order. First, the coherence criterion should not be confused with the consistency criterion described earlier. Both have to do with the implications of moral principles, but the consistency criterion does not appeal to core moral beliefs; rather, it focuses on whether a principle or set of principles is consistent in what it implies about the morality of actions.

Second, the coherence criterion helps us determine whether a moral principle is well supported by urging us to seek some kind of unity among our core moral beliefs. If we were to make a list of the various core moral beliefs we have about forbidden actions, the list would include beliefs about many different action types (such as torture, lying, fraud, and forgery) as well as beliefs about many concrete actions. Given the great variety of actions classified as forbidden, we might wonder whether any underlying principle could explain why they were forbidden and hence provide insight into the nature of forbidden action. We might be able to formulate a moral principle of the form, "An action is forbidden if and only if C" (where C stands for some feature(s) of an action), that coheres well with the core beliefs in question. Presumably the coherence would be due to the fact that the principle expresses some common feature shared by all forbidden actions—for example, interfering with human well-being. Knowing what this common feature is would help us explain why forbidden actions are forbidden and would disclose to us an underlying unity that we might not previously have recognized. The ability to explain and unify surely counts in favor of a moral principle, and for this reason coherence has some bearing on their correctness.

External Support. The criterion of coherence might be described as having to do with the degree of *internal* support a moral principle receives—that is, support from within the realm of moral considerations. The criterion of *external support* involves the degree to which moral principles receive support from nonmoral assumptions and theories. As J. L. Mackie puts it: "Moral principles and ethical theories do not stand alone: they affect and are affected by beliefs and assumptions which belong to other fields, and not least to psychology, metaphysics, and religion."[6] Not every moral philosopher thinks that such external support is possible or even needed; some do. The issues underlying the controversy between those who do and those who don't are extremely complex and extend well beyond the scope of this introduction. But since a central part of any moral theory consists of providing reasons or support for accepting the principles of that theory, and since many theorists have sought such support by appealing to nonmoral considerations, some discussion of these matters is important.

Philosophers who claim that moral principles need no external support have typically argued that certain moral principles are correct either as a result of the *meanings* of the moral terms mentioned in the principles or because such principles are *self-evident*. For example, some supporters of the divine command theory of right conduct, according to which (roughly) the morality of an action depends on whether or not God commands it, appeal directly to the meanings of such terms as *forbidden* and *obligatory*. They claim that describing an action as forbidden merely acknowledges that God commands us not to do that action. They then argue that the principle, "An action is forbidden if and only if God commands us not to do that action," is correct in virtue of the meaning of the word *forbidden*.

Other philosophers claim that, upon reflection, anyone of reasonable intelligence can grasp the correctness of certain moral principles—that the principles are, in a sense, self-supported or self-evident. Defenders of such a view usually compare moral principles to certain mathematical principles. In Euclidean geometry, for example, such self-evident principles as, "If equals be added to equals, the wholes are equal," and "Things that coincide with one another are equal to one another," are not susceptible to proof, but even so they are accepted and are not thought to need such support. Some philosophers have claimed that basic moral principles are like such mathematical axioms and postulates in this regard: they are in no need of support from other considerations but can immediately be understood to be correct.

For reasons we need not go into here, most contemporary philosophers are suspicious of such appeals to meaning and self-evidence, and they regard external support for moral principles as both possible and important. Theorists who have attempted to find external support for certain moral principles have typically offered arguments premised on perceived facts about the nature of human beings and society. Immanuel Kant, for example, argued that only a certain principle of right conduct, which he called the "categorical imperative," was consistent with our nature as free agents. In his view, the fact that we are free—a deep-going fact about the nature of human beings—supported a certain moral principle. Similarly, J. S. Mill sought to defend a utilitarian moral principle by invoking what he deemed to be universal facts about human motivation—facts having to do with what people desire. Kant and Mill, then, attempted to offer positive external support for the moral principle each sought to defend. Other philosophers have *criticized* moral principles for *failing* to fit with certain facts about human beings. John Rawls, for example, claims that classical utilitarian moral principles conflict with the idea that each human being is, in some interesting sense, separate from all others.

We can formulate the criterion of *external support* in this way: if the principles of one theory fit better with certain nonmoral considerations than do those of another theory, then the first theory is (in this respect) more satisfactory than the second.

EVALUATING THE CRITERIA

We now have six criteria for evaluating theories of right conduct. Consistency, determinacy, livability, and publicity help us judge the *usefulness* of moral principles, and coherence and external support help us judge their *correctness*.

In closing, a few remarks about these criteria are in order. First, it is fairly obvious that the criteria of consistency, determinacy, coherence, and external support are useful for judging theories of value. For example, some people have argued that a hedonistic principle of nonmoral value, according to which states of pleasure alone are intrinsically good, fails to cohere with our firm convictions about the goodness of such things as beauty, knowledge, liberty, and self-expression. Therefore, a separate discussion of the evaluation of theories of value is not necessary for our purposes.

Second, it is worth noticing that most of the criteria are *comparative;* that is, they are formulated in terms of one theory's being more satisfactory than another in some respect.[7] This reflects the fact that, in the end, judging the overall adequacy of a moral theory is a matter of comparing it with its competitors. We select the theory that is best overall—that beats out the competition. But exactly how are we to judge the *overall* adequacy of a moral theory? Do we take the six criteria to be of equal importance, so that in comparing two theories we simply determine which one does better in relation to a majority of the criteria? If not, can we rank the criteria in order of importance, assign some numerical value to each of them, and then use a point system to decide which theory is most satisfactory?

This question about overall adequacy is important and unfortunately quite difficult. Part of the difficulty stems from the fact that not all philosophers would agree about the relative importance of the six criteria. In fact, not all philosophers would agree that the six criteria listed here are the proper ones to use. Some theorists, for example, do not think that livability and publicity are appropriate measures for determining the adequacy of a moral theory.[8] Which criteria one thinks are relevant for evaluating a moral theory and how one ranks those criteria depend largely on one's conception of the aims of moral theorizing; and philosophers do disagree about just what goals or aims moral theorizing is intended to accomplish. Such issues—issues about moral theorizing itself—constitute too broad a subject for this introduction.

There is no decisive answer to the question of how we are to judge the overall adequacy of a moral theory. Obviously, if one theory outperforms a competitor with regard to each of the criteria, it is the more satisfactory theory of the two. But in other cases, where some of the criteria favor one theory and some of them favor a competing theory, judging overall superiority is not so easy. Although this may be disconcerting to someone just beginning the study of moral theory, it might be of some comfort to know that the same sort of problem arises in connection with evaluating scientific theories. Scientists disagree about the specific aims of scientific theorizing, and consequently they have disputes over the evaluative criteria to be used in theory selection and over the relative importance of the criteria they do agree on. But such disputes do not undermine the validity or worth of scientific theorizing, and neither should they be thought to undermine the validity or worth of moral theorizing.[9]

Notes

1.   The first and third cases are adapted from cases presented in John E. Thomas and Wilfrid J. Waluchow, *Well and Good* (Lewiston, N.J.: Broadview Press, 1987). Reprinted by permission of Broadview Press.

2. The terms *good* and *bad* require special comment. Ordinary speakers of English use these terms in evaluating people, actions, and states of affairs generally. However, philosophers typically restrict their application of the terms *good* and *bad* to certain features of people (motives, intentions, character traits) and to various states of affairs that might be brought about through a person's actions. Thus, were we to characterize someone's action as morally good or bad, we would be making a statement about either the motives, intentions, or character of the person responsible for the action, or about the effects of the action.

3. Two comments are in order here. First, versions of the divine command theory and ethical relativism might be either teleological or deontological theories, depending on how they are worked out. For example, one might hold that what is intrinsically valuable depends on what God approves, and then define notions belonging to the theory of right conduct in terms of what is valuable. The result would be a teleological theory. Alternatively, one might hold that right and wrong action is determined by what God commands, and then define value notions in terms of right and wrong. Or again, one might hold that right and wrong are determined by God's commands, that value is determined by what God approves, and that there is no conceptual connection between the notions of right conduct and value. The latter two ways of working out the divine command theory would be classified as deontological views.

    Second, I said earlier that moral theory is concerned with questions about what to do and how to be—that is, with questions about actions and agents. I also said that moral philosophers have characteristically focused most of their attention on questions about what to do—on the theory of right conduct. Recently, however, some moral philosophers have insisted that the emphasis on right conduct is misplaced and that questions about agents—their character—should occupy center stage in moral theorizing. As a result, one sometimes finds the teleological/deontological distinction used only in connection with moral theories whose primary focus is on right conduct. The term *virtue-based ethics* is then reserved for moral theories that make questions about agents central in moral theorizing. See, for example, "On Some Vices of Virtue Ethics," by Robert B. Louden in Chapter 8 of this book.

4. However, some philosophers use this terminology in a more restrictive way. Samuel Scheffler, for example, defines consequentialism as follows: "Consequentialism in its purest form is a moral doctrine which says that the right act in any given situation is the one that will produce the best overall outcome, as judged from an impartial standpoint which gives equal weight to the interests of everyone" (Samuel Scheffler, ed., *Consequentialism and Its Critics* (New York: Oxford University Press, 1988), p. 1). By this definition, ethical egoism (for example) is classed as a nonconsequentialist view.

5. Strictly speaking, the consistency criterion can be defended by appealing to the aim of providing well-supported principles, as well as by appealing to the aim of providing useful principles. We are interested in well-supported

principles because we want some assurance that they are correct. One might well assert that, in order for any principle to be correct, it must be consistent in its implications.

6. J. L. Mackie, *Ethics: Inventing Right and Wrong* (Harmondsworth, Middlesex, England: Penguin Books, 1977), p. 203.

7. I formulated the consistency and publicity criteria in a noncomparative way simply because, in evaluating a moral theory, moral philosophers seem inclined to reject out of hand any theory that leads to inconsistency or fails to satisfy the publicity criterion.

8. See, for example, Derek Parfit, *Reasons and Persons* (New York: Oxford University Press, 1984), ch. 1, §§9, 12, 17.

9. I wish to thank Michael Gorr for his comments on an earlier draft of this essay. In writing the essay I benefitted from William Frankena's *Ethics*, 2d ed. (Englewood Cliffs, N.J.: Prentice-Hall, 1973) and Fred Feldman's *Introductory Ethics* (Englewood Cliffs, N.J.: Prentice-Hall, 1978).

CHAPTER 2

Egoism

THE MYTH OF GYGES
Plato

Plato (428–348 B.C.) was a student of Socrates and a teacher of Aristotle. In a famous passage from The Republic, *Glaucon (one of the characters in the dialogue) argues to Socrates that, by nature, human beings are egoists strongly inclined to pursue their own self-interest. Thus "those who practice justice do so against their will because they lack the power to do wrong." To illustrate his point, Glaucon recounts the story of Gyges.*

So, if you agree, I will do the following: I will renew the argument of Thrasymachus; I will first state what people consider the nature and origin of justice; secondly, that all who practise it do so unwillingly as being something necessary but not good; thirdly, that they have good reason to do so, for, according to what people say, the life of the unjust man is much better than that of the just. . . .

Splendid, he said, then listen while I deal with the first subject I mentioned: the nature and origin of justice.

They say that to do wrong is naturally good, to be wronged is bad, but the suffering of injury so far exceeds in badness the good of inflicting it that when men have done wrong to each other and suffered it, and have had a taste of both, those who are unable to avoid the latter and practise the former decide that it is profitable to come to an agreement with each other neither to inflict injury nor to suffer it. As a result they begin to make laws and covenants, and the law's command they call lawful and just. This, they say, is the origin and essence of justice; it stands between the best and the worst, the best being to do wrong without paying the

From G. M. A. Grube, trans., *Plato's Republic*, (Indianapolis, 1974) by permission of Hackett Publishing Co., Inc., Indianapolis and Cambridge.

penalty and the worst to be wronged without the power of revenge. The just then is a mean between two extremes; it is welcomed and honoured because of men's lack of the power to do wrong. The man who has that power, the real man, would not make a compact with anyone not to inflict injury or suffer it. For him that would be madness. This then, Socrates, is, according to their argument, the nature and origin of justice.

Even those who practise justice do so against their will because they lack the power to do wrong. This we could realize very clearly if we imagined ourselves granting to both the just and the unjust the freedom to do whatever they liked. We could then follow both of them and observe where their desires led them, and we would catch the just man redhanded travelling the same road as the unjust. The reason is the desire for undue gain which every organism by nature pursues as a good, but the law forcibly sidetracks him to honour equality. The freedom I just mentioned would most easily occur if these men had the power which they say the ancestor of the Lydian Gyges possessed. The story is that he was a shepherd in the service of the ruler of Lydia. There was a violent rainstorm and an earthquake which broke open the ground and created a chasm at the place where he was tending sheep. Seeing this and marvelling, he went down into it. He saw, besides many other wonders of which we are told, a hollow bronze horse. There were window-like openings in it; he climbed through them and caught sight of a corpse which seemed of more than human stature, wearing nothing but a ring of gold on its finger. This ring the shepherd put on and came out. He arrived at the usual monthly meeting which reported to the king on the state of the flocks, wearing the ring. As he was sitting among the others he happened to twist the hoop of the ring towards himself, to the inside of his hand, and as he did this he became invisible to those sitting near him and they went on talking as if he had gone. He marvelled at this and, fingering the ring, he turned the hoop outward again and became visible. Perceiving this he tested whether the ring had this power and so it happened: if he turned the hoop inwards he became invisible, but was visible when he turned it outwards. When he realized this, he at once arranged to become one of the messengers to the king. He went, committed adultery with the king's wife, attacked the king with her help, killed him, and took over the kingdom.

Now if there were two such rings, one worn by the just man, the other by the unjust, no one, as these people think, would be so incorruptible that he would stay on the path of justice or bring himself to keep away from other people's property and not touch it, when he could with impunity take whatever he wanted from the market, go into houses and have sexual relations with anyone he wanted, kill anyone, free all those he wished from prison, and do the other things which would make him like a god among men. His actions would be in no way different from those of the other and they would both follow the same path. This, some would say, is a great proof that no one is just willingly but under compulsion, so that justice is not one's private good, since wherever either thought he could do wrong with impunity he would do so. Every man believes that injustice is much more profitable to himself than justice, and any exponent of this argument will say that he is right. The man who did not wish to do wrong with that opportunity, and did not touch other people's property, would be thought by those who knew it to be very foolish and miserable. They would praise him in public, thus deceiving one another, for fear of being wronged. So much for my second topic.

As for the choice between the lives we are discussing, we shall be able to make a correct judgment about it only if we put the most just man and the most unjust man face to face; otherwise we cannot do so. By face to face I mean this: let us grant to the unjust the fullest degree of injustice and to the just the fullest justice, each being perfect in his own pursuit. First, the unjust man will act as clever craftsmen do—a top navigator for example or physician distinguishes what his craft can do and what it cannot; the former he will undertake, the latter he will pass by, and when he slips he can put things right. So the unjust man's correct attempts at wrongdoing must remain secret; the one who is caught must be considered a poor performer, for the extreme of injustice is to have a reputation for justice, and our perfectly unjust man must be granted perfection in injustice. We must not take this from him, but we must allow that, while committing the greatest crimes, he has provided himself with the greatest reputation for justice; if he makes a slip he must be able to put it right; he must be a sufficiently persuasive speaker if some wrongdoing of his is made public; he must be able to use force, where force is needed, with the help of his courage, his strength, and the friends and wealth with which he has provided himself.

Having described such a man, let us now in our argument put beside him the just man, simple as he is and noble, who, as Aeschylus put it, does not wish to appear just but to be so. We must take away his reputation, for a reputation for justice would bring him honour and rewards, and it would then not be clear whether he is what he is for justice's sake or for the sake of rewards and honour. We must strip him of everything except justice and make him the complete opposite of the other. Though he does no wrong, he must have the greatest reputation for wrongdoing so that he may be tested for justice by not weakening under ill repute and its consequences. Let him go his incorruptible way until death with a reputation for injustice throughout his life, just though he is, so that our two men may reach the extremes, one of justice, the other of injustice, and let them be judged as to which of the two is the happier. . . .

PSYCHOLOGICAL EGOISM
James Rachels

James Rachels is dean of the School of Humanities at the University of Alabama and author of several books, including The Elements of Moral Philosophy *(1986). Some philosophers, psychologists, and economists have held that, by nature, people are only capable of self-interested behavior. This doctrine, known as* psychological egoism, *is examined by Rachels. He claims that the arguments most often advanced in favor of psychological egoism are flawed and that, once certain confusions are cleared away, the doctrine loses its appeal. According to Rachels, the most serious error in psychological egoism is that it is an untestable hypothesis.*

Is Unselfishness Possible?

Morality and psychology go together. Morality tells us what we *ought* to do; but there is little point to it if we are not *able* to do as we ought. It may be said that we should love our enemies; but that is empty talk unless we are capable of loving them. A sound morality must be based on a realistic conception of what is possible for human beings.

Almost every system of morality recommends that we behave unselfishly. It is said that we should take the interests of other people into account when we are deciding what to do: we should not harm other people; in fact, we should try to be helpful to them whenever possible—even if it means forgoing some advantage for ourselves.

But are we capable of being unselfish? There is a theory of human nature, once widely held among philosophers, psychologists, and economists, and still held by many ordinary people, that says we are not capable of unselfishness. According to this theory, known as *Psychological Egoism,* each person is so constituted that he will look out only for his *own*

From James Rachels, *The Elements of Moral Philosophy* (New York: Random House, 1986).

interests. Therefore, it is unreasonable to expect people to behave "altruistically." Human nature being what it is, people will respond to the needs of others only when there is something in it for themselves. Pure altruism is a myth—it simply does not exist.

If this view is correct, people are very different from what we usually suppose. Of course, no one doubts that each of us cares very much about his own welfare. But we also believe that we care about others as well, at least to some extent. If Psychological Egoism is correct, this is only an illusion—in the final analysis, we care nothing for other people. Because it so contradicts our usual conception of ourselves, this is a shocking doctrine. Why have so many believed it to be true?

The Strategy of Reinterpreting Motives

Psychological Egoism seems to fly in the face of the facts. It is tempting to respond to it by saying something like this: "*Of course* people sometimes act unselfishly. Jones gave up a trip to the movies, which he would have enjoyed very much, so that he could contribute the money for famine relief. Brown spends his free time doing volunteer work in a hospital. Smith rushed into a burning house to rescue a child. These are all clear cases of unselfish behavior, and if the psychological egoist thinks that such cases do not occur, then he is just mistaken."

Such examples are obvious, and the thinkers who have been sympathetic to Psychological Egoism were certainly aware of them. Yet they have persisted in defending the view. Why? Partly it is because they have suspected that the "altruistic" explanations of behavior are too superficial—it *seems* that people are unselfish, but a deeper analysis of their motives might tell a different story. Perhaps Jones gives money for famine relief because his religion teaches that he will be rewarded in heaven. The man who works as a hospital volunteer may be driven by an inner need to atone for some past misdeed, or perhaps he simply enjoys this work, as other people enjoy playing chess. As for the woman who risks her life to save the child, we all know that such people are honored as heroes; perhaps she is motivated by a desire for public recognition. This technique of reinterpreting motives is perfectly general and may be repeated again and again. For any act of apparent altruism, a way can always be found to eliminate the altruism in favor of some more self-centered motive.

Thomas Hobbes (1588–1679) thought that Psychological Egoism was probably true, but he was not satisfied with such a piecemeal approach. It is not theoretically elegant to deal with each action separately, "after the fact." If Psychological Egoism *is* true, we should be able to give a more general account of human motives, which would establish the theory once and for all. This is what Hobbes attempted to do. His method was to list the possible human motives, concentrating especially on the "altruistic" ones, and show how each could be understood in egoistic terms. Once this project was completed, he would have systematically eliminated altruism from our understanding of human nature. Here are two examples of Hobbes at work:

1.   *Charity*. This is the most general motive that we ascribe to people when we think they are acting from a concern for others. *The Oxford English Dictionary* devotes almost four columns to "charity." It is defined variously as "The Christian love of our fellow-men" and "Benevolence to one's neighbors." But for the psychological egoist, such neighborly love does not exist, and so charity must be understood in a radically different way. In his essay "On Human Nature," Hobbes describes it like this:

There can be no greater argument to a man, of his own power, than to find himself able not only to accomplish his own desires, but also to assist other men in theirs: and this is that conception wherein consisteth *charity*.

Thus charity is a delight one takes in the demonstration of one's powers. The charitable man is demonstrating to himself, and to the world, that he is more capable than others. He can not only take care of himself, he has enough left over for others who are not so able as he. He is really just showing off his own superiority.

Of course Hobbes was aware that the charitable man may not *believe* that this is what he is doing. But we are not the best judges of our own motivations. It is only natural that we would interpret our actions in a way that is flattering to us (that is no more than the psychological egoist would expect!), and it is flattering to think that we are "unselfish." Hobbes's account aims to provide the *real* explanation of why we act as we do, not the superficial flattering account that we naturally want to believe.

2.   *Pity*. What is it to pity another person? We might think it is to sympathize with them, to feel unhappy about their misfortunes. And acting from this sympathy, we might try to help them. Hobbes thinks this is all right, as far as it goes, but it does not go far enough. The *reason* we are disturbed by other people's misfortunes is that we are reminded that the same thing might happen to us! "Pity," he says, "is imagination or fiction of future calamity to ourselves, proceeding from the sense of another man's calamity."

This account of pity turns out to be more powerful, from a theoretical point of view, than it first appears. It can explain very neatly some peculiar facts about the phenomenon. For example, it can explain why we feel greater pity when a good person suffers than when an evil person suffers. Pity, on Hobbes's account, requires a sense of identification with the person suffering—I pity you when I imagine *myself* in your place. But because each of us thinks of himself or herself as a good person, we do not identify very closely with those we think bad. Therefore, we do not pity the wicked in the same way we pity the good—our feelings of pity vary directly with the virtue of the person suffering, because our sense of identification varies in that way.

The strategy of reinterpreting motives is a persuasive method of reasoning; it has made a great many people feel that Psychological Egoism might be true. It especially appeals to a certain cynicism in us, a suspicion that people are not nearly as noble as they seem. But it is not a conclusive method of reasoning, for it cannot *prove* that Psychological Egoism is correct. The trouble is, it only shows that it is *possible* to interpret motives egoistically; it does nothing to show that the egoistic motives are deeper or truer than the altruistic explanations they are intended to replace. At most, the strategy shows that Psychological Egoism is possible. We still need other arguments to show it is true.

Two Arguments in Favor of Psychological Egoism

Two general arguments have often been advanced in favor of Psychological Egoism. They are "general" arguments, in the sense that each one seeks to establish at a stroke that *all* actions, and not merely some limited class of them, are motivated by self-interest. As will be seen, neither argument stands up very well under scrutiny.

1. The first argument goes as follows. If we describe one person's action as selfish and another person's action as unselfish, we are overlooking the crucial fact that in both cases, assuming the action is done voluntarily, *the person is merely doing what he most wants to do*. If Jones gives his money for the cause of famine relief rather than spending it on the movies, that only shows that he wanted to contribute to that cause more than he wanted to go to the movies—and why should he be praised for "unselfishness" when he is only doing what *he* most wants to do? His action is being dictated by his own desires, his own sense of what *he* wants most. Thus he cannot be said to be acting unselfishly. And since exactly the same may be said about *any* alleged act of altruism, we can conclude that Psychological Egoism must be true.

This argument has two primary flaws. First, it rests on the premise that people never voluntarily do anything except what they want to do. But this is plainly false; there are at least two kinds of actions that are exceptions to this generalization. One is actions that we may not want to do but that we do anyway as a means to an end that we want to achieve—for example, going to the dentist to stop a toothache. Such cases may, however, be regarded as consistent with the spirit of the argument, because the ends mentioned (such as stopping the toothache) are wanted.

Still, there are also actions that we do not because we want to nor even because they are means to an end we want to achieve, but because we feel that we *ought* to do them. For example, someone may do something because she had promised to do it, and thus feels obligated, even though she does not want to do it. It is sometimes suggested that in such cases we do the action because, after all, we want to keep our promises; so even here we are doing what we want. However, this will not work. If I have promised to do something and I do not want to do it, then it is simply false to say that I want to keep my promise. In such cases we feel a conflict precisely because we do *not* want to do what we feel obligated to do. If our desires and our sense of obligation *were* always in harmony, it would be a happier world. Unfortunately, we enjoy no such happy situation. It is an all too common experience to be pulled in different directions by desire and obligation. Jones's predicament may be like this: he *wants* to go to the movies, but he feels he *should* give the money for famine relief instead. Thus if he chooses to contribute the money, he is not simply doing what he wants to do. If he did that, he would go to the movies.

The argument has a second flaw. Suppose we were to concede, for the sake of argument, that all voluntary action is motivated by desire, or at least that Jones is so motivated. Even if this were granted, it would not follow that Jones is acting selfishly or from self-interest. For if Jones wants to do something to help starving people, even when it means forgoing his own enjoyments, that is precisely what makes him *un*selfish. What else could unselfishness be, if not wanting to help others, even at some sacrifice to oneself? Another way to put the point is to say that it is the *object* of a want that determines whether it is selfish or not. The mere fact that I am acting on *my* wants does not mean that I am acting selfishly; it depends on *what it is* that I want. If I want only my own good and care nothing for others, then I am selfish; but if I also want other people to be happy and I act on *that* desire, then my action is not selfish.

Therefore, this argument goes wrong in just about every way that an argument can go wrong: the premises are not true, and even if they were true, the conclusion would not follow from them.

2.   The second general argument for Psychological Egoism appeals to the fact that so-called unselfish actions produce a sense of self-satisfaction in the person who does them. Acting "unselfishly" makes people *feel good* about themselves. This has often been noted and has been put in various

ways: "It gives him a clear conscience" or "He couldn't sleep at night if he had done otherwise" or "He would have been ashamed of himself for not doing it" are familiar ways of making the same point. This sense of self-satisfaction is a pleasant state of consciousness, which we desire and seek. Therefore, actions are "unselfish" only at a superficial level of analysis. If we dig deeper, we find that the *point* of acting "unselfishly" is really to achieve this pleasant state of consciousness. Jones will feel much better about himself for having given the money for famine relief—if he had gone to the movies, he would have felt terrible about it—and that is the real point of the action.

According to a well-known story, this argument was once advanced by Abraham Lincoln. A nineteenth-century newspaper reported that

Mr. Lincoln once remarked to a fellow-passenger on an old-time mud coach that all men were prompted by selfishness in doing good. His fellow-passenger was antagonizing this position when they were passing over a corduroy bridge that spanned a slough. As they crossed this bridge they espied an old razor-backed sow on the bank making a terrible noise because her pigs had got into the slough and were in danger of drowning. As the old coach began to climb the hill, Mr. Lincoln called out, "Driver, can't you stop just a moment?" Then Mr. Lincoln jumped out, ran back, and lifted the little pigs out of the mud and water and placed them on the bank. When he returned, his companion remarked: "Now, Abe, where does selfishness come in on this little episode?" "Why, bless your soul, Ed, that was the very essence of selfishness. I should have had no peace of mind all day had I gone on and left that suffering old sow worrying over those pigs. I did it to get peace of mind, don't you see?"

Lincoln was a better President than philosopher. His argument is vulnerable to the same sorts of objections as the previous one. Why should we think, merely because someone derives satisfaction from helping others, that this makes him selfish? Isn't the unselfish person precisely the one who *does* derive satisfaction from helping others, whereas the selfish person does not? If Lincoln "got peace of mind" from rescuing the piglets, does this show him to be selfish or, on the contrary, doesn't it show him to be compassionate and good-hearted? (If a person were truly selfish, why should it bother his conscience that others suffer—much less pigs?) Similarly, it is nothing more than sophistry to say, because Jones finds satisfaction in giving for famine relief, that he is selfish. If we say this rapidly, while thinking about something else, perhaps it will sound all right; but if we speak slowly and pay attention to what we are saying, it sounds plain silly.

Moreover, suppose we ask *why* Jones derives satisfaction from contributing for famine relief. The answer is, it is because Jones is the kind of person who cares about other people: even if they are strangers to him, he doesn't want them to go hungry, and he is willing to take action to help them. If Jones were not this kind of person, then he would take no special pleasure in assisting them; and as we have already seen, this is the mark of unselfishness, not selfishness.

There is a general lesson to be learned here, having to do with the nature of desire and its objects. If we have a positive attitude toward the attainment of some goal, then we may derive satisfaction from attaining it. But the *object* of our attitude is *the attainment of that goal;* and we must want to attain the goal *before* we can find any satisfaction in it. We do not first desire some sort of "pleasurable consciousness" and then try to figure out how to achieve it. Rather, we desire all sorts of different things— money, a new car, to be a better chess player, to get a promotion in our work, and so on—and because we desire these things, we derive satisfaction from getting them. And so if someone desires the welfare and happiness of other people, he will derive satisfaction from helping them; but this does not mean that those good feelings are the *object* of his desire. *They* are not what he is after. Nor does it mean that he is in any way selfish on account of having those feelings.

These two arguments are the ones most commonly advanced in defense of Psychological Egoism. It is a measure of the weakness of the theory that stronger arguments have not been forthcoming.

Clearing Away Some Confusions

One of the most powerful theoretical motives is a desire for simplicity. When we set out to explain something, we would like to find as *simple* an explanation as possible. This is certainly true in the sciences—the simpler a scientific theory, the greater its appeal. Consider phenomena as diverse as planetary motion, the tides, and the way objects fall to the surface of the earth when released from a height. These appear, at first, to be very different; it would seem that we would need a multitude of different principles to explain them all. Who would suspect that they could all be explained by a single simple principle? Yet the theory of gravity does just that. The theory's ability to bring diverse phenomena together under a single explanatory principle is one of its great virtues. It makes order out of chaos.

In the same way, when we think about human conduct, we would like to find one principle that explains it all. We want a single simple formula, if we can find one, that would unite the diverse phenomena of human behavior, in the way that simple formulas in physics bring together apparently diverse phenomena. Since it is obvious that self-regard is an overwhelmingly important factor in motivation, it is only natural to wonder whether all motivation might not be explained in terms of it. And so the idea of Psychological Egoism is born.

But, most philosophers and psychologists would agree today, it is stillborn. The fundamental idea behind Psychological Egoism cannot even be expressed without falling into confusion; and once these confusions have been cleared away, the theory no longer seems even plausible.

The first confusion is between selfishness and self-interest. When we think about it, the two are clearly not the same. If I see a physician because I am feeling poorly, I am acting in my own self-interest, but no one would think of calling me "selfish" on account of it. Similarly, brushing my teeth, working hard at my job, and obeying the law are all in my self-interest, but none of these are examples of selfish conduct. This is because selfish behavior is behavior that ignores the interests of others, in circumstances in which their interests ought not to be ignored. The concept of "selfishness" has a definite evaluative flavor; to call people selfish is not just to describe their action but to criticize it. Thus you would not be called selfish for eating a normal meal in normal circumstances (although this would surely be in your self-interest); but you would be called selfish for hoarding food while others are starving.

A second confusion is between self-interested behavior and the pursuit of pleasure. We do lots of things because we enjoy them, but that does not mean we are acting from self-interest. The man who continues to smoke cigarettes even after learning about the connection between smoking and cancer is surely not acting from self-interest, not even by his own standards—self-interest would dictate that he quit smoking at once—and he is not acting altruistically either. He *is*, no doubt, smoking for the pleasure of it, but this only shows that undisciplined pleasure seeking and acting from self-interest are very different. This is what led Joseph Butler, the leading eighteenth-century critic of egoism, to remark, "The thing to be lamented is, not that men have so great regard to their own good or interest in the present world, for they have not enough."

Taken together, the last two paragraphs show (a) that it is false that all actions are selfish and (b) that it is false that all actions are done from self-interest. When we brush our teeth, at least in normal circumstances, we are not acting selfishly; therefore not all actions are selfish. And when we smoke cigarettes, we are not acting out of self-interest; therefore not all actions are done from self-interest. It is worth noting that these two points do not depend on examples of altruism; even if there were no such thing as altruistic behavior, Psychological Egoism would, according to these arguments, *still* be false!

A third confusion is the common but false assumption that a concern for one's own welfare is incompatible with any genuine concern for others. Since it is obvious that everyone (or very nearly everyone) does desire his or her own well-being, it might be thought that no one can really be concerned for the well-being of others. But again, this is surely a false dichotomy. There is no inconsistency in desiring that everyone, including oneself *and* others, be happy. To be sure, it may happen on occasion that our interests conflict with the interests of others, in the sense that both cannot be satisfied. In these cases we have to make hard choices. But even in these cases we sometimes opt for the interests of others, especially when the others are our friends and family. But more important, not all cases are like this. Sometimes we are able to promote the welfare of others when our own interests are not involved at all. In those circumstances, not even the strongest self-regard need prevent us from acting considerately toward others.

Once these confusions are cleared away, there seems little reason to think Psychological Egoism is a plausible theory. On the contrary, it seems decidedly implausible. If we simply observe people's behavior with an open mind, we find that much of it is motivated by self-regard, but by no means all of it. There may indeed be one simple formula, as yet undiscovered, that would explain all of human behavior—but Psychological Egoism is not it.

The Deepest Error in Psychological Egoism

The preceding discussion may seem relentlessly negative—even objectionably so. "If Psychological Egoism is so obviously confused," you may ask, "and if there are no plausible arguments in its favor, why have so many intelligent people been attracted to it?" It is a fair question. Part of the answer, I think, is the almost irresistible urge toward theoretical simplicity; another part is the attraction of what appears to be a hard-headed, deflationary attitude toward human pretensions. But there is a deeper reason: Psychological Egoism was accepted by many thinkers because it appeared to them to be *irrefutable*. And in a certain sense, they were right. Yet in another sense, the theory's immunity from refutation is its deepest flaw.

To explain, let me first tell a (true) story that might appear to be far from our subject.

A few years ago a group of investigators led by Dr. David Rosenham, professor of psychology and law at Stanford University, had themselves admitted as patients to various mental institutions. The hospital staffs did not know there was anything special about them; the investigators were thought to be simply patients. The investigators' purpose was to see how they would be treated.

The investigators were perfectly "sane," whatever that means, but their very presence in the hospitals created the assumption that they were mentally disturbed. Although they behaved normally—they did nothing to feign illness—they soon discovered that everything they did was interpreted as a sign of some sort of mental problem. When some of them were found to be taking notes on their experiences, entries were made in their records such as "patient engages in writing behavior." During one interview, one "patient" confessed that although he was closer to his mother as a small child, he became more attached to his father as he grew older—a perfectly normal turn of events. But this was taken as evidence of "unstable relationships in childhood." Even their protestations of normalcy were turned against them. One of the real patients warned them: "Never tell a doctor that you're well. He won't believe you. That's called a 'flight into health.' Tell him you're still sick, but you're feeling a lot better. That's called insight."

No one on the hospital staffs ever caught on to the hoax. The real patients, however, did see through it. One of them told an investigator, "You're not crazy. You're checking up on the hospital." And so he was.

What the investigators learned was that *once a hypothesis is accepted, everything may be interpreted to support it*. The hypothesis was that the pseudopatients were mentally disturbed; once that became the controlling assumption, it did not matter how they behaved. Everything they did would be construed so as to fit the assumption. But the "success" of this technique of interpretation did not prove the hypothesis was true. If anything, it was a sign that something had gone wrong.

The hypothesis that the pseudopatients were disturbed was faulty because, at least for the hospital staffs, it was *untestable*. If a hypothesis purports to say something about the world, then there must be some conditions that could verify it and some that conceivably could refute it. Otherwise, it is meaningless. Consider this example: suppose someone says "Kareem Abdul-Jabbar cannot get into my Volkswagen." We know perfectly well what this means, because we can imagine the circumstances that would make it true and the circumstances that would make it false: to test the statement, we take the car to Kareem, invite him to step inside, and see what happens. If it turns out one way, the statement is true; if it turns out the other way, the statement is false. The problem with the hypothesis about the pseudopatients' mental health, as it was applied within the hospital setting, was that nothing could have refuted it.

Such hypotheses may be immune from refutation, but their immunity is purchased at too dear a price—they no longer say anything significant about the world.

Psychological Egoism is involved in this same error. All our experience tells us that people act from a great variety of motives: greed, anger, lust, love, and hate, to name only a few. Sometimes, people think only of themselves. At other times, they do not think of themselves at all and act from a concern for others. The common distinction between self-regard and unselfishness gets its meaning from this contrast. But then Psychological Egoism tells us that there is *really* only one motive, self-regard, and this seems a new and fascinating revelation. We must have been wrong. But as the theory unfolds, it turns out that we were not wrong at all. The psychological egoist does not deny that people act in the variety of ways they have always appeared to act in. In the ordinary sense of the term, people are still, sometimes, unselfish. In effect, the psychological egoist has only announced his determination to *interpret* people's behavior in a certain way, *no matter what they do*. Therefore, *nothing that anyone could do could possibly count as evidence against the hypothesis*. The thesis is irrefutable, but for that very reason it turns out to have no factual content. It is not a new and fascinating revelation at all.

I am not saying that the hypothesis of the pseudopatients' mental illness or the hypothesis of Psychological Egoism are meaningless in themselves. The trouble is not so much with the hypotheses as with the people who manipulate the facts to fit them. The staffs of the mental institutions, and the estimable Hobbes, *could* have allowed some facts to count as falsifying their assumptions. Then, their hypotheses would have been meaningful but would have been seen to be plainly false. That is the risk one must take. Paradoxically, if we do not allow some way in which we might be mistaken, we lose all chance of being right.

A CRITIQUE OF ETHICAL EGOISM
Paul W. Taylor

Paul W. Taylor is professor of philosophy at the Graduate School and University Center, City University of New York. Ethical egoism is a moral theory that makes the pursuit of self-interest the supreme end of conduct. Taylor distinguishes three types of ethical egoism: universal, individual, and personal. Against universal ethical egoism, he charges that it leads to inconsistent moral conclusions. Individual ethical egoism, while not inconsistent, is unable to explain the unique treatment claimed as a right by the egoist. Personal ethical egoism turns out not to be a moral theory at all. Taylor concludes that ethical egoism, in all its varieties, is an unacceptable moral theory.

Ethical egoism is a normative theory. Its basic tenet is that self-interest is the sole valid standard of right conduct. This standard may be explained as follows. To know in any given case which of the alternatives open to a person is the one he morally ought to do, we proceed thus. We calculate, first, the probable consequences that would result if the person were to follow one alternative; next, the probable consequences that would result if he were to choose a second alternative; and so on for every alternative open to him. We then ask ourselves, Which of the acts possible will result in furthering the self-interest of the person to a greater extent than any of the others? In other words, which of the alternatives will bring about more things that the person would like and fewer that he would dislike over his life span as a whole than any other alternative? When we have answered this question, we know what the person ought to do. For we know which act is the best alternative, as judged by the standard of his self-interest.

It should be noted at this point, however, that there are three types of ethical egoism and that the foregoing account describes only one of them. The three may be designated "universal ethical egoism," "individual ethical egoism," and "personal ethical egoism." Here is what differentiates them. Does the ethical egoist say, "*Every* person ought to do what will most further *his own* self-interest"; or does he say, "*Every* person ought to do what will most further *my* self-interest"; or does he say only, "*I* ought to do what will most further *my* self-interest"? In the first case we have universal egoism: the standard of right action is the agent's or doer's self-interest, no matter who the agent is. This is the version of ethical egoism given in the preceding paragraph. According to the individual ethical egoist, on the other hand, the standard of right action is not the agent's self-interest, but that of the ethical egoist himself. Thus if the population of the world consisted of four people, A, B, C, and D, universal ethical egoism would hold that A ought to further A's self-interest, B ought to further B's, and C and D each ought to further his

From *Principles of Ethics: An Introduction* by Paul W. Taylor © 1975 by Dickenson Publishing Company, Inc. Reprinted by permission of Wadsworth, Inc.

own. From the point of view of individual ethical egoism, however, we would have to know which of the four people was the individual ethical egoist before we could know what any of them ought to do. Suppose he were A. Then the theory states that A ought to further A's self-interest, B ought to further A's self-interest, and so should C and D. Finally, the theory of personal ethical egoism is simply the view that the egoist alone ought to further his self-interest. It does not say anything about what other people ought to do. Thus if the personal egoist were A, then according to his theory A ought to further A's self-interest, but his theory would not tell B, C, and D what they ought or ought not to do.

This chapter will be concerned mainly with universal ethical egoism, since it is this form of the theory that has seriously been advocated by both ancient and modern philosophers. . . .

What objections might be raised against the theory of universal ethical egoism, and what replies might be given to those objections? The most frequent criticism of universal ethical egoism is that it must be false because it contains an *internal inconsistency*. The argument goes as follows. The universal ethical egoist says that each person should promote his own self-interest. There will be many situations, however, in which a conflict of interest occurs between the egoist and others. In such situations, if others pursue their ends the egoist himself will be hindered or prevented from pursuing his own, and vice versa. Yet according to his theory, an action ought to be done whenever it furthers the interests of the agent, *whoever that agent may be*. It follows that in all cases of conflict of interest between the egoist himself and others, the principle of universal ethical egoism entails contradictory ought-statements. For it entails that another person ought to do a certain action (because it would promote his interests) and at the same time it entails that he ought not to, since his doing it would interfere with the egoist's pursuit of his own interests. Similarly, if the egoist's action would benefit him, then according to his theory he ought to do it. However, in a situation where his action conflicts with another's self-interest, that other would *correctly* judge that the action ought not to be done. Thus the two contradictory judgments: "The egoist ought to do the act" and "The egoist ought not to do the act" would both be true of the same action. It follows, therefore, that universal ethical egoism is internally inconsistent.

The egoist's reply to this argument is that, according to his theory, he need not *assert* that others ought to pursue their interests when doing so conflicts with the promotion of his own. He can simply keep quiet about the matter. Indeed, if he is to further his interests in the most effective way possible he should publicly urge others to be altruistic, since by following his counsel they will not interfere with him but, on the contrary, will help him attain his goals. If, then, he is true to the egoist principle that he ought to do everything that will most effectively further his own ends, he will not advocate publicly that everyone be an ethical egoist. Instead, he will declare that all persons should be altruists—at least with regard to the way they treat him!

It has seemed to the critics of egoism, however, that this reply does not get rid of the inconsistency. They point out that it follows from the theory of universal egoism that *each and every person* ought to think in the way described above. Thus everyone ought to urge others to be altruistic as a means to promoting his self-interest. And since each person's pursuit of self-interest requires that he not become altruistic himself, the theory implies that no one should be an altruist. Hence, every individual ought to do something (namely, promote his own self-interest by getting others to be altruistic) and at the same time ought to prevent another from doing what that other ought to do (namely, getting others to be altruistic without becoming altruistic himself).

The logical consequence of universal ethical egoism thus appears to be that everyone should do a certain sort of thing while actually it is impossible that everyone do it successfully. If one person succeeds in doing it (that is, succeeds in getting another to be altruistic while remaining egoistic himself), someone else must fail to do it (if he happens to be the person whom the other has successfully made altruistic). Ethical egoism need not be *advocated* universally for this internal inconsistency to arise. It is an inconsistency that arises from everyone's *practicing* ethical egoism by *not* advocating that everyone become an ethical egoist.

It should be noted that these considerations apply to what we have called "universal ethical egoism." The other two forms of ethical egoism, which were designated by the terms "individual" and "personal," can escape the foregoing difficulties, since neither claims that every person should promote his own self-interest. The "individual" ethical egoist holds that *he* should promote his own self-interest and that all others should also promote his, the ethical egoist's, self-interest. There is nothing internally inconsistent with everyone's putting this principle into practice. The "personal" ethical egoist, on the other hand, asserts that *he* should promote his self-interest and simply has nothing to say, one way or the other, concerning what anyone else ought to do. Here also, no contradiction is involved in what the personal ethical egoist claims ought to be done.

Can we accept, then, either of these forms of ethical egoism as a justifiable normative system? That there remain certain problems which each of them has to face becomes clear from the following reflections.

Consider, first, the position of the individual ethical egoist. He says that his interests ought to be furthered not only by his own actions but also by those of everyone else. One implication of his view is that his wishes, desires, and needs have a right to be fulfilled even at the cost of frustrating the wants of others. His ultimate principle, in other words, entails an inequality of rights among persons. We can then formulate a challenge which will reasonably be addressed to the egoist by all others: "Why should your self-interest count more than anyone else's? On what grounds do your wants and needs make a higher claim to fulfillment than those of anyone else? Unless you can show that you merit special consideration, there is no reason why others owe you a duty (namely, to further your interests) which you do not owe to them. And your theory itself offers no basis for your claim to special consideration, since anyone else can propose the same ultimate principle on his own behalf and thus endow his interests with a higher claim to fulfillment than yours. Your theory provides no *reasons* why you should be given unique treatment." It is difficult to see how the egoist could reply to this challenge. As long as others knew that it was contrary to their interests to accept his principle, they would need to be shown why they should accept it before they could have a reason to do the actions it required of them. But the only way the individual egoist could justify others' accepting his principle would be by pointing out some *characteristic* of himself that made him deserving of special consideration. If he were to do this, however, the possession of the given characteristic would be the supreme principle of his system, not the principle of egoism itself. He would then have to admit that if anyone else were found to have the attribute in question, that person's interest would have a claim to fulfillment equal to his own. And this would be giving up individual ethical egoism.

Let us look, next, at the position of personal ethical egoism. The personal egoist escapes the foregoing criticism since he does not claim that others ought to promote his self-interest. He simply says that he ought to do those actions that will most benefit him, and makes no ought-statements about anyone else's actions (not even the statement that they ought not to interfere with or frustrate him in the pursuit of his interests). It is important to realize that the principle of personal ethical egoism does not provide any basis for judging the rightness or wrongness of the conduct of any individual other than the egoist himself. Once we see clearly that personal ethical egoism has this implication, we see how it is possible to raise the following objection to it. (It is an objection, be it noted, which cannot be raised against the theories of universal or individual ethical egoism.)

How can personal ethical egoism be considered a normative ethical system at all? Since it tells only one person in the world what *he* ought and ought not to do but remains completely silent about the actions of everyone else, it turns out to be nothing more than a private policy of action adopted by one person with regard to himself alone. It is a policy by which he can guide his own conduct, but it cannot serve to guide anyone else's. Consequently it does not qualify as a moral principle. Even if everyone were to accept the principle, it would leave all but one person completely in the dark about what they morally ought or ought not to do. It may indeed be *consistent* for someone to adopt the principle for himself and use it as a policy governing his own actions. But such a personal policy cannot provide others with moral reasons for or against doing anything they please.

This argument assumes that an ethical system must give an account of *moral* reasons for action and that a *moral* reason for action cannot be merely a personal policy adopted by one individual as a guide to his own conduct alone. If a statement about the properties or consequences of an action constitutes a moral reason for (or against) the action, then it must be a reason for *anyone's* performing (or refraining from) that kind of conduct, whenever *anyone* is in a situation in which doing and refraining from an action of the given kind are alternatives open to him. Whether this view of a moral reason for action is itself acceptable is an issue that requires further inquiry into normative ethical systems.

EGOISM, ALTRUISM, AND SOCIOBIOLOGY
Peter Singer

Peter Singer currently teaches philosophy at La Trobe University in Victoria, Australia. His works include Animal Liberation *(1975) and* The Expanding Circle *(1981). Singer appeals to recent work in sociobiology to argue that humans are not psychological egoists by nature. He argues that there are good reasons for supposing that evolution favors genuinely altruistic behavior, and he illustrates this point by reference to a puzzle called the "prisoner's dilemma."*

Every human society has some code of behavior for its members. This is true of nomads and city-dwellers, of hunter-gatherers and of industrial civilizations, of Eskimos in Greenland and Bushmen in Africa, of a tribe of twenty Australian aborigines and of the billion people that make up China. Ethics is part of the natural human condition.

That ethics is natural to human beings has been denied. More than three hundred years ago Thomas Hobbes wrote in his *Leviathan:*

During the time men live without a common Power to keep them all in awe they are in that condition called War; and such a war, as is of every man against every other man. . . . To this war of every man against every man, this also is consequent; that nothing can be Unjust. The notions of Right and Wrong, Justice and Injustice have there no place.

Hobbes's guess about human life in the state of nature was no better than Rousseau's idea that we were naturally solitary. It is not the force of the state that persuades us to act ethically. The state, or some other form of social power, may reinforce our tendency to observe an ethical code, but that tendency exists before the social power is established. The primary role Hobbes gave to the state was always suspect on philosophical grounds, for it invites the question why, having agreed to set up a power to enforce the law, human beings would trust each other long enough to make the agreement work. Now we also have biological grounds for rejecting Hobbes's theory.

Occasionally there are claims that a group of human beings totally lacking any ethical code has been discovered. The Ik, a northern Uganda tribe described by Colin Turnbull in *The Mountain People,* is the most recent example. The biologist Garrett Hardin has even claimed that the Ik are an incarnation of Hobbes's natural man, living in a state of war of every Ik against every other Ik. The Ik certainly were, at the time of Turnbull's visit, a most unfortunate people. Originally nomadic hunters and gatherers, their hunting ground was turned into a national park. They were forced to become farmers in an arid mountain area in which they had difficulty supporting themselves; a prolonged drought and consequent famine was the final blow. As a result, according to Turnbull, Ik society collapsed. Parents turned their three-year-old children out to fend for themselves, the strong took food from the mouths of the weak, the sufferings of the old and sick were a source of laughter, and anyone who helped another was considered a fool. The Ik, Turnbull says, abandoned family, cooperation, social life, love, religion, and everything else except the pursuit of self-interest. They teach us that our much vaunted human values are, in Turnbull's words, "luxuries that can be dispensed with."

The idea of a people without human values holds a certain repugnant fascination. *The Mountain People* achieved a rare degree of fame for a work of anthropology. It was reviewed in *Life,* talked about over cocktails, and turned into a stage play by the noted director Peter Brook. It was also severely criticized by some anthropologists. They pointed out the subjective nature of many of Turnbull's observations, the vagueness of his data, contradictions between *The Mountain People* and an earlier report Turnbull had published (in which he described the Ik as fun-loving, helpful, and "great family people"), and contradictions within *The Mountain People* itself. In reply Turnbull admitted that "the data in the book are inadequate for anything approaching proof" and recognized the existence of evidence pointing toward a different picture of Ik life.

Even if we take the picture of Ik life in *The Mountain People* at face value, there is still ample evidence that Ik society has an ethical code. Turnbull refers to disputes over the theft of berries which reveal that, although stealing takes place, the Ik retain notions of private property and the wrongness of theft. Turnbull mentions the Ik's attachment to the mountains and the reverence with which they speak of Mount Morungole, which seems to be a sacred place for them. He observes that the Ik like to sit together in groups and insist on living together in villages. He describes a code that has to be followed by an Ik husband who intends to beat his wife, a code that gives the wife a chance to leave first. He reports that the obligations of a pact of mutual assistance known as *nyot* are invariably carried out. He tells us that there is a strict prohibition on Ik killing each other or even drawing blood. The Ik may let each other starve, but they apparently do not think of other Ik as they think of any non-human animals they find—that is, as potential food. A normal well-fed reader will take the prohibition of cannibalism for granted, but under the circumstances in which the Ik were living human flesh would have been a great boost to the diets of stronger Ik; that they refrain from this source of food is an example of the continuing strength of their ethical code despite the crumbling of almost everything that had made their lives worth living.

Under extreme conditions like those of the Ik during famine, the individual's need to survive becomes so dominant that it may seem as if all other values have ceased to matter, when in fact they continue to exercise an influence. If any conditions can be worse than those the Ik endured, they were the conditions of the inmates of Soviet labor camps and, more horrible still, the Nazi death camps. Here too, it has been said that "the doomed devoured each other," that "all trace of human solidarity vanished," that all values were erased and every man fought for himself. Nor should it be surprising if this were so, for the camps deliberately and systematically dehumanized their inmates, stripping them naked, shaving their hair, assigning them numbers, forcing them to soil their clothing with excrement, letting them know in a hundred ways that their lives were of no account, beating them, torturing them, and starving them. The astonishing thing is that despite all this, life in the camps was *not* every man for himself. Again and again, survivors' reports show that prisoners helped each other. In Auschwitz prisoners risked their lives to pick up strangers who had fallen in the snow at roll call; they built a radio and disseminated news to keep up morale; though they were starving, they shared food with those still more needy. There were also ethical rules in the camps. Though theft occurred, stealing from one's fellow prisoners was strongly condemned and those caught stealing were punished by the prisoners themselves. As Terrence Des Pres observes in *The Survivor*, a book based on reports by those who survived the camps: "The assumption that there was no moral or social order in the camps is wrong. . . . Through innumerable small acts of humanness, most of them covert but everywhere in evidence, survivors were able to maintain societal structures workable enough to keep themselves alive and morally sane.". . .

Early in the previous chapter, we accepted a definition of altruism in terms of behavior—"altruistic behavior is behavior which benefits others at some cost to oneself"—without inquiring into motivation. Now we must note that when people talk of altruism they are normally thinking not simply of behavior but also of motivation. To be faithful to the generally accepted meaning of the term, we should redefine altruistic behavior as behavior which benefits others at some initial cost to oneself, and is motivated by the desire to benefit others. To what extent human beings are altruistically motivated is a question I shall consider in a later chapter. Meanwhile we should note that according to the common meaning of the term, which I shall use from now on, an act may in fact benefit me in the long run, and yet—perhaps because I didn't foresee that the act would redound to my advantage—still be altruistic because my intention was to benefit someone else.

Robert Trivers has offered a sociobiological explanation for our moral preference for altruistic motivation. People who are altruistically motivated will make more reliable partners than those motivated by self-interest. After all, one day the calculations of self-interest may turn out differently. Looking at the shabby clothes I have left on the beach, a self-interested potential rescuer may decide that the prospects of a sizable reward are dim. In an exchange in which cheating is difficult to detect, a self-interested partner is more likely to cheat than a partner with real concern for my welfare. Evolution would therefore favor people who could distinguish self-interested from altruistic motivation in others, and then select only the altruistic as beneficiaries of their gifts or services.

Psychologists have experimented with the circumstances that lead people to behave altruistically, and their results show that we are more ready to act altruistically toward those we regard as genuinely altruistic than to those we think have ulterior motives for their apparently altruistic acts. As one review of the literature concludes: "When the legitimacy of the apparent altruism is questioned, reciprocity is less likely to prevail." Another experiment proved something most of us know from our own attitudes: we find genuine altruism a more attractive character trait than a pretense of altruism covering self-interested motives.

Here an intriguing and important point emerges; if there are advantages in being a partner in a reciprocal exchange, and if one is more likely to be selected as a partner if one has genuine concern for others, there is an evolutionary advantage in having genuine concern for others. (This assumes, of course, that potential partners can see through a pretense of altruism by those who are really self-interested—something that is not always easy, but which we spend a lot of time trying to do, and often can do. Evolutionary theory would predict that we would get better at detecting pretense, but at the same time the performance of the pretenders would improve, so the task would never become a simple one.)

This conclusion is highly significant for understanding ethics, because it cuts across the tendency of sociobiological reasoning to explain behavior in terms of self-interest or the interests of one's kin. Properly understood, sociobiology does not imply that behavior is actually motivated by the desire to further one's own interests or those of one's kin. Sociobiology says nothing about motivation, for it remains on the level of the objective consequences of types of behavior. That a piece of behavior in fact benefits oneself does not mean that the behavior is motivated by self-interest, for one might be quite unaware of the benefits to oneself the behavior will bring. Nevertheless, it is a common assumption that sociobiology implies that we are motivated by self-interest, not by genuine altruism. This assumption gains credibility from some of the things sociobiologists write. We can now see that sociobiology itself can explain the existence of genuinely altruistic motivation. The implications of this I shall take up in a later chapter, but it may be useful to make the underlying mechanism more explicit. This can be done by reference to a puzzle known as the Prisoner's Dilemma.

In the cells of the Ruritanian secret police are two political prisoners. The police are trying to persuade them to confess to membership in an illegal opposition party. The prisoners know that if neither of them confesses, the police will not be able to make the charge stick, but they will be interrogated in the cells for another three months before the police give up and let them go. If one of them confesses, implicating the other, the one who confesses will be released immediately but the other will be sentenced to eight years in jail. If both of them confess, their helpfulness will be taken into account and they will get five years in jail. Since the prisoners are interrogated separately, neither can know if the other has confessed or not.

The dilemma is, of course, whether to confess. The point of the story is that circumstances have been so arranged that if either prisoner reasons from the point of view of self-interest, she will find it to her advantage to confess; whereas taking the interests of the two prisoners together, it is obviously in their interests if neither confesses. Thus the first prisoner's self-interested calculations go like this: "If the other prisoner confesses, it will be better for me if I have also confessed, for then I will get five years instead of eight; and if the other prisoner does not confess, it will still be better for me if I confess, for then I will be released immediately, instead of being interrogated for another three months. Since we are interrogated separately, whether the other prisoner confesses has nothing to do with whether I confess—our choices are entirely independent of each other. So whatever happens, it will be better for me if I confess." The second prisoner's self-interested reasoning will, of course, follow exactly the same route as the first prisoner's, and will come to the same conclusion. As a result, both prisoners, if self-interested, will confess, and both will spend the next five years in prison. There was a way for them both to be out in three months, but because they were locked into purely self-interested calculations, they could not take that route.

What would have to be changed in our assumptions about the prisoners to make it rational for them both to refuse to confess? One way of achieving this would be for the prisoners to make an agreement that would bind them both to silence. But how could each prisoner be confident that the other would keep the agreement? If one prisoner breaks the agreement, the other will be in prison for a long time, unable to punish the cheater in any way. So each prisoner will reason: "If the other one breaks the agreement, it will be better for me if I break it too; and if the other one keeps the agreement, I will still be better off if I break it. So I will break the agreement."

Without sanctions to back it up, an agreement is unable to bring two self-interested individuals to the outcome that is best for both of them, taking their interests together. What has to be changed to reach this result is the assumption that the prisoners are motivated by self-interest alone. If, for instance, they are altruistic to the extent of caring as much for the interests of their fellow prisoner as they care for their own interests, they will reason thus: "If the other prisoner does not confess it will be better for us both if I do not confess, for then between us we will be in prison for a total of six months, whereas if I do confess the total will be eight years; and if the other prisoner does confess it will still be better if I do not confess, for then the total served will be eight years, instead of ten. So whatever happens, taking our interests together, it will be better if I don't confess." A pair of altruistic prisoners will therefore come out of this situation better than a pair of self-interested prisoners, *even from the point of view of self-interest*.

Altruistic motivation is not the only way to achieve a happier solution. Another possibility is that the prisoners are conscientious, regarding it as morally wrong to inform on a fellow prisoner; or if they are able to make an agreement, they might believe they have a duty to keep their promises. In either case, each will be able to rely on the other not confessing and they will be free in three months.

The Prisoner's Dilemma shows that, paradoxical as it may seem, we will sometimes be better off if we are not self-interested. Two or more people motivated by self-interest alone may not be able to promote their interests as well as they could if they were more altruistic or more conscientious.

The Prisoner's Dilemma explains why there could be an evolutionary advantage in being genuinely altruistic instead of making reciprocal exchanges on the basis of calculated self-interest. Prisons and confessions may not have played a substantial role in early human evolution, but other forms of cooperation surely did. Suppose two early humans are attacked by a sabertooth cat. If both flee, one will be picked off by the cat; if both stand their ground, there is a very good chance that they can fight the cat off; if one flees and the other stands and fights, the fugitive will escape and the fighter will be killed. Here the odds are sufficiently like those in the Prisoner's Dilemma to produce a similar result. From a self-interested point of view, if your partner flees your chances of survival are better if you flee too (you have a 50 percent chance rather than none at all) and if your partner stands and fights you still do better to run (you are sure of escape if you flee, whereas it is only probable, not certain, that together you and your partner can overcome the cat). So two purely self-interested early humans would flee, and one of them would die. Two early humans who cared for each other, however, would stand and fight, and most likely neither would die. Let us say, just to be able to put a figure on it, that two humans cooperating can defeat a sabertooth cat on nine out of every ten occasions and on the tenth occasion the cat kills one of them. Let us also say that when a sabertooth cat pursues two fleeing humans it always catches one of them, and which one it catches is entirely random, since differences in human running speed are negligible in comparison to the speed of the cat. Then one of a pair of purely self-interested humans would not, on average, last more than a single encounter with a sabertooth cat; but one of a pair of altruistic humans would on average survive ten such encounters.

If situations analogous to this imaginary sabertooth cat attack were common, early humans would do better hunting with altruistic comrades than with self-interested partners. Of course, an egoist who could find an altruist to go hunting with him would do better still; but altruists who could not detect—and refuse to assist—purely self-interested partners would be selected against. Evolution would therefore favor those who are genuinely altruistic to other genuine altruists, but are not altruistic to those who seek to take advantage of their altruism. We can add, again, that the same goal could be achieved if, instead of being altruistic, early humans were moved by something like a sense that it is wrong to desert a partner in the face of danger.

CHAPTER 3

Relativism

A DEFENSE OF ETHICAL RELATIVISM
Ruth Benedict

Ruth Benedict (1887–1948) was a pioneering American anthropologist and wrote Patterns of Culture *(1935), an important work in comparative anthropology. Benedict argues that careful study of the cultural practices of different peoples supports the idea that what is and is not behaviorally normal is culturally determined. She argues for a similar point in connection with such moral distinctions as good and bad, and right and wrong. She suggests that phrases like "it is morally good" should be understood as being synonymous with "it is habitual."*

Modern social anthropology has become more and more a study of the varieties and common elements of cultural environment and the consequences of these in human behavior. For such a study of diverse social orders primitive peoples fortunately provide a laboratory not yet entirely vitiated by the spread of a standardized worldwide civilization. Dyaks and Hopis, Fijians and Yakuts are significant for psychological and sociological study because only among these simpler peoples has there been sufficient isolation to give opportunity for the development of localized social forms. In the higher cultures the standardization of custom and belief over a couple of continents has given a false sense of the inevitability of the particular forms that have gained currency, and we need to turn to a wider survey in order to check the conclusions we hastily base upon this near-universality of familiar customs. Most of the simpler cultures did not gain the wide currency of the one which, out of our experience, we identify with human nature, but this was for various historical reasons,

From "Anthropology and the Abnormal," by Ruth Benedict, *The Journal of General Psychology*, 1934, vol. 10, pp. 59–82. Reprinted by permission of Helen Dwight Ried Educational Foundation. Published by Heldref Publications, Washington, D.C.

and certainly not for any that gives us as its carriers a monopoly of social good or of social sanity. Modern civilization, from this point of view, becomes not a necessary pinnacle of human achievement but one entry in a long series of possible adjustments.

These adjustments, whether they are in mannerisms like the ways of showing anger, or joy, or grief in any society, or in major human drives like those of sex, prove to be far more variable than experience in any one culture would suggest. In certain fields, such as that of religion or of formal marriage arrangements, these wide limits of variability are well known and can be fairly described. In others it is not yet possible to give a generalized account, but that does not absolve us of the task of indicating the significance of the work that has been done and of the problems that have arisen.

One of these problems relates to the customary modern normal-abnormal categories and our conclusions regarding them. In how far are such categories culturally determined, or in how far can we with assurance regard them as absolute? In how far can we regard inability to function socially as diagnostic of abnormality, or in how far is it necessary to regard this as a function of the culture?

As a matter of fact, one of the most striking facts that emerges from a study of widely varying cultures is the ease with which our abnormals function in other cultures. It does not matter what kind of "abnormality" we choose for illustration, those which indicate extreme instability, or those which are more in the nature of character traits like sadism or delusions of grandeur or of persecution, there are well-described cultures in which these abnormals function at ease and with honor, and apparently without danger or difficulty to the society.

The most notorious of these is trance and catalepsy. Even a very mild mystic is aberrant in our culture. But most peoples have regarded even extreme psychic manifestations not only as normal and desirable, but even as characteristic of highly valued and gifted individuals. This was true even in our own cultural background in that period when Catholicism made the ecstatic experience the mark of sainthood. It is hard for us, born and brought up in a culture that makes no use of the experience, to realize how important a role it may play and how many individuals are capable of it, once it has been given an honorable place in any society. . . .

Cataleptic and trance phenomena are, of course, only one illustration of the fact that those whom we regard as abnormals may function adequately in other cultures. Many of our culturally discarded traits are selected for elaboration in different societies. Homosexuality is an excellent example, for in this case our attention is not constantly diverted, as in the consideration of trance, to the interruption of routine activity which it implies. Homosexuality poses the problem very simply. A tendency toward this trait in our culture exposes an individual to all the conflicts to which all aberrants are always exposed, and we tend to identify the consequences of this conflict with homosexuality. But these consequences are obviously local and cultural. Homosexuals in many societies are not incompetent, but they may be such if the culture asks adjustments of them that would strain any man's vitality. Wherever homosexuality has been given an honorable place in any society, those to whom it is congenial have filled adequately the honorable roles society assigns to them. Plato's *Republic* is, of course, the most convincing statement of such a reading of homosexuality. It is presented as one of the major means to the good life, and it was generally so regarded in Greece at that time.

The cultural attitude toward homosexuals has not always been on such a high ethical plane, but it has been very varied. Among many American Indian tribes there exists the institution of the berdache, as the French called them. These men-women were men who at puberty or thereafter took the dress and the occupations of women. Sometimes they married other men and lived with them. Sometimes they were men with no inversion, persons of weak sexual endowment who chose this role to avoid the jeers of the women. The berdaches were never regarded as of first-rate supernatural power, as similar men-women were in Siberia, but rather as leaders in women's occupations, good healers in certain diseases, or, among certain tribes, as the genial organizers of social affairs. In any case, they were socially placed. They were not left exposed to the conflicts that visit the deviant who is excluded from participation in the recognized patterns of his society.

The most spectacular illustrations of the extent to which normality may be culturally defined are those cultures where an abnormality of our culture is the cornerstone of their social structure. It is not possible to do justice to these possibilities in a short discussion. A recent study of an island of northwest Melanesia by Fortune describes a society built upon traits which we regard as beyond the border of paranoia. In this tribe the exogamic groups look upon each other as prime manipulators of black magic, so that one marries always into an enemy group which remains for life one's deadly and unappeasable foes. They look upon a good garden crop as a confession of theft, for everyone is engaged in making magic to induce into his garden the productiveness of his neighbors'; therefore no secrecy in the island is so rigidly insisted upon as the secrecy of a man's harvesting of his yams. Their polite phrase at the acceptance of a gift is, "And if you now poison me, how shall I repay you this present?" Their preoccupation with poisoning is constant; no woman ever leaves her cooking pot for a moment untended. Even the great affinal economic exchanges that are characteristic of this Melanesian culture area are quite altered in Dobu since they are incompatible with this fear and distrust that pervades the culture. They go farther and people the whole world outside their own quarters with such malignant spirits that all-night feasts and ceremonials simply do not occur here. They have even rigorous religiously enforced customs that forbid the sharing of seed even in one family group. Anyone else's food is deadly poison to you, so that communality of stores is out of the question. For some months before harvest the whole society is on the verge of starvation, but if one falls to the temptation and eats up one's seed yams, one is an outcast and a beachcomber for life. There is no coming back. It involves, as a matter of course, divorce and the breaking of all social ties.

Now in this society where no one may work with another and no one may share with another, Fortune describes the individual who was regarded by all his fellows as crazy. He was not one of those who periodically ran amok and, beside himself and frothing at the mouth, fell with a knife upon anyone he could reach. Such behavior they did not regard as putting anyone outside the pale. They did not even put the individuals who were known to be liable to these attacks under any kind of control. They merely fled when they saw the attack coming on and kept out of the way. "He would be all right tomorrow." But there was one man of sunny, kindly disposition who liked work and liked to be helpful. The compulsion was too strong for him to repress it in favor of the opposite tendencies of his culture. Men and women never spoke of him without laughing; he was silly and simple and definitely crazy. Nevertheless, to the ethnologist used to a culture that has, in Christianity, made his type the model of all virtue, he seemed a pleasant fellow. . . .

. . . Among the Kwakiutl it did not matter whether a relative had died in bed of disease, or by the hand of an enemy, in either case death was an affront to be wiped out by the death of another person. The fact that one had been caused to mourn was proof that one had been put upon. A chief's sister and her daughter had gone up to Victoria, and either because they drank bad whiskey or because their boat capsized they never came back. The chief called together his warriors, "Now I ask you, tribes, who shall wail? Shall I do it or shall another?" The spokesman answered, of course, "Not you, Chief. Let some other of the tribes." Immediately they set up the war pole to announce their intention of wiping out the injury, and gathered a war party. They set out, and found seven men and two children asleep and killed them. "Then they felt good when they arrived at Sebaa in the evening."

The point which is of interest to us is that in our society those who on that occasion would feel good when they arrived at Sebaa that evening would be the definitely abnormal. There would be some, even in our society, but it is not a recognized and approved mood under the circumstances. On the Northwest Coast those are favored and fortunate to whom that mood under those circumstances is congenial, and those to whom it is repugnant are unlucky. This latter minority can register in their own culture only by doing violence to their congenial responses and acquiring others that are difficult for them. The person, for instance, who, like a Plains Indian whose wife has been taken from him, is too proud to fight, can deal with the Northwest Coast civilization only by ignoring its strongest bents. If he cannot achieve it, he is the deviant in that culture, their instance of abnormality.

This head-hunting that takes place on the Northwest Coast after a death is no matter of blood revenge or of organized vengeance. There is no effort to tie up the subsequent killing with any responsibility on the part of the victim for the death of the person who is being mourned. A chief whose son has died goes visiting wherever his fancy dictates, and he says to his host, "My prince has died today, and you go with him." Then he kills him. In this, according to their interpretation, he acts nobly because he has not been downed. He has thrust back in return. The whole procedure is meaningless without the fundamental paranoid reading of bereavement. Death, like all the other untoward accidents of existence, confounds man's pride and can only be handled in the category of insults.

Behavior honored upon the Northwest Coast is one which is recognized as abnormal in our civilization, and yet it is sufficiently close to the attitudes of our own culture to be intelligible to us and to have a definite vocabulary with which we may discuss it. The megalomaniac paranoid trend is a definite danger in our society. It is encouraged by some of our major preoccupations, and it confronts us with a choice of two possible attitudes. One is to brand it as abnormal and reprehensible, and is the attitude we have chosen in our civilization. The other is to make it an essential attribute of ideal man, and this is the solution in the culture of the Northwest Coast.

These illustrations, which it has been possible to indicate only in the briefest manner, force upon us the fact that normality is culturally defined. An adult shaped to the drives and standards of either of these cultures, if he were transported into our civilization, would fall into our categories of abnormality. He would be faced with the psychic dilemmas of the socially unavailable. In his own culture, however, he is the pillar of society, the end result of socially inculcated mores, and the problem of personal instability in his case simply does not arise.

No one civilization can possibly utilize in its mores the whole potential range of human behavior. Just as there are great numbers of possible phonetic articulations, and the possibility of language depends on a selection and standardization of a few of these in order that speech communication may be possible at all, so the possibility of organized behavior of every sort, from the fashions of local dress and houses to the dicta of a people's ethics and religion, depends upon a similar selection among the possible behavior traits. In the field of recognized economic obligations or sex tabus this selection is as nonrational and subconscious a process as it is in the field of phonetics. It is a process which goes on in the group for long periods of time and is historically conditioned by innumerable accidents of isolation or of contact of peoples. In any comprehensive study of psychology, the selection that different cultures have made in the course of history within the great circumference of potential behavior is of great significance.

Every society, beginning with some slight inclination in one direction or another, carries its preference farther and farther, integrating itself more and more completely upon its chosen basis, and discarding those types of behavior that are uncongenial. Most of those organizations of personality that seem to us most uncontrovertibly abnormal have been used by different civilizations in the very foundations of their institutional life. Conversely the most valued traits of our normal individuals have been looked on in differently organized cultures as aberrant. Normality, in short, within a very wide range, is culturally defined. It is primarily a term for the socially elaborated segment of human behavior in any culture; and abnormality, a term for the segment that that particular civilization does not use. The very eyes with which we see the problem are conditioned by the long traditional habits of our own society.

It is a point that has been made more often in relation to ethics than in relation to psychiatry. We do not any longer make the mistake of deriving the morality of our locality and decade directly from the inevitable constitution of human nature. We do not elevate it to the dignity of a first principle. We recognize that morality differs in every society, and is a convenient term for socially approved habits. Mankind has always preferred to say, "It is morally good," rather than "It is habitual," and the fact of this preference is matter enough for a critical science of ethics. But historically the two phrases are synonymous.

The concept of the normal is properly a variant of the concept of the good. It is that which society has approved. A normal action is one which falls well within the limits of expected behavior for a particular society. Its

variability among different peoples is essentially a function of the variability of the behavior patterns that different societies have created for
themselves, and can never be wholly divorced from a consideration of
culturally institutionalized types of behavior.

Each culture is a more or less elaborate working-out of the potentiali-
ties of the segment it has chosen. In so far as a civilization is well
integrated and consistent within itself, it will tend to carry farther and
farther, according to its nature, its initial impulse toward a particular type
of action, and from the point of view of any other culture those elabora-
tions will include more and more extreme and aberrant traits.

Each of these traits, in proportion as it reinforces the chosen behavior
patterns of that culture, is for that culture normal. Those individuals to
whom it is congenial either congenitally, or as the result of childhood sets,
are accorded prestige in that culture, and are not visited with the social
contempt or disapproval which their traits would call down upon them in
a society that was differently organized. On the other hand, those individuals whose characteristics are not congenial to the selected type of
human behavior in that community are the deviants, no matter how
valued their personality traits may be in a contrasted civilization.

The Dobuan who is not easily susceptible to fear of treachery, who
enjoys work and likes to be helpful, is their neurotic and regarded as silly.
On the Northwest Coast the person who finds it difficult to read life in
terms of an insult contest will be the person upon whom fall all the
difficulties of the culturally unprovided for. The person who does not find
it easy to humiliate a neighbor, nor to see humiliation in his own experience, who is genial and loving, may, of course, find some unstandardized
way of achieving satisfactions in his society, but not in the major pat-
terned responses that his culture requires of him. If he is born to play an
important role in a family with many hereditary privileges, he can succeed only by doing violence to his whole personality. If he does not
succeed, he has betrayed his culture; that is, he is abnormal.

I have spoken of individuals as having sets toward certain types of
behavior, and of these sets as running sometimes counter to the types of
behavior which are institutionalized in the culture to which they belong.
From all that we know of contrasting cultures it seems clear that differences of temperament occur in every society. The matter has never been
made the subject of investigation, but from the available material it would
appear that these temperament types are very likely of universal recur-
rence. That is, there is an ascertainable range of human behavior that
is found wherever a sufficiently large series of individuals is observed.
But the proportion in which behavior types stand to one another in different societies is not universal. The vast majority of individuals

in any group are shaped to the fashion of that culture. In other words, most individuals are plastic to the moulding force of the society into which they are born. In a society that values trance, as in India, they will have supernormal experience. In a society that institutionalizes homosexuality, they will be homosexual. In a society that sets the gathering of possessions as the chief human objective, they will amass property. The deviants, whatever the type of behavior the culture has institutionalized, will remain few in number, and there seems no more difficulty in moulding the vast malleable majority to the "normality" of what we consider an aberrant trait, such as delusions of reference, than to the normality of such accepted behavior patterns as acquisitiveness. The small proportion of the number of the deviants in any culture is not a function of the sure instinct with which that society has built itself upon the fundamental sanities, but of the universal fact that, happily, the majority of mankind quite readily take any shape that is presented to them. . . .

SITUATIONAL, CULTURAL, AND ETHICAL RELATIVISM
William Tolhurst

William Tolhurst is associate professor of philosophy at Northern Illinois University. He has published articles in the fields of ethics and aesthetics. Tolhurst distinguishes three sorts of relativist views having to do with morality: situational relativism, cultural relativism, and ethical relativism. He argues that standard attempts to support ethical relativism by appeal to either situational relativism or cultural relativism fail.

M inimal acquaintance with other cultures suffices to show that there is widespread disagreement concerning how people ought to live. In some societies cannibalism has been approved while in ours it is viewed with disgust. We prohibit polygamy, while some think it to be permissible or even preferable to monogamy.[1] This divergence in attitude inevitably gives rise to conflict. Members of one culture believe their practices

Commissioned for this anthology, © William Tolhurst, 1989.

to be objectively correct and judge the practices of other cultures to be morally wrong. But when we become fully aware of the extent of this disagreement, we often find ourselves judging the practices of other societies to be as appropriate for them as the practices of our society are for us. Further reflection on why this is so has led some to conclude that there are no absolute standards of morality. The obvious fact of widespread moral disagreement has been taken to show that standards of morality are internal to the culture in which they operate, that there is no objective external point of view from which to evaluate a culture's internal standards. In this discussion my aim will be to examine some of the reasons which have been given for thinking that all moral norms are culturally relative.

In order to do this it will be useful to begin by distinguishing three different claims which are mentioned in the preceding paragraph. The first of these is the thesis that there is widespread disagreement between cultures concerning right and wrong. I shall call this view **cultural relativism (CR)**. The second claim says that what is right in one cultural context may be wrong in another. Since this is the thesis that what is right in one situation may be wrong in another, I shall refer to it as **situational relativism (SR)**. The final claim holds that the ultimate ethical standards for evaluating whether an action is ethically acceptable are the moral beliefs operative in the culture in which it is performed; I shall refer to it as **ethical relativism (ER)**. A more precise statement of each of these three is as follows:

CR: The moral beliefs of some cultures often conflict with the moral beliefs of other cultures.

SR: Acts which are right when performed in one culture may be wrong when performed in another.

ER: Acts are right if (and only if) they are permitted by the moral beliefs of the cultures in which they are performed.

The main concern of my discussion will be just how these three claims are related to one another. More specifically I shall be considering whether CR and SR provide any reason for accepting ER.

1.   The Argument from Cultural Relativism to Ethical Relativism

It has been held that the fact of widespread moral disagreement between cultures provides a good reason for accepting ethical relativism. Before we can consider whether this is so, we must note an important difference between the two claims. Cultural relativism is a descriptive claim; it says that the moral beliefs of people in some cultures conflict with the moral beliefs held by people in other cultures. It does not tell us whether the beliefs of those who disagree are correct or incorrect, nor does it say anything about how we should go about determining whether a moral belief is correct. Ethical relativism, by contrast, does provide us with a way to determine this. It says that a person's moral belief is correct if (and only if) it accords with the moral standards generally accepted in that person's culture. In doing so, ethical relativism provides us with a general theory of what it is that makes an action, or social practice, right or wrong. Thus ethical relativism is a normative doctrine; it provides us with a clear standard for determining how we ought to act in any situation.

The evidence for cultural relativism is overwhelming; a minimal acquaintance with the findings of anthropologists suffices to show that the moral beliefs of one culture can differ widely from those of another. The real issue concerns the significance of this disagreement. Those who infer that ethical relativism is correct from the fact of moral disagreement take this disagreement to show that all of the apparently conflicting moral beliefs are correct *for the culture in which they are held*.

One basis for questioning this inference is the fact that many moral disagreements are based on disagreements concerning matters of nonmoral fact. The moral beliefs of a culture are often based on widely held nonmoral beliefs. Let us imagine a culture in which most people approve of capital punishment only because they believe that it is a uniquely effective deterrent to criminals. Let us suppose further that it can be shown that capital punishment will not in fact increase deterrence and lower crime.[2] In such a case, the widely held belief that capital punishment is morally proper would be open to serious criticism despite the fact that most of the people in this culture accept it. In cases where two cultures disagree about a moral issue because the members of one culture are mistaken with regard to a matter of nonmoral fact, there is no good reason to take the moral beliefs of both cultures to be equally correct.

In general we cannot infer from the fact that a belief is widely held that it is in fact true. We now judge many of the nonmoral beliefs of other times and cultures to be incorrect and we seem to have good reasons for doing so. Insofar as the moral beliefs of a culture can be based on mistaken nonmoral beliefs, we can have good reasons for questioning the propriety of inferring ethical relativism from cultural relativism. Thus I conclude that the argument from cultural relativism is not, as it stands, a good reason for accepting ethical relativism.

One way to repair the argument would be to distinguish fundamental moral disagreements from nonfundamental moral disagreements. This distinction is based on a further distinction between fundamental moral beliefs and nonfundamental moral beliefs. The basic idea is that some moral beliefs are based on (or inferred from) other beliefs which one holds. For example, if one were to ask someone in our culture why it is wrong to set cats on fire for the fun of it, one might be told that doing this causes unnecessary suffering and that it is wrong to cause unnecessary suffering. In this case the moral belief that it is wrong to set cats on fire is derived from more fundamental beliefs. One of these more fundamental beliefs is the nonmoral belief that setting cats on fire causes them to suffer. Another is the moral belief that it is wrong to cause unnecessary suffering. Since the belief concerning the wrongness of incinerating cats is based on a nonmoral belief, we can see that it is not one of the person's fundamental moral beliefs. If the belief that it is wrong to cause un- necessary suffering is not based on other nonmoral beliefs, we may say that it is fundamental. Thus we may define a fundamental moral belief and a fundamental moral disagreement as follows:

A moral belief is fundamental if, and only if, it is not based on any nonmoral belief.

A moral disagreement is fundamental if, and only if, it is not based on a disagreement concerning a matter of nonmoral fact.

Given these distinctions between fundamental and nonfundamental moral beliefs and disagreements we can define more sophisticated ver- sions of cultural relativism and ethical relativism.

CR': The fundamental moral beliefs of some cultures often conflict with the fundamental moral beliefs of other cultures.

ER': Acts are right if (and only if) they are permitted by the fundamental moral beliefs of the cultures in which they are performed.

The defender of ethical relativism can grant that the moral beliefs of a particular culture can be open to criticism, but only from the internal standard provided by more fundamental moral beliefs held by the mem- bers of the culture. However, the argument from CR' to ER' is still highly problematic. Although the initial version of cultural relativism is obviously true, the same cannot be said for CR'. One could hold that *all* crosscultural moral disagreement stems from disagreement concerning matters of nonmoral fact. In order to show that this is not the case, the proponent of the argument from CR' to ER' would have to provide a great deal more evidence than is readily available from a cursory examination of the differences between cultures.

For example, in our culture it is generally accepted that people have an obligation to respect and care for the well-being of their parents regardless of how old their parents are. I shall call this belief the principle of parental care (PPC for short). Let us now suppose that we discover a culture in which people kill their parents as soon as they (the parents) show the slightest sign of becoming infirm. One might be tempted to think that in such a culture PPC is rejected and that here we have a clear case of a serious fundamental moral disagreement. But this is not at all obvious. Further investigation might well reveal that people in this culture believe that there is an afterlife in which one engages in a wide range of physical activities and that the body which one has in the afterlife is the body one had at the time of death. People in this culture kill their parents at a relatively early age in order to ensure that the parents will be able to enjoy this afterlife. They believe that in order to adequately provide for the well-being of their parents it is necessary that they kill their parents. Indeed both we and they can agree on the truth of PPC. Our disagreement concerns what PPC requires us to do in particular situations. Since their practice is based on nonmoral beliefs which we would reject, the disagreement between the imaginary culture and our culture would not be a fundamental one. It is entirely possible that all moral disagreements between cultures can be explained in this manner. If this is so, then CR' would turn out to be false. Since it is extremely difficult to rule out this possibility, it is no easy matter to come up with good evidence for accepting CR'.

But even if it could be shown that there are some fundamental moral disagreements between cultures, it is still not clear why this would show that ER' is true. If the nonmoral beliefs of a culture can be mistaken, then why can't their fundamental moral beliefs be mistaken as well? To show why this is not possible the defender of ER' would have to show why there is an important difference between moral and nonmoral beliefs which renders the former immune from criticism in a way that the latter are not. But if such an argument could be given, it would constitute an independent argument for accepting ethical relativism, one which would not need to appeal to the existence of fundamental moral disagreement.

2.   The Argument from Situational Relativism to Ethical Relativism

A more promising argument for ethical relativism is based on the hypothesis that it is possible for an act to be right in one cultural setting and wrong in another. For example, it is clear that it is morally correct to drive on the right-hand side of the road in the United States and also that it would be morally wrong to do this in Great Britain.[3] If this is so, then it would follow that situational relativism is true. Nonetheless, even if we grant that the morality of an action can vary from one culture to another, this is a curious fact which calls for some explanation. Ethical relativism is a theory of morality which provides an apparently plausible explanation of this otherwise puzzling fact. According to ethical relativism the morality of an act depends on whether it is permitted by the moral conventions of the society in which it is performed. The United States has adopted one convention concerning where one is to drive and Great Britain has adopted another. This argument is very similar to the sorts of arguments which might be given for accepting a scientific theory. One begins by noting a phenomenon which is in need of explanation. One then tries to find an hypothesis that will explain what one has observed. If this hypothesis provides a better explanation than any other available hypothesis, then it is reasonable to accept it. We might summarize the argument as follows:

1. It is possible for an act to be right in one culture and wrong in another. (Situational Relativism)

2. The best explanation of why (1) is true is the hypothesis that ER is true.

3. Therefore, probably ER is true.

This argument is more modest than the first. It is not offered as providing a conclusive reason for accepting ethical relativism, merely as one which shows that it is probably true. Even so, it is highly problematic. The main problem is whether the second step is plausible. Ethical relativism is not the only moral theory which can explain why situational relativism is true. Another theory which offers a competing explanation is utilitarianism. Utilitarianism is a moral theory which holds that whether an action is right depends on how much happiness (and unhappiness) it produces in comparison to the other actions which a person might have performed instead. According to utilitarianism a person has acted rightly whenever her act produces as great a net balance of happiness over unhappiness as was possible under the circumstances.[4] In determining whether this is so, we are to consider the happiness of everyone affected by the action. Since the amount of happiness which an act will produce can vary from one situation to another, utilitarianism provides an alternative explanation of why situational relativism is true. To see how this might work in practice we need only consider how a utilitarian would explain why it is right to drive on the right-hand side of the road in the U.S. and wrong to do this in Britain. A utilitarian would point out that driving on the right rather than the left in the U.S. would avoid accidents and hence avoid causing a great deal of unhappiness while the reverse would be true in Britain. The reason why this is so is the fact that different conventions for where one ought to drive are in effect in each country. Since each of the conventions seems to do an equally good job of promoting the well-being of those affected by them, they are equally permissible and one ought to act in accord with the requirements of whichever one is in force. Thus utilitarianism can also explain why and how social conventions have a role to play in determining what we ought to do. However, it explains this role in a way which does not render the social conventions immune to moral criticism. This is a significant difference between utilitarianism and ER.

Since moral theories like utilitarianism also provide an explanation of situational relativism, it is not obvious that the second step of the above argument for ethical relativism is true. The argument needs to be supplemented by an argument to show why ethical relativism is a *better* explanation than utilitarianism. Thus we may conclude that as it stands the argument is not a very strong reason for accepting ethical relativism.

3.   Conclusion

We have considered two lines of argument for ethical relativism. Both the argument from cultural relativism and the argument from situational relativism fail to provide a good reason for accepting ethical relativism. Nonetheless, for all we have shown thus far it is possible that this theory is true. We have not considered any compelling reasons for thinking that the revised version of the theory (ER') is false and there might be reasons which we have not considered for accepting it. Thus it is still necessary to consider the advantages and disadvantages of this theory as compared with alternative accounts of what makes something right or wrong.[5]

Notes

1.   For another example see William Shaw's discussion of the status of abortion in Spain and Japan in the following selection.
2.   I am well aware that many would deny this. I am only suggesting that it be assumed for the sake of the argument.
3.   It should be noted that it is widely held that the morality of an action can vary from one situation to another within a culture. Some would hold that sexual intercourse is morally permissible under circumstances where the participants are married (to each other) but not under circumstances where they are not. (I am indebted to Mylan Engel for this example.)

4.   In those circumstances where it is not possible to produce more happiness than unhappiness, the theory says that we should produce as small a net balance of unhappiness over happiness as possible.
5.   This will be done in the selection by William Shaw.

A CRITIQUE OF ETHICAL RELATIVISM
William H. Shaw

William H. Shaw is associate professor of philosophy at San Jose State University. After reviewing some of the reasons why ethical relativism seems attractive as a moral theory, Shaw argues that the view encounters serious difficulties. In the first place, criticism and reform of the moral principles and practices of society's morality makes no sense if one accepts ethical relativism. Furthermore, to avoid unclarity, the relativist must answer such questions as what percentage of a society must agree on some moral issue before the shared belief becomes part of the society's morality. Yet, as Shaw notes, the relativist will have a difficult time answering this and related questions. Finally, since according to ethical relativism, the moralities of different groups are equally valid, we cannot make sense of the possibility of moral progress.

The peoples and societies of the world are diverse; their institutions, fashions, ideas, manners, and mores vary tremendously. This is a simple truth. Sometimes an awareness of this diversity and of the degree to which our own beliefs and habits mirror those of the culture around us stimulates self-examination. In the realm of ethics, familiarity with strikingly different cultures has led many people to suppose that morality itself is relative to particular societies, that right and wrong vary from culture to culture.

This view is generally called "ethical relativism"; it is the normative theory that what is right is what the culture says is right. What is right in one place may be wrong in another, because the only criterion for distinguishing right from wrong—the only ethical standard for judging an action—is the moral system of the society in which the act occurs. Abortion, for example, is condemned as immoral in Catholic Spain, but practiced as a morally neutral form of birth control in Japan. According to the ethical relativist, then, abortion is wrong in Spain but morally permissible in Japan. The relativist is not saying merely that the Spanish believe abortion is abominable and the Japanese do not; that is acknowledged by everyone. Rather, the ethical relativist contends that abortion is immoral in Spain because the Spanish believe it to be immoral and morally permissible in Japan because the Japanese believe it to be so. There is no absolute ethical standard, independent of cultural context, no criterion of right and wrong by which to judge other than that of particular societies. In short, mortality is relative to society.

A different sort of relativist might hold that morality is relative, not to the culture, but to the individual. The theory that what is right and wrong is determined by what a person thinks is right and wrong, however, is not very plausible. The main reason is that it collapses the distinction between thinking something is right and its actually being right. We have all done things we thought were right at the time, but later decided were wrong. Our normal view is that we were mistaken in our original thinking; we believed the action to have been right, but it was not. In the relativist view under consideration, one would have to say that the action in question was originally right, but later wrong as our thinking changed—surely a confused and confusing thing to say! Furthermore, if we accept this view, there would be no point in debating ethics with anyone, for whatever he thought right would automatically be right for him, and whatever we thought right would be right for us. Indeed, if right were determined solely by what we took to be right, then it would not be at all clear what we are doing when we try to decide whether something is right or wrong in the first place—since we could never be mistaken! Certainly this is a muddled doctrine. Most likely its proponents have meant to emphasize that each person must determine for himself as best he can what actually is right or to argue that we ought not to blame people for acting according to their sincere moral judgments. These points are plausible, and with some qualifications, perhaps everyone would accept them, but they are not relativistic in the least.

The theory that morality is relative to society, however, is more plausible, and those who endorse this type of ethical relativism point to the diverseness of human values and the multiformity of moral codes to support their case. From our own cultural perspective, some seemingly "immoral" moralities have been adopted: polygamy, homosexuality, stealing, slavery, infanticide, and the eating of strangers have all been tolerated or even encouraged by the moral system of one society or another. In light of this, the ethical relativist feels that there can be no non-ethnocentric standard by which to judge actions. We feel the individuals in some remote tribe are wrong to practice infanticide, while other cultures are scandalized that we eat animals. Different societies have different rules; what moral authority other than society, asks the relativist, can there be? Morality is just like fashion in clothes, beauty in persons, and legality in action—all of which are relative to, and determined by, the standards of a particular culture.

In some cases this seems to make sense. Imagine that Betty is raised in a society in which one is thought to have a special obligation to look after one's maternal aunts and uncles in their old age, and Sarah lives in a society in which no such obligation is supposed. Certainly we are inclined to say that Betty really does have an obligation that Sarah does not. Sarah's culture, on the other hand, may hold that if someone keeps a certain kind of promise to you, you owe him or her a favor, or that children are not required to tell the truth to adults. Again, it seems plausible that different sorts of obligations arise in Sarah's society; in her society, promisees really do owe their promisors and children are not wrong to lie, whereas this might not be so in other cultures.

Ethical relativism explains these cases by saying that right and wrong are determined solely by the standards of the society in question, but there are other, nonrelativistic ways of accounting for these examples. In Betty's society, people live with the expectation that their sister's offspring will look after them; for Betty to behave contrary to this institution and to thwart these expectations may produce bad consequences—so there is a reason to think she has this obligation other than the fact that her society thinks she has it. In Sarah's world, on the other hand, no adult expects children to tell the truth; far from deceiving people, children only amuse them with their tall tales. Thus, we are not required to be ethical relativists in order to explain why moral obligations may differ according to the social context. And there are other cases in which ethical relativism seems implausible. Suppose Betty's society thinks that it is wicked to engage in intercourse on Sundays. We do not believe it wrong of her to do so just because her society thinks such conduct is impermissible. Or suppose her culture thinks that it is morally reprehensible to wear the fur of rare animals. Here we may be inclined to concur, but if we think it is wrong of her to do this, we do not think it so because her society says so. In this example and the previous one, we look for some reason why her conduct should be considered immoral. The fact that her society thinks it so is not enough.

Ethical relativism undermines any moral criticism of the practices of other societies as long as their actions conform to their own standards. We cannot say that slavery in a slave society like that of the American South of the last century was immoral and unjust as long as that society held it to be morally permissible. Slavery was right for them, although it is wrong for us today. To condemn slave owners as immoral, says the relativist, is to attempt to extend the standards of our society illegitimately to another culture. But this is not the way we usually think. Not only do we wish to say that a society is mistaken if it thinks that slavery (or cannibalism, cruelty, racial bigotry) is morally permissible, but we also think we have justification for so saying and are not simply projecting ethnocentrically the standards of our own culture. Indeed, far from mirroring those standards in all our moral judgments, we sometimes criticize certain principles or practices accepted by our own society. None of this makes sense from the relativist's point of view. People can be censured for not living up to their society's moral code, but that is all; the moral code itself cannot be criticized. Whatever a society takes to be morally right really is right for it. Reformers who campaign against the "injustices" of their society are only encouraging people to be immoral—that is, to depart from the moral standards of their society—unless or until the majority of society agrees with the reformers. The minority can never be right in moral matters; to be right it must become the majority.

This raises some puzzles for the theory of ethical relativism. What proportion of a society must believe, say, that abortion is permissible for it to be morally acceptable in that society—90 percent? 75 percent? 51 percent? If the figure is set high (say 75 percent) and only 60 percent of the society condone abortion, then it would not be permissible; yet it would seem odd for the relativist to say that abortion was therefore wrong, given that a majority of the population believes otherwise. Without a sufficient majority either way, abortion would be neither morally permissible nor impermissible. On the other hand, if the figure is set lower, then there will be frequent moral flip-flops. Imagine that last year abortion was thought wrong by 51 percent of the populace, but this year only 49 percent are of that opinion; that means, according to the relativist, that it was wrong last year, but is now morally permissible—and things may change again. Surely, though, something is wrong with majority rule in matters of morality. In addition one might wonder what is to count, for the relativist, as a society. In a large and heterogeneous nation like the United States, are right and wrong determined by the whole country; or do smaller societies like Harlem, San Francisco, rural Iowa, or the Chicano community in Los Angeles set their own moral standards? But if these are cohesive enough to count as morality generating societies, what about such "societies" as outlaw bikers, the drug culture, or the underworld? And what, then, does the relativist say about conflicts between these group moralities or between them and the morality of the overall society? Since an individual may be in several overlapping "societies" at the same time, he may well be receiving conflicting moral instructions—all of which, it would seem, are correct according to the relativist.

These are all questions the relativist must answer if he is to make his theory coherent. To raise them is not to refute relativism, of course, since the relativist may be able to explain satisfactorily what he means by "society," how its standards relate to those of other groups, and what is to count as moral approval by a given society. However the relativist attempts to refine his theory, he will still be maintaining that what is right is determined by what the particular society, culture, or group takes to be right and that this is the only standard by which an individual's actions can be judged. Not only does the relativist neglect to give us a reason for believing that a society's own views about morality are conclusive as to what is actually right and wrong, but also his theory does not square with our understanding of morality and the nature of ethical discourse. By contending that the moralities of different societies are all equally valid, the relativist holds that there can be no nonethnocentric ground for preferring one moral code to another, that one cannot speak of moral progress. Moralities may change, but they do not get better or worse. If words mean anything, however, it seems clear that a society that applauded the random torture of children would be immoral, even if it thought such a practice were right. It would simply be mistaken, and disastrously so. Since this is the case, ethical relativism must be false as a theory of normative ethics. . . .

THE IDEAL OF A RATIONAL MORALITY
Marcus G. Singer

Marcus G. Singer is professor of philosophy at the University of Wisconsin–Madison. He is author of Generalization in Ethics *(1961), as well as many articles on ethics. In the following selection, Singer argues, against the ethical relativist, that our critical moral judgments presuppose that there is what he calls a "critical morality"—a set of standards that we can use to evaluate an individual's or group's moral code. He then sets forth some of the central provisions of a rational morality.*

From *Proceedings and Addresses of the American Philosophical Association* 60, 1986. Copyright © 1986 by Marcus G. Singer. Reproduced by permission of the American Philosophical Association.

I

In 1924 there appeared a symposium volume entitled "Our Changing Morality"; among the authors was Bertrand Russell, who contributed a piece called "Styles in Ethics". The book dealt mainly with changes in the status of women and attitudes towards marriage, divorce, and sexual relations. Now there is no doubt that sexual morality has changed and has been changing, and if the authors thought it had changed a great deal by 1924, they, as we all know now, hadn't seen anything yet, and maybe, in the same parlance, we haven't seen anything yet either—though it is hard to imagine what else there is to see. However, if morality is changing, how can there be a single true morality? Indeed, can there be any true morality?

There can. There can because the concept of morality is systematically ambiguous. It can mean either positive morality, or personal morality, or true or rational morality.

What is called positive morality could also go under the name of conventional or received or accepted or customary morality, and, by a sort of anomaly, positive morality is largely negative. Positive morality is the customary or accepted morality of a given group at a given time. This also is an ambiguous conception. The positive morality of a given group consists in the rules or principles or standards the members of the group generally follow in their conduct, whether or not they profess to or are even aware of them. But it also consists in the standards the group professes to follow or believes it follows, whether it actually does or not. As we all know, practice does not always follow precept, and precept does not always determine practice. For some purposes it would be important to emphasize this ambivalence; I shall not stress it at the moment. By positive morality I mean some combination of these. Thus the positive morality of a group is its conventional morality, in the sense of the standards most members of the group normally follow or profess to follow or believe they follow or think they should follow, in their own conduct and in their criticism of their own conduct and the conduct and character of others. The precepts of positive morality are the precepts that are taught to the young and supported by characteristic forms of social pressure, such as expressions of approval or disapproval, acceptance or ostracism. There is no doubt there is such a thing, even though we are not always aware of what it is until we find ourselves criticizing it.

When we criticize the morality of our own society, we do so, at least in the first instance, on the basis of our own personal moral standards, which perhaps we think should become the standards of the group but which clearly are not in actuality. One's personal morality consists in one's own ideas of right and wrong, which sometimes do guide one's conduct, and if they do not guide one's conduct, at least they guide one's judgment of others. Here also we must distinguish between the standards one professes to follow and the standards one actually does follow, and here also by personal morality I shall mean some combination of these. But personal morality must be distinguished from positive morality because we recognize that our personal morality is not always congruent with the morality of the group to which we belong. If a group has attained that level of civilization at which individuality is discernible, it will contain people who have ideas of right and wrong not always congruent with that of the group, which sometimes puts them in the position of being critical of or in conflict with the group to which they belong. And of course a person's morality is not just a set of principles; it is a complex of conduct, character, and values—that is, things a person regards as important. It includes the person's moral beliefs, but is not restricted to them. It reflects the person's character and is expressed in the person's conduct, both overtly and in more subtle forms. One's morality is expressed in one's conduct even in cases where it does not determine the conduct, where, for instance, one acts contrary to one's morality. For such conduct gives rise to feelings of guilt or shame or remorse, which are expressions of one's morality (as on occasion they are expressions of one's fear of breaching positive morality or public opinion). But in distinguishing one's personal morality from the morality of one's society the emphasis is on the standards that are part of one's own idea of right and wrong, whether in agreement with one's society or not.

I doubt if any would deny the distinction between positive and personal morality, and the account I have given is fairly standard. [There are of course problems about how exactly they are to be defined, as there are problems about how they interrelate and how they ought to.] I have not distinguished between manners, morals, and mores, nor have I said anything about the role played by customs, traditions, and laws. Nor will I. What I must get to is the existence of rational morality, which may seem more dubious. Yet its reality is not far to seek. It is a presupposition of any criticism of positive morality, past or present. It is presupposed in our critical moral judgments, those based or thought to be based on reasons, that there is a rational or true morality that our judgments represent. The existence of rational morality should be manifest to anyone who has ever had a change of mind on a moral matter. "I used to think that was all right, and now I see that it is wrong" [or, "I used to think that was wrong, and now I no longer think so"] represents the form of such a change of mind. What one is thinking in such a case is that the judgment previously made is false, though once believed true, and that it is corrected by the judgment that is now held and believed true. Thus one has a conception of a more rational morality which, though elusive, is an essential presupposition of the process of thinking about one's change of view, or even having one. Where one has a belief that the positive morality of one's group (which, say, approves of slavery or torture or a caste system or apartheid or a lower wage scale for females than for males) is unjust or wrong or unjustified, one has a belief that this conventional morality ought to change and that the change ought to be in the direction of a more rational, equitable, justified arrangement. What one thinks in such a case is not just that conventional morality does not correspond to one's own personal morality (though confusion on this matter is rife in practice, with some thinking that that is sufficient for refutation, when all that it does is pit one outlook against another), but that it cannot be approved of at the bar of rational morality.

Thus, whenever one criticizes some precept or practice, not with mere irritation or aversion or anger but on the basis of reasons, one is appealing to an idea of a rational morality which provides the basis for the criticism. And at least a glimpse of this rational morality is provided to anyone who has ever changed his or her mind on a moral matter for what one regards as good reason. "I was mistaken," one thinks, "I was in error. It is hard to realize this, and even harder to admit it. But if I am to be honest with myself, if I am to be able to maintain a sense of my own integrity, I must admit that I was mistaken, I was in error." In thinking this one is necessarily thinking that something that was once and perhaps for a long time a part of one's personal morality has to this extent changed, and that the change is in the direction of a more rational or correct morality.

What is essential to this process is that the change of mind be thought to be rationally based, that it not be conceived of as something resting solely on whim. What I am claiming is that we cannot make sense of a change of moral *belief* or *judgment* or *opinion* apart from the conception of a rational or true morality. A change in one's tastes or preferences is of a different order and is not a change of moral belief. I used not to like broccoli, now I do; I used to like squash, now I don't; at an early age I liked strawberry ice cream, and after a while no longer did. (And I am not wholly inconstant in my food tastes: I am not now and never have been a liker of Brussels sprouts.) But whether or not I think I understand the causes of this change of taste, I do not for a moment think of it as something rationally based or that my later preferences are more rational or correct than my previous ones. [There are, to be sure, cases in between, where a change in taste is brought about by a conviction that some substance is harmful, as where one gives up smoking; in my own case, I used to prefer milk to whiskey, and it is not too many years ago that I came to see how childish that preference was. No doubt opinions on this latter point will differ; still these are changes that are not merely changes in taste or preference but are mixed.]

In matters of taste or preference, as distinct from matters of judgment and opinion, the concepts of truth and falsity, of being correct or incorrect, are not involved. [The conception of "good" and "bad" taste provides a complication here, but I am thinking primarily of taste in the primary sense, not in the aesthetic sense.] If I think I am "changing my mind" (to use the conventional characterization), I do not think of it in terms of a change in likes or dislikes or preference or inclination. I think that I have progressed from believing something false to believing something true, or at least to believing something more rationally based. Thus, in changing one's mind and in having the idea that one previously was mistaken in what one believed, one has the conception of a rational morality which is presupposed in the very process of thinking about and attempting to describe the change in opinion. Thus it is evident that the idea of a rational morality is involved both when we think some criticism of positive morality is rationally based—and not just something we don't like—and also when we recognize the phenomenon of changing our minds on a moral matter, which itself involves a change in our personal morality. [And these three conceptions of morality, so different and yet in some ways so similar, may well involve one another.]

II

Positive morality, then, is the morality we find around us. We are born into a culture and acquire its moral outlook as we acquire its language. We are in this sense creatures of traditions and institutions, and morality is one of the institutions that mold us. The existence of positive morality is a social fact, as indubitable as any social fact can be, even though just what it requires or permits is not always clear or indubitable, and in some cultures, such as ours, is easily confused with public opinion, which is variable, unstable, and transitory, and can be played upon by demagogues, propagandists, and advertisers. The more heterogeneous the society the more complex or confused the requirements of positive morality are. We are also born, or enter freely, into various groups or associations or sub-cultures, and these can have moralities different in important respects from that of the wider society. This creates conflicts and engenders moral problems, and helps generate a sense of personal or individual morality, which sometimes only appears to be individual but is really only another species of positive morality, that of a subculture. It turns out to be hard to avoid the influence of positive morality, and may not be avoidable altogether.

Is morality an institution? It is often said to be. But it is also said to be the basis on which institutions can be judged or criticized, and it is hard to see how it can play both roles at once. Our distinction enables us to see. Positive morality is an institution; personal morality is a social and psychological fact, hardly an institution, except in the impossible case of a society of absolute individualists. But rational morality is not and cannot be an institution. It is the basis for all fundamental criticism of social institutions, including the institution of positive morality. In his *On Liberty* Mill was criticizing not just law and not just opinion, but also the positive morality of his time and place, as he did in *The Subjection of Women*. But he did this from a position partly inside the society and partly outside, a perspective supplied in part by the positive morality of his society, which allowed such fundamental criticism to take place, and partly by the perspective of his complicated form of utilitarianism, which was put forward not as itself a form of positive morality but as something to modify it and eventually to replace it—and a very radical replacement it would have been.

The rules of positive morality and the attitudes they engender are often narrow, vicious, stupid, and cruel. They can be the results of ignorance, superstition, prejudice, fear, and folly, can embody taboos and dessicated habits, can be oppressive, intolerant, and unjust. But we can make such judgments only from the perspective provided by a more rational morality. Positive morality cannot by itself distinguish fundamental moral rules, essential to the survival of the society and the welfare of its members (such as the rules prohibiting murder, assault, mayhem, enslavement, rape, robbery, and gross dishonesty), from local rules, which vary across time and space and which constitute the part of morality that is felt as changing, sometimes giving rise to feelings of being adrift. But there is also no doing without positive morality. It is because we are brought up in a culture that has a morality that we are enabled to acquire a morality of our own and hence the capacity to improve on the morality of the group. No doubt an individual can do without a morality, for a time, as an individual can do without a language, but no society can. One of the tests of any proposed change in morality is whether it could serve as the morality of a group and work and find acceptance, in actual practice and not just in the imagination of the theorist. The received morality is what is generally accepted and conformed to, almost as something natural and certainly as something habitual. Nothing can replace it that is not capable of becoming habitual and seeming natural. . . .

III

The ideal of a rational and true morality, then, is presupposed in our critical moral judgments, those based on reasons, and also in the phenomenon of changing our minds on a moral matter, where this is regarded as not a matter of whim or taste but as something resting on reasons. The expression "changing our minds" is a curious one, containing a curious ambiguity. It sounds like something we do deliberately and on volition, like changing our shoes or our selection from a dinner menu. Sometimes, when we are merely choosing a course of amusement, or are in a situation where there is no question that we can choose what to do—as in choosing to go to the circus or the opera or the zoo or stay home instead—we can decide one way one moment and then "change our minds" the next, and this is a matter of volition or whim, having no more basis in reason or necessity than choosing to change our clothes. But when we are exercising judgment about what is true or what is right, the language of "changing our minds," though perfectly natural, is nonetheless deceptive. The true relation is that our minds are changed, but we do not choose to change them. Though our judgment may in the end actually rest on whim, we cannot think so or we could not think of it as a judgment on a matter of what is true or what is right. We necessarily think of it as something over which we have no control but must go along with. If you and I are discussing some matter on which we disagree, and I come to think that you were right and I was wrong, I may describe the phenomenon that occurs by saying "I have changed my mind," but that is just a façon de parler; you have changed my mind, or, rather, your argument has, and I have no more control over that, as distinct from the admission of it, than I do over your argument itself. Here is genuine necessity, the true home of determinism, the power of reason.

It is something of this phenomenon, with which every philosopher has to be familiar, that I have in mind in talking about rational morality. But so far we have caught merely a glimpse of it, and we want more than a glimpse. More than a glimpse can be gotten, and I go on to give some account of its contents, principles, structure, and limits.

The following are some central provisions of a rational morality:

1. A rational morality rests on principles, which provide its basis.

2. These principles are capable of rational proof, though this proof might not be evident to all who are rational.

3. Some of these principles are fundamental, others subsidiary, established by reference to the fundamental principles.

4. It contains rules of conduct, more specific than principles, which in turn rest on reasons, reasons that relate to the principles.

5. The principles of a rational morality allow for different rules for different conditions, and provide the basis for determining justified exceptions to the rules.

6. But some of the rules are fundamental and changeless, as long as human beings retain certain essential features, such as being mortal, capable of being deceived and taken advantage of, capable of feeling pain. Such rules relate to the condition of being human, a presupposition of their applicability.

7. The rules and principles of a rational morality must be acceptable in human conditions and relate to human purposes, not to purposes that are made up *a priori* having no relation to the realities of human life. This is consistent with great variety of human conditions and purposes and values, as it is consistent with certain uniformities.

8. The principles and fundamental rules of rational morality must apply to all human beings in all societies, and can be excepted or inoperative only under conditions that they themselves allow for.

9. Judgments made in a rational morality are made on the basis of reasons and on knowledge of the relevant facts—though this is perhaps a feature of rational moral persons rather than of a rational morality itself.

10. It is not necessary that specific moral judgments on concrete cases made within a rational morality be conclusively supported or even in agreement. Often conclusive reasons will not be available, as a matter of principle. Thus it may be reasonable for one person to think that some action is right in some situation, and for another to think something else right in that same situation; given that each judgment is reasonable, there will be reasons for each; given the impossibility of attaining conclusive reasons (which would rule out variability of judgment), each would be justified in acting, and judging, on his or her own judgment.

11. The rules and principles of a rational morality leave a realm of moral freedom, where it is open to each person to decide and act as he or she thinks best or wants or is inclined, without breaching any rule or principle of rational morality. This will occur even in situations that are felt to be moral and to generate moral problems.

That is to say, there is a realm of moral freedom where each person must decide individually what to do, and no right answer can be deduced or otherwise obtained from the principles. The opposite state is one of moral fanaticism, where it is supposed that in every situation there is just one course of action that is morally right and that this is or must be uniquely determined by the principles. This is the fallacy of exclusive rightness.

12. It follows that in a rational morality in most situations what specifically ought to be done, as distinct from what ought not to be done, is not deducible from the principles. One must decide. . . .

At times I have spoken of the *existence* of rational morality, at other times of the *ideal*. Is it in existence or is it an ideal? In part, both. When I speak of its existence, I do not mean that there is some place, say Rationalia, where rational morality is accepted and practiced. I mean that the idea of it is available to us, that the idea is not self-contradictory and neither fiction nor figment, and that there are occasions when it is embodied in conduct and character. But mainly I want to emphasize its status as an ideal. It is not now fully existent and most likely cannot become fully existent. When we talk about positive or personal morality, we are talking about something that already exists. But rational morality can never exist as the morality that people have in the way positive and personal morality do. When we talk about rational morality we are talking about something that does not as such already exist but that, to some degree and to some extent, ought to. We can describe it in general terms and delineate its general features. The progress of moral philosophy itself is an attempt to carry out this project, and we cannot predict the specific results of future inquiry. (If we could we could get them now.) And clearly rational morality is better than existing positive and personal codes, and in that sense desirable. Hence rational morality is ideal because it is not now actual, is better than what is actual, worth aiming at, and capable of some realization, even if not in full. . . .

CHAPTER 4

The Divine
Command Theory

GOOD AND DUTY DETERMINED
BY THE WILL OF GOD
Carl F. H. Henry

Carl F. H. Henry is an American theologian and author of numerous books and articles, including Personal Christian Ethics *(1957) from which the following selection is taken. Henry presents a version of the divine command theory according to which the goodness of something and the rightness of an action depend on God's will. "There exists no intrinsic good that is distinguishable from the will of God and to which God must conform."*

An Oxford Tutor recently acknowledged that only by a return to the Hebrew-Christian belief in the will of God as the foundation of ethics can we gain "assistance in the elucidation of an otherwise insoluble problem"—that of "achieving a real union of the two fundamental concepts of moral philosophy, duty and value."[1] Thrust into the ethical stalemate of our age, his judgment is a pertinent reminder of the uniqueness and importance of the biblical view that the good is what God does and wills.

"To the Israelites," L. A. Garrard remarks, "God is the ultimate source of all moral obligation. The only absolute duty is to do his will."[2] Hebrew-Christian ethics unequivocally defines moral obligation as man's duty to God. "The conception of moral duty and moral value as founded *in the nature of man* may have been implicit, but it was not developed as

From *Christian Personal Ethics* by Carl F. Henry, copyright 1957, Wm. B. Eerdmans, Grand Rapids, Michigan. Used by permission of the publisher.

the primary foundation of moral conduct. Man's chief duty is to obey God. . . . The emphasis is placed on *obedience*." So writes Clifford Barrett of the Hebrew-Christian ethic.[3] And in this acknowledgment he is decidedly correct. The good in Hebrew-Christian theistic ethics is not that which is adapted to human nature, but it is that to which the Creator obliges human nature.

The doctrine that the good is to be identified with the will of God cuts across secular ethics at almost every point. It protests against Utilitarianism, and its validation of the good by an appeal to consequences alone. It indicts Kant's supposition that duty and obligation rest upon a wholly immanental basis. According to Kant, the human will alone imposes man's duties upon him and affirms for him the categorical imperative. This theory of morality mediated to the modern man the artificial hope that the objectivity of the moral order could be maintained by a deliberate *severance* of duty and the good *from* the will of God. The Hebrew-Christian ethical perspective also challenges the many species of humanistic ethics so influential in the Western world today. Biblical ethics discredits an autonomous morality. It gives theonomous ethics its classic form—the identification of the moral law with the Divine will. In Hebrew-Christian revelation, distinctions in ethics reduce to what is good or what is pleasing, and to what is wicked or displeasing to the Creator-God alone. The biblical view maintains always a dynamic statement of values, refusing to sever the elements of morality from the will of God. . . .

Yet the failure to identify duty and the good with the will of God is characteristic of idealistic ethics both in ancient and in modern times. Even those moral philosophies that professed hostility to an autonomous ethic and championed the transcendent objectivity of the moral order regarded the good as something given to God. They viewed the good as something to which God was bound rather than as something legislated by him. This prepared the way for an objectionable doctrine of the "good in itself." The good then is superior to God. It is a content which is externally addressed to him as it is to us. This thesis runs through Oriental religion as well as early Western philosophy. It underlies the Zoroastrian notion that Ormazd becomes supreme through his furtherance of the good. This view assumes the existence of an ethical law superior to God himself. It is found also in the Hindu conception of the law of Karma. God is the author of sovereign causality in an impersonal moral universe. Yet not even he can interefere with its autonomous operation now that it is in movement.[4] The same idea becomes influential in Western thought through the moral philosophy of Plato, as expressed in the *Euthyphro*. Plato did not clearly identify the Idea of the Good with

God, but it stood at the apex of the Divine Ideas. Hence the good can only be regarded as confronting the eternal spiritual world.

This notion of an "intrinsic good" is alien to biblical theology. The God of Hebrew-Christian revelation is the ground of ethics. He is the supreme rule of right. He defines the whole content of morality by his own revealed will. It is not merely because "in God is the perfect realization of the Ideal Righteousness,"[5] but because God legislates the nature of the good that biblical ethics is a radical departure from the pagan view of the moral order. The distinction between intrinsic and instrumental goods may be a grossly misleading distinction. In the proper context it is quite acceptable. Scripture would solidly back the idea that the good is not to be prized merely for the sake of consequences or for the rewards it gives. That is an unacceptable variation of an instrumental good. The fear of punishment and the desire for reward may be acceptable as secondary motivations in the ethical life, but they can hardly bear the whole weight of a healthy moral outlook. The good must be good for an intrinsic reason that is apparent from an analysis of the nature of the good.

This artificial view of an instrumental good is overcome by showing clearly that the will of God is the only intrinsic good. Since the good is divinely-willed, and since God attaches rewards to its fulfillment, it is both intrinsically and instrumentally good. The good is not prized more highly if its instrumental aspects are disparaged and it is viewed as a purely intrinsic good. It is the will of God that defines the nature of intrinsic goodness. There exists no intrinsic good that is distinguishable from the will of God and to which God must conform. . . .

The question what makes an act a duty has been answered ambiguously throughout the whole history of ethics. The view that finds in consequences or good results the obligatory basis of our actions, and conceives the ethical act merely as instrumentally good is inadequate. The view that regards an action itself as intrinsically good with total indifference to its consequences, and derives goodness from obligation, is equally inadequate. Both views fail to grasp the fact that obligation and virtue, goodness and happiness, find their common ground in the Divine will. They also fail to recognize that the notions of duty and goodness cannot be analyzed so as to enforce their interlocking nature when this fundamental reference is ignored. Why should man be obliged to do what is regarded as intrinsically good without regard to the consequences? Why is he obliged to do what leads to good consequences if he is in doubt regarding the basic rightness of his action? Speculative ethics furnishes a running commentary on this tension and fails to resolve it. . . .

The moral law that lays an imperative on the human conscience is nothing more or less than the manifested will of God. For man nothing is good but union with the sovereign holy will of God. Sin therefore must not be defined primarily as social irresponsibility. Rather, it is repudiation of a Divine claim. David's words "against thee only have I sinned" (Psa. 51:4) echo the penitent's confession at its deepest level. Since God fashioned man to bear his moral likeness, nothing other than the fulfillment of this Divine purpose is man's supreme good. This purpose of God is the moral standard by which man throughout all history will be judged. Society in all its breadth and depth is responsible to the will of God. According to Christianity, to be morally good is to obey God's commands. The performance of God's will alone constitutes man's highest good. The rule of life is to "seek first the kingdom of God and his righteousness" (Mt. 6:33). . . .

Notes

1. L. A. Garrard, *Duty and the Will of God* (Oxford: Blackwell, 1938), pp. 51f.
2. *Ibid.*, p. 58.
3. Clifford C. Barrett, *Ethics* (New York: Harper, 1933), p. 49.
4. Vinjamuri E. Devadutt, in *Biblical Authority for Today*, Alan Richardson and Wolfgang Schweitzer, eds. (Philadelphia: Westminster, n.d.), p. 67.
5. George Walker, *The Idealism of Christian Ethics*, p. 30.

MORALITY WITHOUT GOD
John Arthur

John Arthur is associate professor of philosophy and director of the Program in Law and Society at State University of New York, Binghampton. Arthur considers the commonly held belief that morality somehow depends on religion. Against this he first argues that religion is unnecessary in order either to act morally or to attain moral understanding. After rejecting the idea that God is necessary in order to make sense of morality's being objective, Arthur considers the divine command theory, according to which morality depends on God's will. As Arthur points out, this theory implies that morality is arbitrary (it just so happens that God

From *Morality and Moral Controversies*, 2nd edition, John Arthur, ed., (Prentice-Hall, Inc., 1986) pp. 10–15. Copyright © John Arthur, 1986. Reprinted by permission of John Arthur.

forbids cruelty; He has no reason for doing so). Furthermore, if we accept
the divine command theory, we cannot make sense of the idea that God is
good. But if morality is independent of God's will, so that God discovers
rather than creates morality, then God's powers are limited. So either
way—whether morality is dependent on or independent of God—there
are difficulties. (We find expression of this dilemma in Plato's dialogue,
Euthyphro.) Having examined the various claims about the connection
between morality and religion, Arthur concludes by suggesting how
theists and atheists might agree on what moral rules should be adopted by
society.

The issue which I address in this paper is the nature of the connection, if any, between morality and religion. I will argue that although there are a variety of ways the two could be connected, in fact morality is independent of religion, both logically and psychologically. First, however, it will be necessary to say something about the subjects: just what are we referring to when we speak of morality and of religion?

A useful way to approach the first question—the nature of morality—is to ask what it would mean for a society to exist without a moral code. What would such a society look like? How would people think? And behave? The most obvious thing to say is that its members would never feel any moral responsibilities or any guilt. Words like duty, rights, fairness, and justice would never be used, except in the legal sense. Feelings such as that I ought to remember my parents' anniversary, that he has a moral responsibility to help care for his children after the divorce, that she has a right to equal pay for equal work, and that discrimination on the basis of race is unfair would be absent in such a society. In short, people would have no tendency to evaluate or criticize the behavior of others, nor to feel remorse about their own behavior. Children would not be taught to be ashamed when they steal or hurt others, nor would they be allowed to complain when others treat them badly.

Such a society lacks a moral code. What, then, of religion? Is it possible that a society such as the one I have described would have religious beliefs? It seems clear that it is possible. Suppose every day these same people file into their place of worship to pay homage to God (they may believe in many gods or in one all-powerful creator of heaven and earth). Often they can be heard praying to God for help in dealing with their problems and thanking Him for their good fortune. Whenever a disaster befalls them, the people assume that God is angry with them; when things go well they believe He is pleased. Frequently they give sacrifices to God, usually in the form of money spent to build beautiful temples and churches.

To have a moral code, then, is to tend to evaluate (perhaps without even expressing it) the behavior of others and to feel guilt at certain actions when we perform them. Religion, on the other hand, involves beliefs in supernatural power(s) that created and perhaps also control nature, along with the tendency to worship and pray to those supernatural forces or beings. The two—religion and morality—are thus very different. One involves our attitudes toward various forms of behavior (lying and killing, for example), typically expressed using the notions of rules, rights, and obligations. The other, religion, typically involves a different set of activities (prayer, worship) together with beliefs about the supernatural.

We come, then, to the central question: What is the connection, if any, between a society's moral code and its religious beliefs? Many people have felt that there must be a link of some sort between religious beliefs and morality. But is that so? What sort of connection might there be? In what follows I distinguish various ways in which one might claim that religion is necessary for a moral code to function in society. I argue, however, that such connections are not necessary, and indeed that often religion is detrimental to society's attempt to encourage moral conduct among its members.

One possible role which religion might play in morality relates to motives people have. Can people be expected to behave in any sort of decent way towards one another without religious faith? Religion, it is often said, is necessary so that people will DO right. Why might somebody think that? Often, we know, doing what is right has costs: you don't cheat on the test, so you flunk the course; you return the lost billfold, so you don't get the contents. Religion can provide motivation to do the right thing. God rewards those who follow His commands by providing for them a place in heaven and by insuring that they prosper and are happy on earth. He also punishes with damnation those who disobey. Other people emphasize less selfish ways in which religious motives may encourage people to act rightly. God is the creator of the universe and has ordained that His plan should be followed. How better to live one's life than to participate in this divinely ordained plan? Only by living a moral life, it is said, can people live in harmony with the larger, divinely created order.

But how are we to assess the relative strength of these various motives for acting morally, some of which are religious, others not? How important is the fear of hell or the desire to live as God wishes in motivating people? Think about the last time you were tempted to do something you knew to be wrong. Surely your decision not to do so (if that was your decision) was made for a variety of reasons: "What if I get caught? What if somebody sees me—what will he or she think? How will I feel afterwards? Will I regret it?" Or maybe the thought of cheating just doesn't occur to you. You were raised to be an honest person, and that's what you want to be—period. There are thus many motives for doing the right thing which have nothing whatsoever to do with religion. Most of us in fact do worry about getting caught, about being blamed and looked down on by others. We also may do what is right just for that reason, because it's our duty, or because we don't want to hurt others. So to say that we need religion to act morally is mistaken; indeed it seems to me that most of us, when it really gets down to it, don't give much of a thought to religion when making moral decisions. All those other reasons are the ones which we tend to consider, or else we just don't consider cheating and stealing at all. So far, then, there seems to be no reason to suppose that people can't be moral yet irreligious at the same time.

Another oft-heard argument that religion is necessary for people to do right questions whether people would know how to do the right thing without the guidance of religion. In other words, however much people may *want* to do the right thing, it is only with the help of God that true moral understanding can be achieved. People's own intellect is simply inadequate to this task; we must consult revelation for help.

Again, however, this argument fails. Just consider what we would need to know in order for religion to provide moral guidance. First we must be sure that there is a God. And then there's the question of which of the many religions is true. How can anybody be sure his or her religion is the right one? After all, if you had been born in China or India or Iran your religious views would almost certainly not have been the ones you now hold. And even if we can somehow convince ourselves that the Judeo-Christian God is the real one, we still need to find out just what it is He wants us to do. Revelation comes in at least two forms, according to theists, and not even Christians agree which form is real. Some hold that God tells us what he wants by providing us with His words: the Ten Commandments are an example. Many even believe, as Billy Graham once said, that the entire *Bible* was written by God using 39 secretaries. Others doubt that every word of the *Bible* is literally true, believing instead that it is merely an historical account of the *events* in history whereby God revealed Himself. So on this view revelation is not understood as statements made by God but, instead, as His intervening into historical events, such as leading His people from Egypt, testing Job, and sending His son as an example of the ideal life. But if we are to use revelation as a guide we must know what is to count as revelation—words given us by God, events, or both? Supposing that we could somehow solve all those puzzles, the problems of relying on revelation are still not over. Even if we can agree on who God is and on how and when He reveals Himself, we still must interpret that revelation. Some feel that the *Bible* justifies various forms of killing, including war and capital punishment, on the basis of such statements as "An eye for an eye." Others, emphasizing such sayings as "Judge not lest ye be judged" and "Thou shalt not kill," believe the *Bible* demands absolute pacifism. How are we to know which interpretation is correct?

Far from providing a short-cut to moral understanding, looking to revelation for guidance just creates more questions and problems. It is much simpler to address problems such as abortion, capital punishment, and war directly than to seek answers in revelation. In fact, not only is religion unnecessary to provide moral understanding, it is actually a hindrance. (My own hunch is that often those who are most likely to appeal to Scripture as justification for their moral beliefs are really just rationalizing positions they already believe.)

Far from religion being necessary for people to do the right thing, it often gets in the way. People do not need the motivation of religion; they for the most part are not motivated by religion as much as by other factors; and religion is of no help in discovering what our moral obligations are. But others give a different reason for claiming morality depends on religion. They think religion, and especially God, is necessary for morality because without God there could BE no right or wrong. The idea was expressed by Bishop R. C. Mortimer: "God made us and all the world. Because of that He has an absolute claim on our obedience. . . . From [this] it follows that a thing is not right simply because we think it is. . . . It is right because God commands it."[1]

What Mortimer has in mind can best be seen by comparing moral rules with legal ones. Legal statutes, we know, are created by legislatures. So if there had been no law passed requiring that people limit the speed they travel then there would be no such legal obligation. Without the commands of the legislature statutes simply would not exist. The view defended by Mortimer, often called the divine command theory, is that God has the same relation to moral law as the legislature does to statutes. Without God's commands there would be no moral rules.

Another tenet of the divine command theory, besides the belief that God is the author of morality, is that only the divine command theory is able to explain the objective difference between right and wrong. This point was forcefully argued by F. C. Copleston in a 1948 British Broadcasting Corporation radio debate with Bertrand Russell.

RUSSELL. But aren't you now saying in effect "I mean by God whatever is good or the sum total of what is good—the system of what is good, and, therefore, when a young man loves anything that is good he is loving God." Is that what you're saying, because if so, it wants a bit of arguing.

COPLESTON. I don't say, of course, that God is the sum total or system of what is good . . . but I do think that all goodness reflects God in some way and proceeds from Him, so that in a sense the man who loves what is truly good, loves God even if he doesn't advert to God. But still I agree that the validity of such an interpretation of man's conduct depends on the recognition of God's existence, obviously. . . . Let's take a look at the Commandant of the [Nazi] concentration camp at Belsen. That appears to you as undesirable and evil and to me too. To Adolph Hitler we suppose it appeared as something good and desirable. I suppose you'd have to admit that for Hitler it was good and for you it is evil.

RUSSELL. No, I shouldn't go so far as that. I mean, I think people can make mistakes in that as they can in other things. If you have jaundice you see things yellow that are not yellow. You're making a mistake.

COPLESTON. Yes, one can make mistakes, but can you make a mistake if it's simply a question of reference to a feeling or emotion? Surely Hitler would be the only possible judge of what appealed to his emotions.

RUSSELL. . . . you can say various things about that; among others, that if that sort of thing makes that sort of appeal to Hitler's emotions, then Hitler makes quite a different appeal to my emotions.

COPLESTON. Granted. But there's no objective criterion outside feeling then for condemning the conduct of the Commandant of Belsen, in your view. . . . The human being's idea of the content of the moral law depends certainly to a large extent on education and environment, and a man has to use his reason in assessing the validity of the actual moral ideas of his social group. But the possibility of criticizing the accepted moral code presupposes that there is an objective standard, that there is an ideal moral order, which imposes itself. . . . It implies the existence of a real foundation of God.[2]

God, according to Copleston, is able to provide the basis for the distinction, which we all know to exist, between right and wrong. Without that objective basis for defining human obligation we would have no real reason for condemning the behavior of anybody, even Nazis. Morality would be little more than an expression of personal feeling.

Before assessing the divine command theory, let's first consider this last point. Is it really true that only the commands of God can provide an objective basis for moral judgments? Certainly many philosophers . . . have felt that morality rests on its own, perfectly sound footing; to prejudge those efforts or others which may be made in the future as unsuccessful seems mistaken. And, second, if it were true that there is no nonreligious basis for claiming moral objectivity, then perhaps that means there simply is no such basis. Why suppose that there *must* be such a foundation?

What of the divine command theory itself? Is it reasonable, even though we need not do so, to equate something's being right with its being commanded by God? Certainly the expressions "is commanded by God" and "is morally required" do not *mean* the same thing; atheists and agnostics use moral words without understanding them to make any reference to God. And while it is of course true that God (or any other moral being for that matter) would tend to want others to do the right thing, this hardly shows that being right and being commanded by God are the same thing. Parents want their children to do the right thing, too, but that doesn't mean they, or anybody else, can make a thing right just by commanding it!

I think that, in fact, theists themselves if they thought about it would reject the divine command theory. One reason is because of what it implies. Suppose we grant (just for the sake of argument) that the divine command theory is correct. Notice what we have now said: Actions are right just because they are commanded by God. And the same, of course, can be said about those deeds which we believe are wrong. If God hadn't commanded us not to do them, they would not be wrong. (Recall the comparison made with the commands of the legislature, which would not be law except for the legislature having passed a statute.)

But now notice this. Since God is all-powerful, and since right is determined solely by His commands, is it not possible that He might change the rules and make what we now think of as wrong into right? It would seem that according to the divine command theory it is possible that tomorrow God will decree that virtues such as kindness and courage have become vices while actions which show cruelty and cowardice are the right actions. Rather than it being right for people to help each other out and prevent innocent people from suffering unnecessarily, it would be right to create as much pain among innocent children as we possibly can! To adopt the divine command theory commits its advocate to the seemingly absurd position that even the greatest atrocities might be not only acceptable but morally required if God were to command them.

Plato made a similar point in the dialogue *Euthyphro*. Socrates is asking Euthyphro what it is that makes the virtue of holiness a virtue, just as we have been asking what makes kindness and courage virtues. Euthyphro has suggested that holiness is just whatever all the gods love.

SOCRATES. Well, then, Euthyphro, what do we say about holiness? Is it not loved by all the gods, according to your definition?

EUTHYPHRO. Yes.

SOCRATES. Because it is holy, or for some other reason?

EUTHYPHRO. No, because it is holy.

SOCRATES. Then it is loved by the gods because it is holy: it is not holy because it is loved by them?

EUTHYPHRO. It seems so.

SOCRATES. . . . Then holiness is not what is pleasing to the gods, and what is pleasing to the gods is not holy as you say, Euthyphro. They are different things.

EUTHYPHRO. And why, Socrates?

SOCRATES. Because we are agreed that the gods love holiness because it is holy: and that it is not holy because they love it.[3]

Having claimed that virtues are what is loved by the gods why does Euthyphro so readily agree that the gods love holiness *because* it's holy? One possibility is that he is assuming whenever the gods love something they do so with good reason, not just arbitrarily. If something is pleasing to gods, there must be a reason. To deny this and say that it is simply the gods' love which makes holiness a virtue would mean that the gods have no basis for their opinions, that they are arbitrary. Or to put it another way, if we say that it is simply God's loving something that makes it right, then what sense does it make to say God wants us to do right? All that could mean is that God wants us to do what He wants us to do. He would have no reason for wanting it. Similarly "God is good" would mean little more than "God does what He pleases." Religious people who find this an unacceptable consequence will reject the divine command theory.

But doesn't this now raise another problem? If God approves kindness because it is a virtue, then it seems that God discovers morality rather than inventing it. And haven't we then suggested a limitation on God's power, since He now, being a good God, must love kindness and command us not to be cruel? What is left of God's omnipotence?

But why should such a limitation on God be unacceptable for a theist? Because there is nothing God cannot do? But is it true to say that God can do absolutely anything? Can He, for example, destroy Himself? Can God make a rock so heavy that He cannot lift it? Or create a universe which was never created by Him? Many have thought that God's inability to do these sorts of things does not constitute a genuine limitation on His power because these are things which cannot logically be done. Thomas Aquinas, for example, wrote that, "whatever implies contradiction does not come within the scope of divine omnipotence, because it cannot have the aspect of possibility. Hence it is more appropriate to say that such things cannot be done than that God cannot do them."[4] Many theists reject the view that there is nothing which God cannot do.

But how, then, ought we to understand God's relationship to morality if we reject the divine command theory? Can religious people consistently maintain their faith in God the Creator and yet deny that what is right is right because He commands it? I think the answer to this is "yes." First, note that there is still a sense in which God could change morality (assuming, of course, there is a God). Whatever moral code we decide is best (most justified), that choice will in part depend on such factors as how we reason, what we desire and need, and the circumstances in which we find ourselves. Presumably, however, God could have constructed us or our environment very differently, so that we didn't care about freedom, weren't curious about nature, and weren't influenced by others' suffering. Or perhaps our natural environment could be altered so that it is less hostile to our needs and desires. If He had created either nature or us that way, then it seems likely that the most justified moral code might be different in important ways from the one it is now rational for us to support. In that sense, then, morality depends on God whether or not one supports the divine command theory.

In fact, it seems to me that it makes little difference for ethical questions whether a person is religious. The atheist will treat human nature simply as a given, a fact of nature, while the theist may regard it as the product of divine intention. But in any case the right thing to do is to follow the best moral code, the one that is most justified. Instead of relying on revelation to discover morality, religious and nonreligious people alike can inquire into which system is best.

In sum, I have argued first that religion is neither necessary nor useful in providing moral motivation or guidance. My objections to the claim that without God there would be no morality are somewhat more complex. First, it is wrong to say that only if God's will is at its base can morality be objective. The idea of the best moral code—the one fully rational persons would support—may prove to provide sound means to evaluate one's own code as well as those of other societies. Furthermore, the divine command theory should not be accepted even by those who are religious. This is because it implies what clearly seems absurd, namely that God might tomorrow change the moral rules and make performing the most extreme acts of cruelty an obligation we all should meet. And, finally, I discussed how the theist and atheist might hope to find common ground about the sorts of moral rules to teach our children and how we should evaluate each other's behavior. Far from helping resolve moral disputes, religion does little more than sow confusion. Morality does not need religion and religion does not need morality.

Notes

1. R. C. Mortimer, *Christian Ethics* (London: Hutchinson's University Library, 1950) pp. 7–8.
2. This debate was broadcast on the Third Program of the British Broadcasting Corporation in 1948.
3. Plato, *Euthyphro* tr. H. N. Fowler (Cambridge Mass.: Harvard University Press, 1947).
4. Thomas Aquinas, *Summa Theologica*, Part I, Q. 25, Art. 3.

THE THEOLOGICAL FRONTIER OF ETHICS
J. L. Mackie

J. L. Mackie (1914–1982) was a fellow in philosophy at University College, Oxford, and the author of many articles and books. The following is taken from his widely read Ethics: Inventing Right and Wrong *(1977). In it, Mackie attempts to resolve the* Euthyphro *dilemma described in the above selection by Arthur. He suggests that the dilemma can be avoided by arguing that in one sense morality is independent of God's will, and in another sense it is not. We might take moral qualities to be independent of God's will in the sense that the rightness of an action, for example, depends on facts about human beings. Yet we can still hold that God's commands provide us the reason for doing what is right and avoiding what is wrong. In this view, morality is not arbitrary, because it is rooted in facts about human nature. Moreover, God plays an important role in adding an "objectively prescriptive" dimension to morality.*

The possible relations between morality and religion are brought sharply into focus by a dilemma first presented in Plato's dialogue

Euthyphro. Does God love what is good, or command what is right, because it is good or right, or is it good or right because he loves or commands it? That is, do human actions, dispositions, and so on have whatever moral qualities they do have independently of any divine command or approbation, so that when God commands or approves of them he is himself responding to the qualities he finds in them; or are there no moral distinctions independent of and antecedent to God's will, so that his will constitutes whatever moral qualities there are, and to be good or right is simply to be approved of or commanded by God?

The second alternative would have the consequence that the description of God himself as good would reduce to the rather trivial statement that God loves himself, or likes himself the way he is. It would also seem to entail that obedience to moral rules is merely prudent but slavish conformity to the arbitrary demands of a capricious tyrant. Realizing this, many religious thinkers have opted for the first alternative. But this seems to have the almost equally surprising consequence that moral distinctions do not depend on God any more than, say, arithmetical ones, hence that ethics is autonomous and can be studied and discussed without reference to religious beliefs, that we can simply close the theological frontier of ethics.

But the dilemma has these stark alternative consequences only if we assume that moral qualities come in one piece, as unanalysable atomic units, which must simply be assigned to one place or another, as being either wholly independent of or wholly constituted by the will of God. In fact we can take them apart. It might be that there is one kind of life which is, in a purely descriptive sense, most appropriate for human beings as they are—that is, that it alone will fully develop rather than stunt their natural capacities and that in it, and only in it, can they find the fullest and deepest satisfaction. It might then follow that certain rules of conduct and certain dispositions were appropriate (still purely descriptively) in that they were needed to maintain this way of life. All these would then be facts as hard as any in arithmetic or chemistry, and so logically independent of any command or prescriptive will of God, though they might be products of the creative will of God which, in making men as they are, will have made them such that this life, these rules, and these dispositions are appropriate for them. But, further, God might require men to live in this appropriate way, and might enjoin obedience to the related rules. This would add an objectively prescriptive element to what otherwise were hard, descriptive, truths, but in a quite non-mysterious way: these would be literally commands issued by an identifiable authority. Finally, it might be that though it is a hard fact that this life, these rules, and these dispositions are appropriate for men, this fact is not completely accessible to direct human investigation; men cannot by observation and experiment discover exactly what life is ultimately most satisfying for them; but given that God knows this, desires that they should so live, and has somehow revealed corresponding explicit instructions to them, men can reasonably resort to such revelations to infer this indirectly, so as to complete their determination of this required and ultimately satisfying life.

This theory is at least coherent; and in the face of it the dilemma falls apart. The descriptive component of moral distinctions is logically independent of God's will: God approves of this way of life because it is, in a purely descriptive sense, appropriate for men. But the prescriptive component of those distinctions is constituted by God's will. The picture of God as an arbitrary tyrant is replaced by the belief that he demands of his creatures only that they should live in what will be, for them, the most satisfying way. We can then say that God is good meaning, descriptively, just this; any prescriptive or evaluative component in 'good' *as applied to God* will be subjective, it will express *our* approval of the sort of thing God does; the God-based objectively prescriptive element in moral terms as applied to human actions can have no non-trivial application to God.

The fact that we can thus employ the descriptive/prescriptive distinction to clarify what is, I believe, a fairly orthodox view and resolve what would otherwise be an embarrassing dilemma should make theists more tolerant than many of them are of the use of this distinction in ethics. But what concerns us more is that if this theistic position were not only coherent but also correct it could make a significant difference to moral philosophy. . . .

. . . It therefore matters a lot for moral philosophy whether any such theistic view is correct: the theological frontier of ethics remains open.

CHAPTER 5

The Natural Law Theory

TREATISE ON LAW
St. Thomas Aquinas

Aquinas (1225–1274) is one of the most important figures in Western intellectual history. In the following passage from his Summa Theologica, *he presents a classical version of the natural law theory of morality. Aquinas defines law as "an ordinance of reason for the common good, promulgated by him who has care of the community." He then distinguishes four sorts of law: eternal, natural, human, and divine. Natural law is the part of God's eternal law that involves how human beings ought to conduct themselves. The first precept of natural law is that "good is to be done and promoted, evil is to be avoided." Human beings have natural inclinations to seek their own good, including such things as self-preservation, continuance of the species, education, and living in society. Such ends, then, are good for human beings, and the first precept of natural law enjoins us to preserve and maintain them. Thus, for Aquinas, basic moral precepts are derived from facts about human nature.*

QUESTION 90

First Article: Whether law is something pertaining to reason?

. . . It belongs to the law to command and to forbid. But it belongs to reason to command, as was stated above. Therefore law is something pertaining to reason. . . . Law is a rule and measure of acts, whereby man is induced to act or is restrained from acting; for *lex (law)* is derived from *ligare (to bind)*, because it binds one to act. Now the rule and measure of

From Anton C. Pegis, ed., *Basic Writings of St. Thomas Aquinas* (New York: Random House, 1945). Reprinted by permission of the A. C. Pegis Estate.

human acts is the reason, which is the first principle of human acts, as is evident from what has been stated above. For it belongs to the reason to direct to the end, which is the first principle in all matters of action. . . .

Second Article: Whether law is always directed to the common good?

. . . Isidore says that *laws are enacted for no private profit, but for the common benefit of the citizens.* . . . As we have stated above, law belongs to that which is a principle of human acts, because it is their rule and measure. Now as reason is a principle of human acts, so in reason itself there is something which is the principle in respect of all the rest. Hence to this principle chiefly and mainly law must needs be referred. Now the first principle in practical matters, which are the object of the practical reason, is the last end: and the last end of human life is happiness or beatitude, as we have stated above. Consequently, law must needs concern itself mainly with the order that is in beatitude. Moreover, since every part is ordained to the whole as the imperfect to the perfect, and since one man is a part of the perfect community, law must needs concern itself properly with the order directed to universal happiness. Therefore the Philosopher, in the above definition of legal matters, mentions both happiness and the body politic, since he says that we call those legal matters *just which are adapted to produce and preserve happiness and its parts for the body politic.* For the state is a perfect community, as he says in *Politics i.* . . . Since law is chiefly ordained to the common good, any other precept in regard to some individual work must needs be devoid of the nature of a law, save in so far as it regards the common good. Therefore every law is ordained to the common good. . . .

Third Article: Whether the reason of any man is competent to make laws?

. . . Isidore says, and the *Decretals* repeat: *A law is an ordinance of the people, whereby something is sanctioned by the Elders together with the Commonalty.* Therefore not everyone can make laws. . . . A law, properly speaking, regards first and foremost the order to the common good. Now to order anything to the common good belongs either to the whole people, or to someone who is the viceregent of the whole people. Hence the making of a law belongs either to the whole people or to a public personage who has care of the whole people; for in all other matters the directing of anything to the end concerns him to whom the end belongs. . . .

As was stated above, a law is in a person not only as in one that rules, but also, by participation, as in one that is ruled. In the latter way, each one is a law to himself, in so far as he shares the direction that he receives from one who rules him. Hence the same text goes on: *Who show the work of the law written in their hearts* (Rom. 2:15).

Fourth Article: Whether promulgation is essential to law?

. . . It is laid down in the *Decretals* that *laws are established when they are promulgated.* . . . As was stated above, a law is imposed on others as a rule and measure. Now a rule or measure is imposed by being applied to those who are to be ruled and measured by it. Therefore, in order that a law obtain the binding force which is proper to a law, it must needs be applied to the men who have to be ruled by it. But such application is made by its being made known to them by promulgation. Therefore promulgation is necessary for law to obtain its force. . . . Law is nothing else than an ordinance of reason for the common good, promulgated by him who has the care of the community. . . .

The natural law is promulgated by the very fact that God has instilled it into man's mind so as to be known by him naturally. . . .

QUESTION 91

First Article: Whether there is an eternal law?

. . . As we have stated above, law is nothing else but a dictate of practical reason emanating from the ruler who governs a perfect community. Now it is evident, granted that the world is ruled by divine providence, as was stated in the First Part, that the whole community of the universe is governed by the divine reason. Therefore the very notion of the government of things in God, the ruler of the universe, has the nature of a law. And since the divine reason's conception of things is not subject to time, but is eternal, according to *Prov.* 8:23, therefore it is that this kind of law must be called eternal. . . .

Promulgation is made by word of mouth or in writing, and in both ways the eternal law is promulgated, because both the divine Word and the writing of the Book of Life are eternal. . . .

Second Article: Whether there is in us a natural law?

. . . The *Gloss* on *Rom.* 2:14 (*When the Gentiles, who have not the law, do by nature those things that are of the law*) comments as follows: *Although they have no written law, yet they have the natural law, whereby each one knows, and is conscious of, what is good and what is evil.* . . . As we have stated above, law, being a rule and measure, can be in a person in two ways: in one way, as in him that rules and measures; in another way, as in that which is ruled and measured, since a thing is ruled and measured in so far as it partakes of the rule or measure. Therefore, since all things subject to divine providence are ruled and measured by the eternal law, as was stated above, it is evident that all things partake in some way in the eternal law, in so far as, namely, from its being imprinted on them, they derive their respective inclinations to their proper acts and ends. Now among all others, the rational creature is subject to divine providence in a more excellent way, in so far as it itself partakes of a share of providence, by being provident both for itself and for others. Therefore it has a share of the eternal reason, whereby it has a natural inclination to its proper act and end; and this participation of the eternal law in the rational creature is called the natural law. Hence the Psalmist, after saying (*Ps*. 4:6): *Offer up the sacrifice of justice*, as though someone asked what the works of justice are, adds: *Many say, Who showeth us good things?* in answer to which question he says: *The light of Thy countenance, O Lord, is signed upon us*. He thus implies that the light of natural reason, whereby we discern what is good and what is evil, which is the function of the natural law, is nothing else than an imprint on us of the divine light. It is therefore evident that the natural law is nothing else than the rational creature's participation of the eternal law.

Third Article: Whether there is a human law?

. . . Augustine distinguishes two kinds of law, the one eternal, the other temporal, which he calls human. . . . As we have stated above, a law is a dictate of the practical reason. . . . Accordingly, we conclude that, just as in the speculative reason, from naturally known indemonstrable principles we draw the conclusions of the various sciences, the knowledge of which is not imparted to us by nature, but acquired by the efforts of reason, so too it is that from the precepts of the natural law, as from common and indemonstrable principles, the human reason needs to proceed to the more particular determination of certain matters. These particular determinations, devised by human reason, are called human laws, provided that the other essential conditions of law be observed, as was stated above. Therefore Tully says in his *Rhetoric* that *justice has its source in nature; thence certain things came into custom by reason of their utility; afterwards these things which emanated from nature, and were approved by custom, were sanctioned by fear and reverence for the law*. . . . Just as on the part of the speculative reason, by a natural participation of divine wisdom, there is in us the knowledge of certain common principles, but not a proper knowledge of each single truth, such as that contained in the divine wisdom, so, too, on the part of the practical reason, man has a natural participation of the eternal law, according to certain common principles, but not as regards the particular determinations of individual cases, which are, however, contained in the eternal law. Hence the need for human reason to proceed further to sanction them by law.

Fourth Article: Whether there was any need for a divine law?

. . . Besides the natural and the human law it was necessary for the directing of human conduct to have a divine law. And this for four reasons. First, because it is by law that man is directed how to perform his proper acts in view of his last end. Now if man were ordained to no other end than that which is proportionate to his natural ability, there would be no need for man to have any further direction, on the part of his reason, in addition to the natural law and humanly devised law which is derived from it. But since man is ordained to an end of eternal happiness which exceeds man's natural ability, as we have stated above, therefore it was necessary that, in addition to the natural and the human law, man should be directed to his end by a law given by God.

Secondly, because, by reason of the uncertainty of human judgment, especially on contingent and particular matters, different people form different judgments on human acts; whence also different and contrary laws result. In order, therefore, that man may know without any doubt what he ought to do and what he ought to avoid, it was necessary for man to be directed in his proper acts by a law given by God, for it is certain that such a law cannot err.

Thirdly, because man can make laws in those matters of which he is competent to judge. But man is not competent to judge of interior movements, that are hidden, but only of exterior acts which are observable; and yet for the perfection of virtue it is necessary for man to conduct himself rightly in both kinds of acts. Consequently, human law could not sufficiently curb and direct interior acts, and it was necessary for this purpose that a divine law should supervene.

Fourthly, because, as Augustine says, human law cannot punish or forbid all evil deeds, since, while aiming at doing away with all evils, it would do away with many good things, and would hinder the advance of the common good, which is necessary for human living. In order, therefore, that no evil might remain unforbidden and unpunished, it was necessary for the divine law to supervene, whereby all sins are forbidden.

Fifth Article: Whether there is but one divine law?

. . . Things may be distinguished in two ways. First, as those things that are altogether specifically different, *e.g.*, a horse and an ox. Secondly, as perfect and imperfect in the same species, *e.g.*, a boy and a man; and in this way the divine law is distinguished into Old and New. Hence the Apostle (*Gal.* 3:24, 25) compares the state of man under the Old Law to that of a child *under a pedagogue;* but the state under the New Law, to that of a full grown man, who is *no longer under a pedagogue.*

Now the perfection and imperfection of these two laws is to be taken in connection with the three conditions pertaining to law, as was stated above. For, in the first place, it belongs to law to be directed to the common good as to its end, as was stated above. This good may be twofold. It may be a sensible and earthly good, and to this man was directly ordained by the Old Law. Hence it is that, at the very outset of the Law, the people were invited to the earthly kingdom of the Chananaceans (*Exod.* 3:8, 17). Again it may be an intelligible and heavenly good, and to this, man is ordained by the New Law. Therefore, at the very beginning of His preaching, Christ invited men to the kingdom of heaven, saying (*Matt.* 4:17): *Do penance, for the kingdom of heaven is at hand.* Hence Augustine says that *promises of temporal goods are contained in the Old Testament, for which reason it is called old; but the promise of eternal life belongs to the New Testament.*

Secondly, it belongs to law to direct human acts according to the order of justice; wherein also the New Law surpasses the Old Law, since it directs our internal acts, according to *Matt.* 5:20: *Unless your justice abound more than that of the Scribes and Pharisees, you shall not enter into the kingdom of heaven.* Hence the saying that *the Old Law restrains the hand, but the New Law controls the soul.*

Thirdly, it belongs to law to induce men to observe its commandments. This the Old Law did by the fear of punishment, but the New Law, by love, which is poured into our hearts by the grace of Christ, bestowed in the New Law, but foreshadowed in the Old. Hence Augustine says that *there is little difference between the Law and the Gospel—fear* [timor] *and love* [amor]. . . .

QUESTION 94

Second Article: Whether the natural law contains several precepts, or only one?

. . . The precepts of the natural law are to the practical reason what the first principles of demonstrations are to the speculative reason, because both are self-evident principles. Now a thing is said to be self-evident in two ways: first, in itself; secondly, in relation to us. Any proposition is said to be self-evident in itself, if its predicate is contained in the notion of the subject; even though it may happen that to one who does not know the definition of the subject, such a proposition is not self-evident. For instance, this proposition, *Man is a rational being*, is, in its very nature, self-evident, since he who says *man*, says *a rational being*; and yet to one who does not know what a man is, this proposition is not self-evident. Hence it is that, as Boethius says, certain axioms or propositions are universally self-evident to all; and such are the propositions whose terms are known to all, as, *Every whole is greater than its part*, and *Things equal to one and the same are equal to one another*. But some propositions are self-evident only to the wise, who understand the meaning of the terms of such propositions. Thus to one who understands that an angel is not a body, it is self-evident that an angel is not circumscriptively in a place. But this is not evident to the unlearned, for they cannot grasp it.

Now a certain order is to be found in those things that are apprehended by men. For that which first falls under apprehension is *being*, the understanding of which is included in all things whatsoever a man apprehends. Therefore the first indemonstrable principle is that *the same thing cannot be affirmed and denied at the same time*, which is based on the notion of *being and not-being*: and on this principle all others are based, as is stated in *Metaph*. iv. Now as *being* is the first thing that falls under the apprehension absolutely, so *good* is the first thing that falls under the apprehension of the practical reason, which is directed to action (since every agent acts for an end, which has the nature of good). Consequently, the first principle in the practical reason is one founded on the nature of good, viz., that *good is that which all things seek after*. Hence this is the first precept of law, that *good is to be done and promoted, and evil is to be avoided*. All other precepts of the natural law are based upon this; so that all the things which the practical reason naturally apprehends as man's good belong to the precepts of the natural law under the form of things to be done or avoided.

Since, however, good has the nature of an end, and evil, the nature of the contrary, hence it is that all those things to which man has a natural inclination are naturally apprehended by reason as being good, and consequently as objects of pursuit, and their contraries as evil, and objects of avoidance. Therefore, the order of the precepts of the natural law is according to the order of natural inclinations. For there is in man, first of all, an inclination to good in accordance with the nature which he has in common with all substances, inasmuch, namely, as every substance seeks the preservation of its own being, according to its nature; and by reason of this inclination, whatever is a means of preserving human life, and of warding off its obstacles, belongs to the natural law. Secondly, there is in man an inclination to things that pertain to him more specially, according to that nature which he has in common with other animals; and in virtue of this inclination, those things are said to belong to the natural law *which nature has taught to all animals*, such as sexual intercourse, the education of offspring, and so forth. Thirdly, there is in man an inclination to good according to the nature of his reason, which nature is proper to him. Thus man has a natural inclination to know the truth about God, and to live in society; and in this respect, whatever pertains to this inclination belongs to the natural law: *e.g.*, to shun ignorance, to avoid offending those among whom one has to live, and other such things regarding the above inclination. . . .

All these precepts of the law of nature have the character of one natural law, inasmuch as they flow from one first precept. . . .

All the inclination of any parts whatsoever of human nature, *e.g.*, of the concupiscible and irascible parts, in so far as they are ruled by reason, belong to the natural law; and are reduced to one first precept, as was stated above. And thus the precepts of the natural law are many in themselves, but they are based on one common foundation. . . .

Third Article: Whether all the acts of the virtues are prescribed by the natural law?

. . . We may speak of virtuous acts in two ways: first, in so far as they are virtuous; secondly, as such and such acts considered in their proper species. If, then, we are speaking of the acts of the virtues in so far as they are virtuous, thus all virtuous acts belong to the natural law. For it has been stated that to the natural law belongs everything to which a man is inclined according to his nature. Now each thing is inclined naturally to an operation that is suitable to it according to its form: *e.g.*, fire is inclined to give heat. Therefore, since the rational soul is the proper form of man, there is in every man a natural inclination to act according to reason; and this is to act according to virtue. Consequently, considered thus, all the acts of the virtues are prescribed by the natural law, since each one's reason naturally dictates to him to act virtuously. But if we speak of virtuous acts, considered in themselves, *i.e.*, in their proper species, thus not all virtuous acts are prescribed by the natural law. For many things are done virtuously, to which nature does not primarily incline, but which, through the inquiry of reason, have been found by men to be conducive to well-living. . . .

Temperance is about the natural concupiscences of food, drink and sexual matters, which are indeed ordained to the common good of nature, just as other matters of law are ordained to the moral common good. . . .

By human nature we may mean either that which is proper to man, and in this sense all sins, as being against reason, are also against nature, as Damascene states; or we may mean that nature which is common to man and other animals, and in this sense, certain special sins are said to be against nature: *e.g.* contrary to sexual intercourse, which is natural to all animals, is unisexual lust, which has received the special name of the unnatural crime. . . .

Fourth Article: Whether the natural law is the same in all men?

. . . As we have stated above, to the natural law belong those things to which a man is inclined naturally; and among these it is proper to man to be inclined to act according to reason. Now it belongs to the reason to proceed from what is common to what is proper, as is stated in *Physics* i. The speculative reason, however, is differently situated, in this matter, from the practical reason. For, since the speculative reason is concerned chiefly with necessary things, which cannot be otherwise than they are, its proper conclusions, like the universal principles, contain the truth without fail. The practical reason, on the other hand, is concerned with contingent matters, which is the domain of human actions; and, consequently, although there is necessity in the common principles, the more we descend towards the particular, the more frequently we encounter defects. Accordingly, then, in speculative matters truth is the same in all men, both as to principles and as to conclusions; although the truth is not known to all as regards the conclusions, but only as regards the principles which are called *common notions*. But in matters of action, truth or practical rectitude is not the same for all as to what is particular, but only as to the common principles; and where there is the same rectitude in relation to particulars, it is not equally known to all.

It is therefore evident that, as regards the common principles whether of speculative or of practical reason, truth or rectitude is the same for all, and is equally known by all. But as to the proper conclusions of the speculative reason, the truth is the same for all, but it is not equally known to all. Thus, it is true for all that the three angles of a triangle are together equal to two right angles, although it is not known to all. But as to the proper conclusions of the practical reason, neither is the truth or rectitude the same for all, nor, where it is the same, is it equally known by all. Thus, it is right and true for all to act according to reason, and from this principle it follows, as a proper conclusion, that goods entrusted to another should be restored to their owner. Now this is true for the majority of cases. But it may happen in a particular case that it would be injurious, and therefore unreasonable, to restore goods held in trust; for instance, if they are claimed for the purpose of fighting against one's country. And this principle will be found to fail the more, according as we descend further towards the particular, *e.g.*, if one were to say that goods held in trust should be restored with such and such a guarantee, or in such and such a way; because the greater the number of conditions added, the greater the number of ways in which the principle may fail, so that it be not right to restore or not to restore.

Consequently, we must say that the natural law, as to the first common principles, is the same for all, both as to rectitude and as to knowledge. But as to certain more particular aspects, which are conclusions, as it were, of those common principles, it is the same for all in the majority of cases, both as to rectitude and as to knowledge; and yet in some few cases it may fail, both as to rectitude, by reason of certain obstacles (just as natures subject to generation and corruption fail in some few cases because of some obstacle), and as to knowledge, since in some the reason is perverted by passion, or evil habit, or an evil disposition of nature. Thus at one time theft, although it is expressly contrary to the natural law, was not considered wrong among the Germans, as Julius Caesar relates.

THE ETHICS OF NATURAL LAW
C. E. Harris

C. E. Harris is associate professor of philosophy at Texas A & M University. In the selection below he presents a version of the natural-law theory, including a discussion of the principle of double effect, which plays an important role in modern natural-law thinking.

What Is Natural Law?   The name *natural law* can be misleading. It implies that ethical laws are like "laws of nature" or scientific laws. An example of a scientific law is Boyle's law in physics, which states that the product of the pressure and the specific volume of a gas at constant temperature is constant. But scientific laws are *descriptive;* they state how phenomena in nature do in fact always behave. Ethical laws, on the other hand, are *prescriptive;* they stipulate how people *should* behave, whether or not they do so. Natural-law theorists assume that human beings have free will and that they can decide whether to act as they ought to act. This discussion implies that the word *law* has more in common with civil laws than with natural laws, because both civil and ethical laws can be disobeyed. Natural phenomena presumably always act according to the laws of nature, whereas people are not necessarily compelled to behave legally or morally.

But the analogy with civil laws can also be misleading, for the point of the term *natural* is to contrast ethical laws with the laws of governments. When the Roman jurists were looking for legal concepts that could apply throughout the Roman empire, they turned to the philosophy of natural law precisely because it proposed that certain ethical laws are "natural" rather than "conventional"; that is, they apply equally to all human beings, regardless of the conventions, customs, or beliefs of their particular society. These natural laws for all human behavior thus could serve as a basis for judging the actions of people throughout the Roman empire. Therefore we can say that *natural law* refers to ethical guidelines or rules that stipulate what people ought to do rather than what they in fact do and that apply equally to all humanity because they are rooted in human nature itself.

The term *natural law* can be misleading because it inevitably brings to mind some kind of ethical legalism—the belief that hard-and-fast guidelines cover every possible detail of conduct. This characterization, however, is unfair to the natural-law tradition. The greatest exponent of natural law, Thomas Aquinas (1225–1274), believed that the basic outlines of proper human behavior are relatively clear. But he also taught that, the closer we come to particular moral judgments, the more prone we are to error and the more room we make for differences of opinion. Some contemporary natural-law theorists even believe that natural law has a historical dimension, so that what is right in one epoch may not be right in another. Whether or not this view is accepted, the lively discussions of ethical issues in the Roman Catholic Church, where natural-law thinking is especially prominent, show that natural-law theorists by no means believe that all ethical problems have already been solved. The word *law* merely refers to the prescriptive character of the rules that should govern human behavior.

The natural-law theorist does, however, believe in an objective standard for morality: Moral truth exists just as scientific truth exists. The natural-law theorist cannot be a radical ethical relativist or an ethical sceptic. He generally believes we know the basic outlines of this standard, but this belief does not mean we have interpreted the implications of this standard correctly in every case. In ethics, as in science, human beings continually search for truth. The belief in objective truth should be no more stifling of human freedom and creativity in ethics than it is in science.

Human Nature and Natural Inclinations   What is the standard of truth in ethics? As an approximation we can say that the standard is human nature. People should do whatever promotes the fulfillment of human nature. Here again we can point out the similarity between natural law and egoism. But natural-law theorists have always believed that the individual alone cannot determine what counts as human nature. How then do we determine what human nature is?

Let us consider some analogous situations that illustrate the difficulty in describing human nature. It is often useful to describe something's nature in terms of its function—that is, in terms of the purpose it serves. For example; we can describe the nature of a pencil in terms of its function or purpose of enabling humans to make marks on paper. A "good" pencil is one that performs this function well—without smudging or scratching or breaking, for example. Similarly, if an automobile's function is to provide transportation, a good automobile is one that provides comfortable and reliable transportation. The function of a tomato plant is to produce tomatoes, and a good tomato plant is one that produces an abundance of tomatoes of high quality.

We can also determine the function of human beings if we confine a person to one particular social role. The function of a farmer is to grow food, and a good farmer produces food efficiently and with proper care for the animals and the land for which he has responsibility. By similar reasoning we can say that a good father is one who attends diligently to the welfare of his children. But now let us take human beings out of their social roles and ask simply "What is the function of a human being?" Here we see the problem faced by those who attempt to base ethics on human nature. Generally speaking, the more complex the animal, the more varied its behavior and presumably the less clearly defined is its "nature." The freedom of action possessed by human beings makes it plausible to argue, as some philosophers have, that human beings are characterized precisely by the fact that they have no set nature or function. How can we make sense out of natural law in the face of these problems?

Fortunately we can take another, more promising approach to discovering what human nature is like. One way to determine the characteristics of a thing is to observe its behavior. In chemistry we learn about the nature of iron by observing how it reacts with other elements. Perhaps we can find out what human nature is like by ascertaining those "natural inclinations," as Aquinas put it, that human beings have in common. To put it another way, perhaps we can discover what human nature is by identifying those goals that human beings generally tend to seek. These values would presumably reflect the structure of our human nature, which natural law directs us to follow. Therefore we shall propose the following statement as the moral standard of natural law:

MS: Those actions are right that promote the values specified by the natural inclinations of human beings.

How do we find out what these natural inclinations are? We might first consult psychologists, sociologists, or anthropologists. Some contemporary natural-law theorists use studies from the social sciences to defend their conclusions. However, the natural-law tradition developed before the rise of the social sciences, and a more informal method of observation was used to discover the basic human inclinations. Most natural-law theorists would maintain that these observations are still valid. We can divide the values specified by natural human inclinations into two basic groups: (1) biological values, which are strongly linked with our bodies and which we share with other animals, and (2) characteristically human values, which are closely connected with our more specifically human aspects. (We will not call this second group uniquely human values because some of the inclinations that point to these values, such as the tendency to live in societies, are not unique to human beings.) We can summarize the values and the natural inclinations that point to them as follows:

1. Biological Values
   a. Life. From the natural inclinations that we and all other animals have to preserve our own existence, we can infer that life is good, that we have an obligation to promote our own health, and that we have the right of self-defense. Negatively, this inclination implies that murder and suicide are wrong.
   b. Procreation. From the natural inclination that we and all animals have to engage in sexual intercourse and to rear offspring, we can infer that procreation is a value and that we have an obligation to produce and rear children. Negatively, this inclination implies that such practices as sterilization, homosexuality, and artificial contraception are wrong.

2. Characteristically Human Values
   a. Knowledge. From the natural tendency we have to know, includ-
      ing the tendency to seek knowledge of God, we can infer that
      knowledge is a value and that we have an obligation to pursue
      knowledge of the world and of God. Negatively, this inclination
      implies that the stifling of intellectual curiosity and the pursuit of
      knowledge is wrong. It also implies that a lack of religion is
      wrong.
   b. Sociability. From the natural tendency we have to form bonds
      of affection and love with other human beings and to associate
      with others in societies, we can infer that friendship and love
      are good and that the state is a natural institution and therefore
      good. We thus have an obligation to pursue close relationships
      with other human beings and to submit to the legitimate au-
      thority of the state. We can also infer that war can be justified
      under certain conditions if it is necessary to defend the state.
      Negatively, this inclination implies that activities that interfere
      with proper human relationships, such as spreading slander
      and lies, are wrong. Actions that destroy the power of the state
      are also wrong, so natural law finds a basis for argument
      against revolution and treason, except when the state is radi-
      cally unjust.

These natural inclinations are reflections of human nature, and the
pursuit of the goods they specify is the way to individual fulfillment.
Aquinas himself makes it clear that the list of values, which in most
respects follows his account, is incomplete; other natural-law theorists
have expanded the list to include such things as play and aesthetic
experience. However the list given here has had the greatest historical
influence, and we shall assume it is basically complete.

The more important issue raised by this list is the potential for conflict
between the various values. What should we do when our need to defend
ourselves requires that we kill someone else? What should we do when
sterilization is necessary to prevent a life-threatening pregnancy? What
should be done when contraception seems necessary in order to limit
family size so that families can properly educate the children they already
have? In each of these examples, one aspect of natural law seems to
conflict with another, and the question arises whether these values have a
hierarchy on which a decision can be based. The answer to this question
brings into focus one of the most important and controversial aspects of
natural law—moral absolutism.

Moral Absolutism and Its Qualifying Principles

Moral Absolutism   Suppose you were on a military convoy from the United States to England during World War II. Your ship was attacked and sunk. Your life raft was carrying 24 persons, although it was designed to carry only 20. You had good reason to believe that the raft would sink unless four people were eliminated, and four people on board were so seriously injured in the catastrophe that they were probably going to die anyhow. Because no one volunteered to jump overboard, you, as the ranking officer on the boat, decided to have them pushed overboard. Were you morally justified in doing so? Many of us would say that under the circumstances you were, but natural-law theorists would say that you were not justified, even if everyone on the raft would have died otherwise.

Consider another wartime example. Suppose you know that some prisoners have information that will save a large number of lives. The only way to obtain the information is to threaten to kill the prisoners, but you know that they will not reveal what they know unless your threat is absolutely serious. To show them how serious you are, you have another prisoner shot before their eyes. As a result of your action, the information is revealed and many lives are saved. Is this action justified? Many people would say that under these extreme circumstances it is justified, but natural-law theorists would say that it is not.

Finally, . . . the traditional natural-law position is that practicing "artificial" contraception, undergoing sterilization, or practicing homosexuality is wrong. For the natural-law theorist, these prohibitions are valid even if the consequences are that parents produce children they cannot afford to educate or that the life of the mother is endangered or if homosexual relationships are the only sexual relationships a person can have with any satisfaction. These examples point out one of the most significant aspects of natural-law theory—namely, its absolutism.

Moral absolutism can refer either to the belief that some objective standard of moral truth exists independently of us or that certain actions are right or wrong regardless of their consequences. Natural law is an absolutist moral theory in both senses, but the second meaning of absolutism is highlighted by the illustrations provided. Natural-law theorists believe that *none of the values specified by natural inclinations may be directly violated*. Innocent people may not be killed for any reason, even if other innocent people can thus be saved. The procreative function that is a part of our biological nature may not be violated by such practices as contraception and sterilization, even if these practices are necessary to preserve other values, such as a child's education or even the mother's life. Similarly, homosexuality violates the value of procreation and is prohibited, even if it is the only kind of sex a person can enjoy.

Natural-law theorists have two reasons to hold that basic values specified by natural inclinations cannot be violated whatever the consequences. First, *basic values cannot be measured or compared;* that is, basic values cannot be quantified or measured by some common unit, so they cannot be traded off for one another. For example, we cannot divide the good of knowledge into units of value and the good of procreation into units of value so that the two can be compared on a common scale. Nor can the good of a single life be compared with the good of a number of lives; thus we cannot say that a single life may be sacrificed to preserve a number of other lives. This idea is sometimes called the "absolute value" or "infinite value" of a human life, suggesting that a human life cannot be weighed against anything else, including another human life. Natural-law theorists also make this point by saying that basic values are *incommensurable*. Because we cannot measure values, we cannot calculate which consequences of an action are more important. Therefore consequences cannot be used to determine the moral status of actions.

Second, consequences cannot be used to determine moral judgments because *we must make moral judgments by evaluating the motives of the person performing the action*. The *motive* of an action is what a person wants to accomplish by performing the action. For example, a person can give money to charity because he wants a good reputation in the community. The consequences of the action are good, but the motive is not morally praiseworthy. Some moral philosophers distinguish between a moral evaluation of the consequences of an action and a moral evaluation of the motives of the person performing the action; with this distinction we can say the action of giving money to charity was praiseworthy but the person giving the money was not praiseworthy, because the motives were bad. Natural-law theorists always place primary emphasis on motives.

Qualifying Principles   Because values are incommensurable and may not ever be directly violated, we may find ourselves in a situation in which any action we could perform violates some value and hence is apparently immoral. For example, self-defense may sometimes require that we override the natural inclination of another human being to self-preservation. If we do nothing, we allow ourselves to be killed; if we defend ourselves, we kill someone else. To avoid this paralysis of action and to gain deeper insight into the dynamics of situations of moral choice, natural-law theorists have developed two ideas that are absolutely crucial in making moral judgments: the principle of forfeiture and the principle of double effect.

According to the *principle of forfeiture,* a person who threatens the life of an innocent person forfeits his or her own right to life. (An *innocent* person is one who has not threatened anyone's life.) Suppose you are a pioneer who is tilling his land. Your wife and small child are in a log cabin on the hill. Two men approach you and express an intent to kill you and your family in order to take the land. Is it morally permissible for you to defend yourself, even to the point of killing them? Natural-law theorists answer the question in the affirmative. Even though you might have to violate the lives of your would-be assailants, they have forfeited their innocence by unjustifiably threatening your life. Therefore they have forfeited their claim to have their lives respected. We can make this point by distinguishing between killing and murder. *Killing* is taking the life of a non-innocent person, whereas *murder* is taking the life of an innocent person. When you take the life of a person who is attempting to kill you, you are killing him but you are not committing murder.

The principle of forfeiture can be used to justify not only acts of individual self-defense, but also war and capital punishment. A defensive war may be justified under certain conditions, even though it involves killing other people, because the aggressors have forfeited their right to life. Similarly, murderers may justly be put to death because they have forfeited their right to life by killing others.

According to the *principle of double effect,* it is morally permissible to perform an action that has two effects, one good and the other bad, if (1) the bad effect is unavoidable if the good effect is to be achieved, (2) the bad effect is unintended—that is, not a direct means to the good effect, and (3) a proportionally serious reason exists for performing the action.

The best way to explain this principle is by example. A pregnant woman who has tuberculosis wants to take a drug that will cure her disease, but the drug has the side effect of aborting the pregnancy. Is taking the drug morally permissible? The principle of double effect justifies taking the drug in this case, because all three of its conditions are met.

First, the bad effect is unavoidable in that the good effect cannot be achieved without also producing the bad effect. Presumably no other drug will cure the woman's tuberculosis and the abortion cannot be prevented once the drug is taken.

Second, the bad effect is unintended in that it is not a direct means to achieving the good effect. We must clarify here what natural-law theorists mean. The bad effect is certainly foreseen; the woman knows the drug will produce an abortion. However, the bad effect is not intended as a direct means to the good effect: An abortion is not a necessary step in curing the tuberculosis; rather, it is an unfortunate and unintended side effect. Evidence that the abortion is unintended even though it is foreseen is that the woman would presumably choose a different treatment that did not kill the fetus if it were equally effective and readily available.

Third, a proportionally serious reason exists for performing the abortion. The death of the fetus is at least balanced by the saving of the mother's life. If the bad effect were serious (as in this case), but the good effect were relatively insignificant, the action would not be justifiable by the principle of double effect, even if the other conditions were met. Here, consequences do play a part in natural-law reasoning. But note that consequences can be considered *only* when the other two conditions have been met.

Two other examples will show more clearly how the principle of double effect works. Suppose I want to turn on a light so that I can read a book on ethics, but I know that turning on the light will electrocute a worker on the floor below. If I cannot get the reading done except by electrocuting the worker, we can say that the electrocution is unavoidable. The bad effect is unintended in that electrocuting a worker is not a direct means to reading philosophy, but rather only an unfortunate and unintended side effect. But the third condition of the principle of double effect is not satisfied. The killing of a human being, even if unintended and unavoidable in the circumstances, is not outweighed by the value of reading a book on ethics. Therefore, turning on the light is not justified by the principle of double effect. The existence of a proportionally serious reason is often difficult to determine, as are the questions of the action's ultimate intention and avoidability. But in this case the application of the principle is clear.

Consider another example. A woman's egg is fertilized in the fallopian tube; as the fertilized egg develops it will rupture the tube, killing both the mother and the fetus. Is an abortion justified by the principle of double effect? The bad effect (the abortion) is unavoidable; the mother's life cannot be saved without it. The bad effect is not unintended, though, since removing the fetus from the fallopian tube is the direct means of saving the mother's life. The principle of proportionality is satisfied, because we have a case of life against life. However, since the second condition is not met, the abortion in this case cannot be justified by the principle of double effect.

This case is, of course, tragic for natural-law theorists, and various attempts have been made to justify the abortion on other grounds. For example, some natural-law theorists argue that the principle of forfeiture can be invoked, since the fetus is actually an aggressor on the life of the mother. Even though the fetus is innocent of any conscious motive to harm its mother, the actual effect of its growth is to threaten the life of its mother. Natural-law theorists sometimes say that the fetus, having no malicious motive, is subjectively innocent but not objectively innocent, because it does threaten the mother's life. Whether this argument justifies an abortion is left to the reader to decide. . . .

Applying the Ethics of Natural Law

We can now apply natural law to some cases involving moral decision . . .

CASE 1: A CASE OF EUTHANASIA

A 36-year-old accountant, married and the father of three young children, is diagnosed as having immunoblastic lymphadenopathy, a fatal malignant tumor of the lymph nodes. He has been receiving a variety of treatments, yet his condition has steadily worsened. He knows that all surgical and medical measures have been exhausted. He suffers daily from excruciating nerve-root pain; he must take addicting doses of narcotics but still is not free from pain. The expenses of his treatment are rapidly exhausting his family's financial resources. His wife and family are beginning to withdraw from him emotionally, in anticipation of his inevitable death. Having reconciled himself to his death, he asks the doctor for the means of killing himself in order to end his pain, the suffering of his family, and the depletion of the funds that are so important for his family's future well-being. Is it morally permissible for the physician to acquiesce in this request?[1]

1.   Obviously, administering a drug to end the accountant's life is a direct action against one of the four fundamental values of natural law—namely, the value of life.

2.   The only question is whether either of the two qualifying principles applies. The accountant is not guilty of any action that would cause him to forfeit his own right to life, so the principle of forfeiture does not apply.

3.   The principle of double effect might be used to justify two kinds of actions the physician could perform to alleviate his patient's suffering. First, it could justify the use of a pain killer, even if the pain killer had the indirect effect of shortening the patient's life. (a) If no other drug could alleviate pain as effectively, the use of that particular drug could be considered unavoidable. (b) The direct intent of administering the pain killer would be to alleviate pain; the tendency of the pain killer to shorten life would be unintended because the shortening of life is not the direct

means to eliminating pain. (c) Although some might argue that an action that shortens life is not justified by the desire to alleviate pain, most natural-law theorists would probably accept the use of the principle of proportionality in this case.

The principle of double effect could also justify the physician's decision not to use "heroic measures" to prolong the accountant's life. Natural-law theorists distinguish between "ordinary" and "extraordinary" means for preserving life. Father Gerald Kelly defines these two terms in the following way:

Ordinary means of preserving life are all medicines, treatments, and operations [that] offer a reasonable hope of benefit for the patient and [that] can be obtained and used without excessive expense, pain, or other inconvenience. . . .

Extraordinary means of preserving life [are] all medicines, treatments, and operations [that] cannot be obtained without excessive expense, pain, or other inconvenience, or [that], if used, would not offer a reasonable hope of benefit.[2]

The failure to use heroic or extraordinary means satisfies all three criteria of double effect. (a) The shortening of life is inevitable if extraordinary means are not used. (b) The shortening of life is unintended, because it is not a direct means to the use of ordinary means, and is simply an unfortunate side effect of the use of ordinary means. (c) The principle of proportionality is satisfied, since the use of extraordinary means would only prolong the accountant's dying process, not restore him to health. Therefore the decision not to use extraordinary means can be justified by the principle of double effect.

But the accountant's request goes far beyond the two measures described here. He is asking the physician to cooperate actively in directly ending his life. (a) The good effect of relieving the accountant's pain cannot be achieved without also producing the bad effect—namely, the accountant's death. So the first criterion is met. (b) However, the accountant's death is the direct means of achieving the release from pain, so the accountant's death is intended. The second criterion is not satisfied. (c) No proportionally serious reason exists for administering the lethal drug, since relief from pain cannot justify directly killing an innocent person, an act that is actually murder.

4.   Because the physician's action in administering a lethal drug to the accountant is a violation of a fundamental value and because the qualifying principles of forfeiture and double effect do not apply, the action is morally impermissible.

CASE 2: THE MORALITY OF OBLITERATION BOMBING
IN WORLD WAR II

During World War II, both the Germans and the Allied Forces bombed civilian residential areas, a practice called "obliteration bombing." Probably the two most famous examples of this practice, in which conventional explosives were used, were the German bombing of London and the Allied bombing of Dresden, Germany. Let us confine ourselves to the fire bombing of Dresden and ask whether this action was permissible by the principles of natural law.

1.   The first question is whether the bombing of Dresden violated the value of life. The answer is that it did, so the action must be morally impermissible unless one of the two qualifying principles applies.

2.   The principle of forfeiture would apply if civilians in wartime can be considered non-innocent. If we assume that the criteria of just-war theory were met—that is, the Allied Forces were fighting a just war and the Germans were not fighting a just war—then the Germans in uniform were non-innocent and attacking them was morally justified. But most civilians in large cities were connected with the war effort in a very indirect way. Many had little direct knowledge of the reasons for war and certainly had no part in starting it. Therefore, the principle of forfeiture does not justify the bombing.

3.   Some have argued that an appeal to the principle of double effect could justify the bombing. According to this argument, the intended effect of the bombing was to destroy war industries, communications, and military installations, whereas the damage to civilian life was unintentional and not a means to the production of the good effect. But a careful analysis of the conditions of the bombing will not sustain this argument. (a) Although killing of civilians truly is sometimes unavoidable when military targets are attacked, the massive civilian deaths in Dresden could have been avoided. (b) If the Allies were engaged in strategic bombing of war plants, with the direct intent to destroy the plants, and if the destruction of human life was unintended and unavoidable, the second condition of the principle of double effect would be satisfied. But, in this case, the maiming and death of hundreds of civilians was an immediate result of the bombing, and the undermining of civilian morale through terror was, on the testimony of military documents themselves, an object of the bombing. This goal of demoralization is impossible without a direct intent to injure and kill civilians. If one intends to create terror, one cannot escape intending the principle means of obtaining that end. Therefore the second condition of double effect is not met. (c) We can also question the allegation that the principle of proportionality was

satisfied by the belief that obliteration bombing would shorten the war. The goal was speculative, futuristic, and problematic, whereas the evil effect was definite, immediate, and widespread. Thus we must conclude that the principle of double effect does not apply.

4.   Because the Allied attack on Dresden involved the destruction of innocent human life and because the qualifying principles of forfeiture and double effect do not apply, we must conclude that the action was morally impermissible by natural-law theory.

CASE 3: THE MORALITY OF HOMOSEXUALITY

James has known since he was five years old that he was somehow different. Even then he enjoyed watching male athletes and seemed to "love" his older male playmates. In high school he was active in sports and his attraction to members of his own sex became obvious to him and to some of his friends. He has never been attracted to women sexually, although he likes some of them as friends, and the thought of sex with a woman has always repelled him. In college he began to associate with other homosexuals. He has talked to several counselors, and he now feels ready to admit to himself and to others, including his family, that he is a homosexual. However he still wonders about the morality of homosexuality, especially because he is a Roman Catholic. Is homosexuality wrong by natural law?

1.   The determination of whether homosexuality violates natural law is more difficult than it might at first appear. The traditional natural-law argument against homosexuality was based on the view that homosexual relationships involve a perversion or misuse of the sexual organs. Because the sex organs are made for procreation, using them for purposes other than this "natural end" is immoral. This same argument also leads to the conclusion that masturbation is immoral, because it uses the sex organs for pleasure rather than procreation. By a similar argument, oral sex and anal sex, even between married partners, is immoral. Thus, it is also wrong for a woman to refuse to breast-feed her child. If female breasts have the natural function of lactation, a mother who decides not to breast-feed her child acts directly against this natural function and does something wrong. This so-called perverted-faculty argument leads to so many absurd conclusions that it is being increasingly rejected. It does not even seem to be in agreement with Thomas Aquinas' basic understanding of natural law. For homosexuality to be immoral by our version of natural law, it must involve a direct action against a fundamental value.

Of course, homosexuals who engage in sexual activity have no intention of producing children; they know that their sexual activity cannot be procreative. But a married heterosexual couple who engage in sex during a nonfertile period also know that they cannot produce children, yet their action is not immoral by natural law. Neither the homosexual nor the married couple has done anything directly to violate the procreative function. The same statement applies to masturbation, oral sex, and anal sex; they do not seem directly to violate the value of procreation.

Some, perhaps many, homosexual acts are immoral because they violate the value of sociability. If the acts are demeaning or destructive or if they involve trickery or deception, they are wrong because they violate the value of loving, supportive human relationships. But the same is true of some heterosexual relationships, even if they occur within marriage. So we must look elsewhere for an argument that homosexual acts are wrong simply because they are homosexual.

Although it seems mistaken to say that homosexuals act directly to violate the value of procreation in the same straightforward sense that the use of contraceptives does, either case involves sex that is closed to the possibility of procreation. In fact, an exclusively homosexual lifestyle is closed to the possibility of procreation in a more decisive way than contraceptive sex or other types of nonprocreative sex by a married couple, because a homosexual's nonprocreative sex lasts throughout a lifetime. Therefore we can say that, although homosexual acts do not constitute a direct violation of the value of procreation, the homosexual lifestyle is antiprocreative.

2.   Since homosexuality is not a direct threat to life, the principle of forfeiture is inapplicable.

3.   James might argue that choosing a homosexual lifestyle is justifiable by the principle of double effect. (a) He might believe that the criterion of unavoidability is met, because it is impossible for him to have a fulfilling sex life without also failing to produce children. (b) He could say that his direct intent is to promote a fulfilling relationship and that any violation of the value of procreation is an unintended side effect. The nonproduction of children is not, after all, a direct means to his end of having a fulfilling sex life; he might even want to have children. (c) He could argue that the principle of proportionality is satisfied because the value of a meaningful relationship outweighs the failure to have children.

The first argument is weak because a fulfilling sex life is not a fundamental value, but the second criterion presents the main problem with this argument. Although it is true that the absence of children is not, as such, a direct means to James's goal of a fulfilling lifestyle, nonprocreative sex is a part of the means to this end. Whether the principle of double effect is applicable depends on the conceptual issue of whether the absence of children or nonprocreative sex is considered the undesirable effect. The absence of children is arguably an unintended side effect, but nonprocreative sex is a means to the desired end.

4.   We have found problems with the argument that homosexual acts violate the value of procreation and with the application of the principle of double effect. However, virtually all natural-law theorists have concluded that homosexual acts are morally impermissible. Ask yourself whether you agree with this conclusion.

Notes

1.   This case was supplied by Harry S. Lipscomb, M.D. Used with permission.
2.   Gerald Kelly, *Medico-Moral Problems* (St. Louis, Mo.: The Catholic Hospital Association. 1958), p. 120. Quoted in Paul Ramsey, *The Patient as Person*, p. 122.

ENDS AND MEANS: DOUBLE EFFECT
Jonathan Glover

Jonathan Glover is a Fellow and tutor in philosophy at New College, Oxford. The following selection is taken from his book, Causing Death and Saving Lives *(1977). Glover raises objections to the principle of double effect. According to the principle, we are forbidden to perform a bad act in order to bring about good consequences, though we may sometimes perform a good act in the knowledge that bad consequences will result. Glover criticizes the principle by pointing out that in many cases it leads to morally absurd conclusions. He further notes that certain crucial distinctions—such as between intended and foreseen consequences of actions and between actions and their consequences—are unclear, and thus he argues that the principle cannot be stated precisely enough to be of much use in our moral deliberations.*

T he objections to killing defended here rest to a large extent on consequences, though not entirely so, because the need to respect someone's autonomy is given some weight independent of good consequences.

This can be seen as accommodating part of what is valued when it is said that we ought always to treat people as ends in themselves and never merely as means.

But many people disapprove of giving the consequences of acts even the restricted, though still important, role that they play in the moral beliefs advocated here. These beliefs will to them still be sufficiently close to traditional utilitarianism to provoke the criticism that, in an objectionable way, 'the end justifies the means'. Those who make this criticism will want some set of principles according to which the relations between the consequences of an act and its morality are more indirect. In discussion of the morality of killing, two such principles are often either cited or else tacitly presupposed. One says that there is a morally significant difference between acts and omissions. . . . The other is the doctrine of double effect.

This doctrine can be summarized crudely as saying that it is always wrong intentionally to do a bad act for the sake of good consequences that will ensue, but that it may be permissible to do a good act in the knowledge that bad consequences will ensue. The doctrine is explained in terms of the difference between intended and foreseen consequences.

G.E.M. Anscombe, who believes in the double-effect doctrine, has illustrated it with the case of killing in self-defence.[1] If you attack me, I may, if necessary, defend myself by striking you so hard that your death results. (The 'if necessary' is important here: I have a duty to use the minimum force necessary.) But, if I know you are searching for me to kill me, I am not morally permitted to arrange for you to be poisoned before you find me.

The explanation usually given of this moral difference is that, where I arrange for you to be poisoned, I must intend your death as a means to my own safety. On the other hand, when I hit you in self-defence, I intend only to prevent you from killing me. If I only knock you unconscious, this will be just as effective. If you do die, this can be a foreseen but unintended consequence of my blow, rather than itself the intended means of my defence.

Some applications to cases of abortion of the double-effect doctrine may be mentioned. The doctrine allows that a pregnant woman with cancer of the womb may have her life saved by removal of the womb, with the foreseen consequence that the foetus dies. But, if the doctor could save only the mother's life by changing the composition of the amniotic fluid and so killing the foetus while still attached to the womb, this would not be permitted. In the second case the death of the foetus would be an intended means; in the first case it would be merely a foreseen consequence.

The double effect doctrine is often criticized on utilitarian grounds. The two abortion cases would each have the same outcome: the death of the foetus and the saving of the mother. A utilitarian is bound to see this moral doctrine as unacceptable: depending on a distinction without a difference. If the death of the mother is a worse outcome than the death of the foetus, it seems to a utilitarian immoral to act as the double effect principle tells us.

Professor Hart has cited another application of the double effect doctrine that is open to similar objection.[2] There was a case in which a man was trapped in the cabin of a blazing lorry, with no hope of being freed. He asked a bystander to shoot him in order to save him from further agony. The bystander did so, but his act would have been condemned by the double effect doctrine. For, according to this view, if it is wrong intentionally to kill an innocent man, it is still wrong to do so even as a means to saving him from pain: better not shoot him, with the foreseen consequence that he will burn to death.

There are also problems of stating the doctrine precisely. How do we draw the line in difficult cases between an intended means and a foreseen inevitable consequence? If, as a political protest, I throw a bomb into a football crowd, causing an explosion and killing several people, are their deaths intended means to my protest or inevitable consequences of it? On what principles do we decide whether the explosion alone is included in the means or whether we must count both explosion and deaths as part of the means? This cannot be decided on the grounds of the virtual inevitability of the deaths if the explosion occurs, for the double effect doctrine tells us that there can be consequences foreseen to be inevitable, yet which do not count as intended means. The matter cannot hinge on whether or not the deaths are desired, for in the forbidden abortion case the death of the foetus is no more desired than it is in the permitted case.

It may be suggested that what is crucial is the 'closeness' of the connection between cause and effect. (Jonathan Bennett has raised the question why 'closeness' should be of any moral importance, aside from its link with the extent to which the effect is either inevitable or desired.[3] A lot of explaining seems called for.) What sort of 'closeness' is in question? Is it closeness in time? If so, having someone poisoned in order to prevent them catching and killing me will turn out not to be forbidden if the poison used is *very* slow-acting. If it is some other form of closeness, how is it specified and what degree of it is required?

The next problem in formulating the doctrine is that of identifying the class of 'bad' acts that can never be justified by appeals to consequences. Some people believe that they know the contents of the list of such bad acts, which has been laid down by an authority, perhaps by God. They have no difficulty in justifying their claim to know which acts are forbidden (apart from familiar problems of saying how they know God exists, how they know what he commands, and why they should obey his commands). If the identification of the class of forbidden acts depends on this kind of appeal to authority, those of us who are unimpressed by such appeals can discard the double effect doctrine at once. But perhaps this is too hasty. Is there any way of identifying the 'bad' acts which can never be justified by good consequences, without appealing to some authority?

These acts cannot be identified by the badness of their consequences in a particular case, for the forbidden and permitted abortions can have the same effects on the interests of all concerned. Perhaps an appeal to the beneficial consequences of a rule is involved. Because it is in general better that people do not take innocent life, a rule is made saying that it must never be done. This raises the problem: why should I obey the rule in cases where to do so does not have the best overall consequences?

There is also a further problem. For there are many things that are in general undesirable, but which are not made the subject of these absolute prohibitions. Lying is in general undesirable, but it is not commonly suggested that it is absolutely wrong to lie, for instance as a means of saving someone's life. So, why killing? Even if killing is 'in itself' worse than lying, this is surely a matter of degree. It seems hard on this basis to justify an absolute prohibition. For suppose killing is a million times worse than lying. If we can lie to avoid someone's death, how can we justify refusing to kill someone where this will save a million lives?

There is a parallel problem of deciding what kinds of foreseen but unintended consequences can be justified by the double effect doctrine. For I cannot, according to the doctrine, perform an act which brings about a small intended benefit, with disproportionately disastrous foreseen consequences. I may not tell the truth about an innocent fugitive's whereabouts to an assassin, with the foreseen consequence that he is murdered. But, having allowed this concession to utilitarian calculation, where is a line to be drawn, and why?

The situation is complicated by the difficulty of deciding where to draw the line between an act and its consequences. If we are on a desert journey and I knowingly use all the drinking water for washing my shirts, my act may be described merely as one of 'washing shirts' or of 'keeping up standards even in the desert', and our being without water may be thought of as a foreseen bad consequence. But it is at least equally acceptable to include the consequence in the description of the act, which may then be described as one of 'using up the last of the water' or of 'putting our lives at risk'. This general problem of distinguishing acts from their consequences is clearly related to the problem already mentioned, of distinguishing intended means from foreseen consequences.

It is crucial for the double effect doctrine that some limit must be set to the re-description of acts in terms of their consequences, for otherwise the doctrine will forbid nothing. Killing the foetus while it is attached to the womb will be permitted under the description 'saving the mother's life'. Eric D'Arcy[4] quotes the jingle 'Imperious Caesar, dead and turned to clay, might stop a hole to keep the wind away', but protests that it would be wrong to describe killing him with that end in view as 'blocking a draught'. D'Arcy's own solution to the problem is to claim that 'certain kinds of act are of such significance that the terms which denote them may not, special contexts apart, be elided into terms which (a) denote their consequences, and (b) conceal, or even fail to reveal, the nature of the act itself'.

This is an attractive claim, for we do feel that there is something wrong with describing Caesar's murder as 'blocking a draught'. Our objection to such an oblique description is presumably because it omits features of great importance to our moral appraisal of the act. But such incompleteness is a matter of degree. Many acts have so many facets of some relevance to moral evaluation that we often have to sacrifice completeness to brevity. In describing a man's act of rushing a seriously injured person to the hospital, we do not have to include in our description of his act the consequence that he broke a promise to meet someone for lunch. We value explicitness of description, and we often disapprove of people slurring over the morally unattractive aspects of actions, especially of their own actions. But the degree of explicitness we think desirable may vary in different contexts, and there may be disagreement as to how incomplete a description can be before it reaches objectionable evasiveness.

If the doctrine of double effect is to have any content, it must stipulate that acts which fall under certain descriptions may never, for purposes of moral evaluation, be described in a way which omits this feature of them. We have seen that the drawing-up of a list of absolutely forbidden acts raises difficulties. A parallel list of un-elidable act-descriptions is likely to be morally just as debatable.

The lack of intuitive plausibility of some of the applications of the double effect doctrine, together with the difficulties both of drawing the key distinctions and of defending their relevance, are good reasons for rejecting it.

Notes

1. G.E.M. Anscombe: 'War and Murder', in W. Stein (ed.): *Nuclear Weapons, A Catholic Response*, London, 1961.
2. H.L.A. Hart: 'Intention and Punishment', *The Oxford Review*, 1967, reprinted in H.L.A. Hart: *Punishment and Responsibility*, Oxford, 1968.
3. Jonathan Bennett: 'Whatever the Consequences', *Analysis*, 1965.
4. Eric D'Arcy: *Human Acts*, Oxford, 1963, Ch. 4, part 3.

MORAL STANDARDS AND THE DISTINGUISHING MARKS OF MAN
Bernard Williams

Bernard Williams is professor of philosophy at the University of California at Berkeley and has authored many books and articles, including Morality: An Introduction *(1972) and* Ethics and the Limits of Philosophy *(1985). Moral theories like the natural-law theory attempt to derive morality from certain distinguishing marks of human beings. About such theories, Williams notes three things: first, some degree of evaluation goes into selecting the distinguishing marks that are made the basis of morality; second, some distinguishing marks of human beings are morally ambiguous in the sense that they are preconditions both for doing evil and for doing good; and third, rationality is often featured as a distinguishing mark of human beings at the expense of our emotional, nonrational sides. Each of these points is the basis for an objection to moral theories like the natural-law theory. Williams concludes that "the attempt to found morality on a conception of the* good *man elicited from considerations of the distinguishing marks of human nature is likely to fail."*

There are more general objections to the procedure of trying to elicit unquestionable moral ends or ideals from distinguishing marks of man's nature. We may mention three. First, a palpable degree of evaluation has already gone into the selection of the distinguishing mark which is given this role, such as rationality or creativity. If one approached without preconceptions the question of finding characteristics which differentiate men from other animals, one could as well, on these principles, end up with a morality which exhorted men to spend as much time as possible in making fire; or developing peculiarly human physical characteristics; or having sexual intercourse without regard to season; or despoiling the environment and upsetting the balance of nature; or killing things for fun.

Second, and very basically, this approach bears out the moral *ambiguity* of distinctive human characteristics (though Aristotle paid some attention, not totally successfully, to this point.) For if it is a mark of a man to employ intelligence and tools in modifying his environment, it is equally a mark of him to employ intelligence in getting his own way and tools in destroying others. If it is a mark of a man to have a conceptualized and fully conscious awareness of himself as one among others, aware that others have feelings like himself, this is a precondition not only of benevolence but (as Nietzsche pointed out) of cruelty as well: the man of sadistic sophistication is not more like other animals than the man of natural affections, but less so. If we offer as the supreme moral imperative that old cry, 'be a man!', it is terrible to think of many of the ways in which it could be taken literally.

Here we seem to encounter a genuine dimension of freedom, to use or neglect the natural endowment, and to use it in one way or another: a freedom which must cut the central cord of the Aristotelian sort of enterprise. Nor can this freedom itself be used as the distinguishing mark of man, and the enterprise mounted again on the basis of that. For this freedom can surely, by its nature, determine no one form of life as against another—as Sartre, in virtue of a central ambiguity already mentioned, perhaps has thought. One might say: if there were a distinctive form of life, that of 'realizing freedom', then there must still be a freedom to reject that, too.

Third, if we revert to that particular case of the *rational* as the distinguishing mark of man: there is a tendency for this approach to acquire a Manichean leaning and emphasize virtues of rational self-control at the expense of all else. There is no reason why such an outlook should *inevitably* follow; apart from anything else, it involves a false and inhuman view of the passions themselves as blind causal forces or merely animal characteristics. To be helplessly in love is in fact as distinctively a human condition as to approve rationally of someone's moral dispositions. But it is easy to see why, in the present direction, Manicheanism looks inviting. If rationality and consistent thought are the preferred distinguishing marks of man, then even if it is admitted that man, as a whole, also has passions, the supremacy of rational thought over them may well seem an unquestionable ideal. This is all the more so, since it is quite obvious that gaining some such control is a basic condition of growing up, and even, at the extreme, of sanity. But to move from that into making such control into *the* ideal, rules out *a priori* most forms of spontaneity. And this seems to be absurd.

All these considerations suggest that the attempt to found morality on a conception of the *good man* elicited from considerations of the distinguishing marks of human nature is likely to fail. I am far from thinking that considerations about human nature, what men are, what it is for men to live in society, do not contribute to a correct view of morality. Of course they do: one could not have any conception of morality at all without such considerations. In particular, they help to delimit the possible content of what could be regarded as a morality. Just as obviously, differing views of human nature (as, for example, some psychoanalytical view) must have differing effects on what views one takes of particular moral requirements and norms. Not merely scientific or semiscientific views must have this effect but also views in the philosophy of mind. Thus a proper philosophical understanding of the nature of the emotions should have a discouraging effect on Manichean views about their management, and philosophical considerations about the nature, indeed the existence, of something called the *will* must have a direct effect on moralities which find in the exercise of the will (against the desires, for instance) a central clue to moral worth.

While all this is true, and while there are very definite limitations on what could be comprehensibly regarded as a system of human morality, there is no direct route from considerations of human nature to a unique morality and a unique moral ideal. It would be simpler if there were fewer things, and fewer distinctively human things, that men can be; or if the characters, dispositions, social arrangements and states of affairs which men can comprehensibly set value on were all, in full development, consistent with one another. But they are not, and there is good reason why they are not: good reason which itself emerges from considerations of human nature.

CHAPTER 6

Kantian Ethical Theory

THE MORAL LAW AND AUTONOMY
OF THE WILL
Immanuel Kant

Kant (1724–1804) is one of the most important philosophers of the Western world. He wrote three major ethical works: Groundwork of the Metaphysic of Morals *(1785),* Critique of Practical Reason *(1788), and* Metaphysic of Morals *(1797). In the selection below, taken from the first of these works, Kant presents and defends the "categorical imperative" as the fundamental principle of right conduct. He begins by claiming that only a* good will*—that is, the disposition to act out of a sense of duty—has unqualified moral worth. He then asks what principle of action guides a good will. He claims that a good will is guided by the idea that one's actions should be acceptable to everyone. Thus, people with a good will act in such a way that the principles of their actions (what Kant calls "maxims") should be universal laws for everyone. The idea of acting on maxims that should become universal laws for everyone's behavior is the fundamental principle of right conduct, Kant's categorical imperative.*

Kant proceeds to illustrate the categorical imperative by showing how it applies to cases of suicide, making a lying promise, letting one's talents rust, and failing to help others in need. He next argues that, since human beings have absolute worth—that is, since they exist as ends in themselves—we can alternatively formulate the categorical imperative as the requirement that we "act as to treat humanity, . . . in every case as an end withal, never as a means only."

Reprinted from *The Foundations of the Metaphysic of Morals*, translated by T. K. Abbott (this translation first published in 1873).

The Good Will

Nothing can possibly be conceived in the world, or even out of it, which can be called good, without qualification, except a Good Will. Intelligence, wit, judgment, and the other *talents* of the mind, however they may be named, or courage, resolution, perseverance, as qualities of temperament, are undoubtedly good and desirable in many respects; but these gifts of nature may also become extremely bad and mischievous if the will which is to make use of them, and which, therefore, constitutes what is called *character*, is not good. It is the same with the *gifts of fortune*. Power, riches, honour, even health, and the general well-being and contentment with one's condition which is called *happiness*, inspire pride, and often presumption, if there is not a good will to correct the influence of these on the mind, and with this also to rectify the whole principle of acting, and adapt it to its end. The sight of a being who is not adorned with a single feature of a pure and good will, enjoying unbroken prosperity, can never give pleasure to an impartial rational spectator. Thus a good will appears to constitute the indispensable condition even of being worthy of happiness.

There are even some qualities which are of service to this good will itself, and may facilitate its action, yet which have no intrinsic unconditional value, but always presuppose a good will, and this qualifies the esteem that we justly have for them, and does not permit us to regard them as absolutely good. Moderation in the affections and passions, self-control, and calm deliberation are not only good in many respects, but even seem to constitute part of the intrinsic worth of the person; but they are far from deserving to be called good without qualification, although they have been so unconditionally praised by the ancients. For without the principles of a good will, they may become extremely bad; and the coolness of a villain not only makes him far more dangerous, but also directly makes him more abominable in our eyes than he would have been without it.

A good will is good not because of what it performs or effects, not by its aptness for the attainment of some proposed end, but simply by virtue of the volition, that is, it is good in itself, and considered by itself is to be esteemed much higher than all that can be brought about by it in favour of any inclination, nay, even of the sum-total of all inclinations. Even if it should happen that, owing to special disfavour of fortune, or the niggardly provision of a step-motherly nature, this will should wholly lack power to accomplish its purpose, if with its greatest efforts it should yet achieve nothing, and there should remain only the good will (not, to be sure, a mere wish, but the summoning of all means in our power), then, like a jewel, it would still shine by its own light, as a thing which has its whole value in itself. Its usefulness or fruitlessness can neither add to or nor take away anything from this value. . . .

. . . Thus the moral worth of an action does not lie in the effect expected from it, nor in any principle of action which requires to borrow its motive from this expected effect. For all these effects—agreeableness of one's condition, and even the promotion of the happiness of others— could have been also brought about by other causes, so that for this there would have been no need of the will of a rational being; whereas it is in this alone that the supreme and unconditional good can be found. The pre-eminent good which we call moral can therefore consist in nothing else than *the conception of law* in itself, *which certainly is only possible in a rational being*, in so far as this conception, and not the expected effect, determines the will. This is a good which is already present in the person who acts accordingly, and we have not to wait for it to appear first in the result.

The Supreme Principle of Morality: The Categorical Imperative

But what sort of law can that be, the conception of which must determine the will, even without paying any regard to the effect expected from it, in order that this will may be called good absolutely and without qualification? As I have deprived the will of every impulse which could arise to it from obedience to any law, there remains nothing but the universal conformity of its actions to law in general, which alone is to serve the will as a principle, *i.e.* I am never to act otherwise than so *that I could also will that my maxim should become a universal law*. Here, now, it is the simple conformity to law in general, without assuming any particular law applicable to certain actions, that serves the will as its principle, and must so serve it, if duty is not to be a vain delusion and a chimerical notion. The common reason of men in its practical judgments perfectly coincides with this, and always has in view the principle here suggested. Let the question be, for example: May I when in distress make a promise with the intention not to keep it? I readily distinguish here between the two significations which the question may have: Whether it is prudent, or whether it is right, to make a false promise? The former may undoubtedly often be the case. I see clearly indeed that it is not enough to extricate myself from a present difficulty by means of this subterfuge, but it must be well considered whether there may not hereafter spring from this lie much greater inconvenience than that from which I now free myself, and as, with all my supposed *cunning*, the consequences cannot be so easily foreseen but that credit once lost may be much more injurious to me than any mischief which I seek to avoid at present, it should be considered whether it would not be more *prudent* to act herein according to a universal maxim, and to make it a habit to promise nothing except with the intention of keeping it. But it is soon clear to me that such a maxim will still only be based on the fear of consequences. Now it is a wholly different thing to be truthful from duty, and to be so from apprehension of injurious consequences. In the first case, the very notion of the action already implies a law for me; in the second case, I must first look about elsewhere to see what results may be combined with it which would affect myself. For to deviate from the principle of duty is beyond all doubt wicked; but to be unfaithful to my maxim of prudence may often be very advantageous to me, although to abide by it is certainly safer. The shortest way, however, and an unerring one, to discover the answer to this question whether a lying promise is consistent with duty, is to ask myself, Should I be content that my maxim (to extricate myself from difficulty by a false promise) should hold good as a universal law, for myself as well as for others? and should I be able to say to myself, "Every one may make a deceitful promise when he finds himself in a difficulty from which he cannot otherwise extricate himself"? Then I presently become aware that while I can will the lie, I can by no means will that lying should be a universal law. For with such a law there would be no promises at all, since it would be in vain to allege my intention in regard to my future actions to those who would not believe this allegation, or if they over-hastily did so, would pay me back in my own coin. Hence my maxim, as soon as it should be made a universal law, would necessarily destroy itself. . . .

Imperatives: Hypothetical and Categorical

Everything in nature works acording to laws. Rational beings alone have the faculty of acting according *to the conception* of laws, that is according to principles, *i.e.* have a *will*. Since the deduction of actions from principles requires *reason*, the will is nothing but practical reason. If reason infallibly determines the will, then the actions of such a being which are recognized as objectively necessary are subjectively necessary also, *i.e.* the will is a faculty to choose *that only* which reason independent of inclination recognizes as practically necessary, *i.e.* as good. But if reason of itself does not sufficiently determine the will, if the latter is subject also to subjective conditions (particular impulses) which do not always coincide with the objective conditions; in a word, if the will does not *in itself* completely accord with reason (which is actually the case with men), then the actions which objectively are recognized as necessary are subjectively contingent, and the determination of such a will according to objective laws is *obligation*, that is to say, the relation of the objective laws to a will that is not thoroughly good is conceived as the determination of the will of a rational being by principles of reason, but which the will from its nature does not of necessity follow.

The conception of an objective principle, in so far as it is obligatory for a will, is called a command (of reason), and the formula of the command is called an Imperative.

All imperatives are expressed by the word *ought* [or *shall*], and thereby indicate the relation of an objective law of reason to a will, which from its subjective constitution is not necessarily determined by it (an obligation). They say that something would be good to do or to forbear, but they say it to a will which does not always do a thing because it is conceived to be good to do it. That is practically *good*, however, which determines the will by means of the conceptions of reason, and consequently not from subjective causes, but objectively, that is on principles which are valid for every rational being as such. It is distinguished from the *pleasant,* as that which influences the will only by means of sensation from merely subjective causes, valid only for the sense of this or that one, and not as a principle of reason, which holds for every one.

A perfectly good will would therefore be equally subject to objective laws (viz., laws of good), but could not be conceived as *obliged* thereby to act lawfully, because of itself from its subjective constitution it can only be determined by the conception of good. Therefore no imperatives hold for the Divine will, or in general for a *holy* will; *ought* is here out of place, because the volition is already of itself necessarily in unison with the law. Therefore imperatives are only formulae to express the relation of objective laws of all volition to the subjective imperfection of the will of this or that rational being, *e.g.* the human will.

Now all *imperatives* command either *hypothetically* or *categorically*. The former represent the practical necessity of a possible action as means to something else that is willed (or at least which one might possibly will). The categorical imperative would be that which represented an action as necessary of itself without reference to another end, *i.e.*, as objectively necessary. . . .

First Formulation of
the Categorical Imperative: Universal Law

There is therefore but one categorical imperative, namely, this: *Act only on that maxim whereby thou canst at the same time will that it should become a universal law.*

Now if all imperatives of duty can be deduced from this one imperative as from their principle, then, although it should remain undecided whether what is called duty is not merely a vain notion, yet at least we shall be able to show what we understand by it and what this notion means.

Since the universality of the law according to which effects are produced constitutes what is properly called *nature* in the most general sense (as to form), that is the existence of things so far as it is determined by general laws, the imperative of duty may be expressed thus: *Act as if the maxim of thy action were to become by thy will a universal law of nature*.

Four Illustrations

We will now enumerate a few duties, adopting the usual division of them into duties to ourselves and to others, and into perfect and imperfect duties.

1.   A man reduced to despair by a series of misfortunes feels wearied of life, but is still so far in possession of his reason that he can ask himself whether it would not be contrary to his duty to himself to take his own life. Now he inquires whether the maxim of his action could become a universal law of nature. His maxim is: From self-love I adopt it as a principle to shorten my life when its longer duration is likely to bring more evil than satisfaction. It is asked then simply whether this principle founded on self-love can become a universal law of nature. Now we see at once that a system of nature of which it should be a law to destroy life by means of the very feeling whose special nature it is to impel to the improvement of life would contradict itself, and therefore could not exist as a system of nature; hence that maxim cannot possibly exist as a universal law of nature, and consequently would be wholly inconsistent with the supreme principle of all duty.

2.   Another finds himself forced by necessity to borrow money. He knows that he will not be able to repay it, but sees also that nothing will be lent to him, unless he promises stoutly to repay it in a definite time. He desires to make this promise, but he has still so much conscience as to ask himself: Is it not unlawful and inconsistent with duty to get out of a difficulty in this way? Suppose, however, that he resolves to do so, then the maxim of his action would be expressed thus: When I think myself in want of money, I will borrow money and promise to repay it, although I know that I never can do so. Now this principle of self-love or of one's own advantage may perhaps be consistent with my whole future welfare; but the question now is, Is it right? I change then the suggestion of self-love into a universal law, and state the question thus: How would it be if my maxim were a universal law? Then I see at once that it could never hold as a universal law of nature, but would necessarily contradict itself. For supposing it to be a universal law that everyone when he thinks himself in

a difficulty should be able to promise whatever he pleases, with the purpose of not keeping his promise, the promise itself would become impossible, as well as the end that one might have in view in it, since no one would consider that anything was promised to him, but would ridicule all such statements as vain pretences.

3.   A third finds in himself a talent which with the help of some culture might make him a useful man in many respects. But he finds himself in comfortable circumstances,and prefers to indulge in pleasure rather than to take pains in enlarging and improving his happy natural capacities. He asks, however, whether his maxim of neglect of his natural gifts, besides agreeing with his inclination to indulgence, agrees also with what is called duty. He sees then that a system of nature could indeed subsist with such a universal law although men (like the South Sea islanders) should let their talents rust, and resolve to devote their lives merely to idleness, amusement, and propagation of their species—in a word, to enjoyment; but he cannot possibly *will* that this should be a universal law of nature, or be implanted in us as such by a natural instinct. For, as a rational being, he necessarily wills that his faculties be developed, since they serve him, and have been given him, for all sorts of possible purposes.

4.   A fourth, who is in prosperity, while he sees that others have to contend with great wretchedness and that he could help them, thinks: What concern is it of mine? Let everyone be as happy as Heaven pleases, or as he can make himself; I will take nothing from him nor even envy him, only I do not wish to contribute anything to his welfare or to his assistance in distress! Now no doubt if such a mode of thinking were a universal law, the human race might very well subsist, and doubtless even better than in a state in which everyone talks of sympathy and good-will, or even takes care occasionally to put it into practice, but, on the other side, also cheats when he can, betrays the rights of men, or otherwise violates them. But although it is possible that a universal law of nature might exist in accordance with that maxim, it is impossible to *will* that such a principle should have the universal validity of a law of nature. For a will which resolved this would contradict itself, inasmuch as many cases might occur in which one would have need of the love and sympathy of others, and in which, by such a law of nature, sprung from his own will, he would deprive himself of all hope of the aid he desires. . . .

Second Formulation of the Categorical Imperative: Humanity as an End in Itself

. . . Now I say: man and generally any rational being *exists* as an end in himself, *not merely as a means* to be arbitrarily used by this or that will, but in all his actions, whether they concern himself or other rational beings, must be always regarded at the same time as an end. All objects of the inclinations have only a conditional worth; for if the inclinations and the wants founded on them did not exist, then their object would be without value. But the inclinations themselves being sources of want are so far from having an absolute worth for which they should be desired, that, on the contrary, it must be the universal wish of every rational being to be wholly free from them. Thus the worth of any object which is *to be acquired* by our action is always conditional. Beings whose existence depends not on our will but on nature's, have nevertheless, if they are nonrational beings, only a relative value as means, and are therefore called *things;* rational beings, on the contrary, are called *persons*, because their very nature points them out as ends in themselves, that is as something which must not be used merely as means, and so far therefore restricts freedom of action (and is an object of respect). These, therefore, are not merely subjective ends whose existence has a worth *for us* as an effect of our action, but *objective ends,* that is things whose existence is an end in itself: an end moreover for which no other can be substituted, which they should subserve *merely* as means, for otherwise nothing whatever would possess *absolute worth;* but if all worth were conditioned and therefore contingent, then there would be no supreme practical principle of reason whatever.

If then there is a supreme practical principle or, in respect of the human will, a categorical imperative, it must be one which, being drawn from the conception of that which is necessarily an end for everyone because it is *an end in itself,* constitutes an *objective* principle of will, and can therefore serve as a universal practical law. The foundation of this principle is: *rational nature exists as an end in itself.* Man necessarily conceives his own existence as being so: so far then this is a *subjective* principle of human actions. But every other rational being regards its existence similarly, just on the same rational principle that holds for me: so that it is at the same time an objective principle, from which as a supreme practical law all laws of the will must be capable of being deduced. Accordingly the practical imperative will be as follows: *So act as to treat humanity, whether in thine own person or in that of any other, in every case as an end withal, never as means only. . . .*

. . . Looking back now on all previous attempts to discover the principle of morality, we need not wonder why they all failed. It was seen that man was bound to laws by duty, but it was not observed that the laws to which he is subject are *only those of his own giving,* though at the same time they are *universal*, and that he is only bound to act in conformity with his own will; a will, however, which is designed by nature to give universal laws. For when one has conceived man only as subject to a law (no matter what), then this law required some interest, either by way of attraction or constraint, since it did not originate as a law from *his own* will, but this will was according to a law obliged by *something else* to act in a certain manner. Now by this necessary consequence all the labour spent in finding a supreme principle of *duty* was irrevocably lost. For men never elicited duty, but only a necessity of acting from a certain interest. Whether this interest was private or otherwise, in any case the imperative must be conditional, and could not by any means be capable of being a moral command. I will therefore call this the principle of *Autonomy* of the will, in contrast with every other which I accordingly reckon as *Heteronomy*.

The Kingdom of Ends

The conception of every rational being as one which must consider itself as giving in all the maxims of its will universal laws, so as to judge itself and its actions from this point of view—this conception leads to another which depends on it and is very fruitful, namely, that of a *kingdom of ends*.

By a *kingdom* I understand the union of different rational beings in a system by common laws. Now since it is by laws that ends are determined as regards their universal validity, hence, if we abstract from the personal differences of rational beings, and likewise from all the content of their private ends, we shall be able to conceive all ends combined in a systematic whole (including both rational beings as ends in themselves, and also the special ends which each may propose to himself), that is to say, we can conceive a kingdom of ends, which on the preceding principles is possible.

For all rational beings come under the *law* that each of them must treat itself and all others *never merely as means*, but in every case *at the same time as ends in themselves*. Hence results a systematic union of rational beings by common objective laws, *i.e.*, a kingdom which may be called a kingdom of ends, since what these laws have in view is just the relation of these beings to one another as ends and means. . . .

KANT'S MORAL THEORY: EXPOSITION AND CRITIQUE
Fred Feldman

Fred Feldman is professor of philosophy at the University of Mas-sachusetts–Amherst. His books include Introductory Ethics *(1978) and* Doing the Best We Can *(1986). Feldman first explains some of the crucial concepts involved in Kant's moral theory and then proceeds to evaluate Kant's four illustrations of the categorical imperative.*

Sometimes our moral thinking takes a decidedly nonutilitarian turn. That is, we often seem to appeal to a principle that is inconsistent with the whole utilitarian standpoint. One case in which this occurs clearly enough is the familiar tax-cheat case. A person decides to cheat on his income tax, rationalizing his misbehavior as follows: "The government will not be injured by the absence of my tax money. After all, compared with the enormous total they take in, my share is really a negligible sum. On the other hand, I will be happier if I have the use of the money. Hence, no one will be injured by my cheating, and one person will be better off. Thus, it is better for me to cheat than it is for me to pay."

In response to this sort of reasoning, we may be inclined to say something like this: "Perhaps you are right in thinking that you will be better off if you cheat. And perhaps you are right in thinking that the government won't even know the difference. Nevertheless, your act would be wrong. For if everyone were to cheat on his income taxes, the government would soon go broke. Surely you can see that you wouldn't want others to act in the way you propose to act. So you shouldn't act in that way." While it may not be clear that this sort of response would be decisive, it should be clear that this is an example of a sort of response that is often given.

There are several things to notice about this response. For one, it is not based on the view that the example of the tax cheat will provoke everyone else to cheat too. If that were the point of the response, then the response might be explained on the basis of utilitarian considerations. We could understand the responder to be saying that the tax cheater has mis-calculated his utilities. Whereas he thinks his act of cheating has high utility, in fact it has low utility because it will eventually result in the

Fred Feldman, *Introductory Ethics,* © 1978, pp. 97–114. Reprinted by permission of Prentice-Hall, Inc., Englewood Cliffs, New Jersey.

collapse of the government. It is important to recognize that the response presented above is not based upon any such utilitarian considerations. This can be seen by reflecting on the fact that the point could just as easily have been made in this way: "Of course, very few other people will know about your cheating, and so your behavior will not constitute an example to others. Thus, it will not provoke others to cheat. Nevertheless, your act is wrong. For if everyone were to cheat as you propose to do, then the government would collapse. Since you wouldn't want others to behave in the way you propose to behave, you should not behave in that way. It would be wrong to cheat."

Another thing to notice about the response in this case is that the responder has not simply said, "What you propose to do would be cheating; hence, it is wrong." The principle in question is not simply the principle that cheating is wrong. Rather, the responder has appealed to a much more general principle, which seems to be something like this: If you wouldn't want everyone else to act in a certain way, then you shouldn't act in that way yourself.

This sort of general principle is in fact used quite widely in our moral reasoning. If someone proposes to remove the pollution-control devices from his automobile, his friends are sure to say "What if everyone did that?" They would have in mind some dire consequences for the quality of the air, but their point would not be that the removal of the pollution-control device by one person will in fact cause others to remove theirs, and will thus eventually lead to the destruction of the environment. Their point, rather, is that if their friend would not want others to act in the way he proposes to act, then it would be wrong for him to act in that way. This principle is also used against the person who refrains from giving to charity; the person who evades the draft in time of national emergency; the person who tells a lie in order to get out of a bad spot; and even the person who walks across a patch of newly seeded grass. In all such cases, we feel that the person acts wrongly not because his actions will have bad results, but because he wouldn't want others to behave in the way he behaves.

A highly refined version of this nonutilitarian principle is the heart of the moral theory of Immanuel Kant.[1] In his *Groundwork of the Metaphysic of Morals*,[2] Kant presents, develops, and defends the thesis that something like this principle is the "supreme principle of morality." Kant's presentation is rather complex; in parts, it is very hard to follow. Part of the trouble arises from his use of a rather unfamiliar technical vocabulary. Another source of trouble is that Kant is concerned with establishing a variety of other points in this little book, and some of these involve fairly complex issues in metaphysics and epistemology. Since our aim here is simply to present a clear, concise account of Kant's basic moral doctrine, we will have to ignore quite a bit of what he says in the book.

Kant formulates his main principle in a variety of different ways. All of the members of the following set of formulations seem to have a lot in common:

I ought never to act except in such a way that I can also will that my maxim should become a universal law.[3]

Act only on that maxim through which you can at the same time will that it should become a universal law.[4]

Act as if the maxim of your action were to become through your will a universal law of nature.[5]

We must be able to will that a maxim of our action should become a universal law—this is the general canon for all moral judgment of action.[6]

Before we can evaluate this principle, which Kant calls the *categorical imperative,* we have to devote some attention to figuring out what it is supposed to mean. To do this, we must answer a variety of questions. What is a maxim? What is meant by "universal law"? What does Kant mean by "will"? Let us consider these questions in turn.

Maxims

In a footnote, Kant defines *maxim* as "a subjective principle of volition."[7] This definition is hardly helpful. Perhaps we can do better. First, however, a little background.

Kant apparently believes that when a person engages in genuine action, he always acts on some sort of general principle. The general principle will explain what the person takes himself to be doing and the circumstances in which he takes himself to be doing it. For example, if I need money, and can get some only by borrowing it, even though I know I won't be able to repay it, I might proceed to borrow some from a friend. My maxim in performing this act might be, "Whenever I need money and can get it by borrowing it, then I will borrow it, even if I know I won't be able to repay it."

Notice that this maxim is *general.* If I adopt it, I commit myself to behaving in the described way *whenever* I need money and the other conditions are satisfied. In this respect, the maxim serves to formulate a general principle of action rather than just some narrow reason applicable in just one case.[8] So a maxim must describe some general sort of situation, and then propose some form of action for the situation. To adopt a maxim is to commit yourself to acting in the described way whenever the situation in question arises.

It seems clear that Kant holds that every action has a maxim, although he does not explicity state this view. When we speak of an action here, we mean a concrete, particular action, or *act-token*, rather than an *act-type*. Furthermore, we must distinguish between genuine actions and what we may call "mere bodily movements." It would be absurd to maintain that a man who scratches himself in his sleep is acting on the maxim "When I itch, I shall scratch." His scratching is a mere bodily movement, and has no maxim. A man who deliberately sets out to borrow some money from a friend, on the other hand, does perform an action. And according to our interpretation of Kant, his action must have a maxim.

It would be implausible to maintain that before we act, we always consciously formulate the maxim of our action. Most of the time we simply go ahead and perform the action without giving any conscious thought to what we're doing, or what our situation is. We're usually too intent on getting the job done. Nevertheless, if we are asked after the fact, we often recognize that we actually were acting on a general policy, or maxim. For example, if you are taking a test, and you set about to answer each question correctly, you probably won't give any conscious thought to your maxim. You will be too busy thinking about the test. But if someone were to ask you to explain what you are doing and to explain the policy upon which you are doing it, you might then realize that in fact you have been acting on a maxim. Your maxim might be, "Whenever I am taking an academic test, and I believe I know the correct answers, I shall give what I take to be the correct answers." So a person may act on a maxim even though she hasn't consciously entertained it.

In one respect, the maxim of an action may be inaccurate: it does not so much represent the actual situation of the action as it does the situation the agent takes himself to be in. Suppose, for example, that I have a lot of money in my savings account but I have forgotten all about it. I take myself to be broke. When I go out to borrow some money from a friend, my maxim might be, "When I am broke and can get money in no other way, I shall borrow some from a friend." In this case, my maxim does not apply to my actual situation. For my actual situation is not one in which I am broke. Yet the maxim does apply to the situation I take myself to be in. For I believe that I am broke, and I believe that I can get money in no other way. So it is important to recognize that a maxim is a general policy statement that describes the sort of situation the agent takes himself to be in when he performs an action, and the sort of action he takes himself to be performing. In fact, both the situation and the action may be different from what the agent takes them to be.

Another point about maxims that should be recognized is this. Externally similar actions may in fact have radically different maxims. Here is an elaborated version of an example given by Kant that illustrates this point.[9] Suppose there are two grocers, Mr. Grimbley and Mr. Hughes. Mr. Grimbley's main goal in life is to get rich. After careful consideration, he has decided that in the long run he'll make more money if he gains a reputation for treating his customers fairly. In other words, he believes that "honesty is the best policy—because it pays." Hence, Mr. Grimbley scrupulously sees to it that every customer gets the correct change. When Mr. Grimbley gives correct change to a customer, he acts on this maxim:

M_1: *When I can gain a good business reputation by giving correct change, I shall give correct change.*

Mr. Hughes, on the other hand, has decided that it would be morally wrong to cheat his customers. This decision has moved him to adopt the policy of always giving the correct change. He doesn't care whether his honest dealings will in the long run contribute to an increase in sales. Even if he were to discover that honesty in business dealings does *not* pay, he would still treat his customers honestly. So Mr. Hughes apparently acts on some maxim such as this:

M_2: *When I can perform a morally right act by giving correct change, I shall give correct change.*

Mr. Grimbley's overt act of giving correct change to a customer looks just like Mr. Hughes's overt act of giving correct change to a customer. Their customers cannot tell, no matter how closely they observe the behavior of Mr. Grimbley and Mr. Hughes, what their maxims are. However, as we have seen, the actions of Mr. Grimbley are associated with a maxim radically different from that associated with the actions of Mr. Hughes.

For our purposes, it will be useful to introduce a concept that Kant does not employ. This is the concept of the *generalized form* of a maxim. Suppose I decide to go to sleep one night and my maxim in performing this act is this:

M_3: *Whenever I am tired, I shall sleep.*

My maxim is stated in such a way as to contain explicit references to me. It contains two occurrences of the word "I." The generalized form of my maxim is the principle we would get if we were to revise my maxim so as to make it applicable to everyone. Thus, the generalized form of my maxim is this:

GM_3:   *Whenever anyone is tired, he will sleep.*

In general, then, we can represent the form of a maxim in this way:

M: Whenever I am ____, *I shall* ____.

Actual maxims have descriptions of situations in the first blank and descriptions of actions in the second blank. The generalized form of a maxim can be represented in this way:

GM: Whenever anyone is ____, *she will* ____.

So much, then, for maxims. Let us turn to our second question, "What is meant by universal law?"

Universal Law

When, in the formulation of the categorical imperative, Kant speaks of "universal law," he seems to have one or the other of two things in mind. Sometimes he seems to be thinking of a *universal law of nature,* and sometimes he seems to be thinking of a *universal law of freedom.*

A *law of nature* is a fully general statement that describes not only how things are, but how things always *must* be. Consider this example: If the temperature of a gas in an enclosed container is increased, then the pressure will increase too. This statement accurately describes the behavior of gases in enclosed containers. Beyond this, however, it describes behavior that is, in a certain sense, necessary. The pressure not only *does* increase, but it *must* increase if the volume remains the same and the temperature is increased. This "must" expresses not logical or moral necessity, but "physical necessity." Thus, a law of nature is a fully general statement that expresses a physical necessity.

A *universal law of freedom* is a universal principle describing how all people ought to act in a certain circumstance. It does not have to be a legal enactment—it needn't be passed by Congress or signed by the president. Furthermore, some universal laws of freedom are not always followed—although they should be. If in fact it is true that all promises ought to be kept, then this principle is a universal law of freedom: If anyone has made a promise, he keeps it. The "must" in a statement such as "If you have made a promise, then you must keep it" does not express logical or physical necessity. It may be said to express moral necessity. Using this concept of moral necessity, we can say that a universal law of freedom is a fully general statement that expresses a moral necessity.

Sometimes Kant's categorical imperative is stated in terms of universal laws of nature, and sometimes in terms of universal laws of freedom. We will consider the "law of nature" version, since Kant appeals to it in discussing some fairly important examples.

Willing

To will that something be the case is more than to merely wish for it to be the case. A person might wish that there would be peace everywhere in the world. Yet knowing that it is not within his power to bring about this wished-for state of affairs, he might refrain from willing that there be peace everywhere in the world. It is not easy to say just what a person does when he wills that something be the case. According to one view, willing that something be the case is something like commanding yourself to make it be the case. So if I will my arm to go up, that would be something like commanding myself to raise my arm. The Kantian concept of willing is a bit more complicated, however. According to Kant, it makes sense to speak of willing something to happen, even if that something is not an action. For example, we can speak of someone willing that everyone keep their promises.

Some states of affairs are impossible. They simply cannot occur. For example, consider the state of affairs of your jumping up and down while remaining perfectly motionless. It simply cannot be done. Yet a sufficiently foolish or irrational person might will that such a state of affairs occur. That would be as absurd as commanding someone else to jump up and down while remaining motionless. Kant would say of a person who has willed in this way that his will has "contradicted itself." We can also put the point by saying that the person has willed inconsistently.

Inconsistency in willing can arise in another, somewhat less obvious way. Suppose a person has already willed that he remain motionless. He does not change this volition, but persists in willing that he remain motionless. At the same time, however, he begins to will that he jump up and down. Although each volition is self-consistent, it is inconsistent to will both of them at the same time. This is a second way in which inconsistency in willing can arise.

It may be the case that there are certain things that everyone must always will. For example, we may have to will that we avoid intense pain. Anyone who wills something that is inconsistent with something everyone must will, thereby wills inconsistently.

Some of Kant's examples suggest that he held that inconsistency in willing can arise in a third way. This form of inconsistency is a bit more complex to describe. Suppose a person wills to be in Boston on Monday and also wills to be in San Francisco on Tuesday. Suppose, furthermore, that because of certain foul-ups at the airport it will be impossible for her to get from Boston to San Francisco on Tuesday. In this case, Kant would perhaps say that the person has willed inconsistently.

In general, we can say that a person wills inconsistently if he wills that p be the case and he wills that q be the case and it is impossible for p and q to be the case together.

The Categorical Imperative

With all this as background, we may be in a position to interpret the first version of Kant's categorical imperative. Our interpretation is this:

CI_1: *An act is morally right if and only if the agent of the act can consistently will that the generalized form of the maxim of the act be a law of nature.*

We can simplify our formulation slightly by introducing a widely used technical term. We can say that a maxim is *universalizable* if and only if the agent who acts upon it can consistently will that its generalized form be a law of nature. Making use of this new term, we can restate our first version of the categorical imperative as follows:

CI_1': *An act is morally right if and only if its maxim is universalizable.*

As formulated here, the categorical imperative is a statement of necessary and sufficient conditions for the moral rightness of actions. Some commentators have claimed that Kant did not intend his principle to be understood in this way. They have suggested that Kant meant it to be understood merely as a necessary but not sufficient condition for morally right action. Thus, they would prefer to formulate the imperative in some way such as this:

CI_1'': *An act is morally right only if its maxim is universalizable.*

Understood in this way, the categorical imperative points out one thing to avoid in action. That is, it tells us to avoid actions whose maxims cannot be universalized. But it does not tell us the distinguishing feature of the actions we should perform. Thus, it does not provide us with a criterion of morally right action. Since Kant explicitly affirms that his principle is "the supreme principle of morality," it is reasonable to suppose that he intended it to be taken as a statement of necessary and sufficient conditions for morally right action. In any case, we will take the first version of the categorical imperative to be CI_1, rather than CI_1''.

It is interesting to note that other commentators have claimed that the categorical imperative isn't a criterion of right action at all. They have claimed that it was intended to be understood as a criterion of correctness for *maxims*.[10] These commentators might formulate the principle in this way:

CI_1''':   *A maxim is morally acceptable if and only if it is universalizable*.

This interpretation is open to a variety of objections. In the first place, it is not supported by the text. Kant repeatedly states that the categorical imperative is the basic principle by which we are to evaluate actions.[11] Furthermore, when he presents his formulations of the categorical imperative, he generally states it as a principle about the moral rightness of action. Finally, it is somewhat hard to see why we should be interested in a principle such as CI_1'''. For it does not constitute a theory about right action, or good persons, or anything else that has traditionally been a subject of moral enquiry. CI_1, on the other hand, competes directly with act utilitarianism, rule utilitarianism, and other classical moral theories.

In order to gain a better insight into the workings of the categorical imperative, it may be worthwhile to compare it with a doctrine with which it is sometimes confused—the golden rule. The golden rule has been formulated in a wide variety of ways.[12] Generally, however, it looks something like this:

GR: *An act is morally right if and only if, in performing it, the agent refrains from treating others in ways in which he would not want the others to treat him*.

According to GR, then, if you wouldn't want others to lie to you, it is wrong to lie to them. If you would want others to treat you with respect, then it is right to treat others with respect.

Kant explicitly rejects the view that his categorical imperative is equivalent to the golden rule.[13] He points out a number of respects in which the two doctrines differ. For one, GR is not applicable to cases in which only one person is involved. Consider suicide. When a person commits suicide, he does not "treat others" in any way; he only "treats himself." Hence, when a person commits suicide, he does not treat others in ways in which he would not want the others to treat him. Therefore, under GR, anyone who commits suicide performs a morally right act. CI_1, on the other hand, may not yield this result. For if a person commits suicide, he does so on a maxim, whether other people are involved or not. Either his maxim is universalizable, or it is not. If it is not, CI_1 entails that his action is not right. If it is, CI_1 entails that his action is right. In this respect, CI_1 is clearly distinct from GR.

Kant also hints at another respect in which the two doctrines differ. Suppose a person considers herself to be utterly self-sufficient. She feels that she has no need of aid from others. GR then has nothing to say against her refraining from extending any kindness to others. After all, she has no objection to being treated in this unkind way by them. So GR entails that her behavior is morally right. CI_1, on the other hand, has no such consequence. Whether this person is willing to be mistreated by others or not, it may still be irrational of her to will that it be a law of nature that no one help anyone else. If so, CI_1 rules out uncharitableness, whether the agent likes it or not.

Similar considerations apply to masochists, whose behavior is not adequately guided by GR. After all, we surely don't want to allow the masochist to torture others simply on the grounds that he wouldn't object to being tortured by them! The unusual desires of masochists do not pose any special threat to CI_1.

So the main difference between GR and CI_1 seems to be this: According to GR, what makes an act right is the fact that the agent would not object to "having it done to himself." This opens the door to incorrect results in cases in which the agent, for some unexpected reason, would not object to being mistreated. According to CI_1, what makes an act right is the fact that the agent's maxim in performing it can be universalized. Thus, even if he would not object to being mistreated by others, his mistreatment of them may be wrong simply because it would be *irrational* to will that everyone should mistreat others in the same way.

Kant's Four Examples

In a very famous passage in Chapter II of the *Groundwork*, Kant presents four illustrations of the application of the categorical imperative.[14] In each case, in Kant's opinion, the act is morally wrong and the maxim is not universalizable. Thus, Kant holds that his theory implies that each of these acts is wrong. If Kant is right about this, then he has given us four positive instances of his theory. That is, he has given us four cases in which his theory yields correct results. Unfortunately, the illustrations are not entirely persuasive.

Kant distinguishes between "duties to self" and "duties to others." He also distinguishes between "perfect" and "imperfect" duties. This gives him four categories of duty: "perfect to self," "perfect to others," "imperfect to self," and "imperfect to others." Kant gives one example of each type of duty. By "perfect duty," Kant says he means a duty "which admits of no exception in the interests of inclination."[15] Kant seems to have in mind something like this: If a person has a perfect duty to perform a certain kind of action, then he must *always* do that kind of action when the opportunity arises. For example, Kant apparently holds that we must always perform the (negative) action of refraining from committing suicide. This would be a perfect duty. On the other hand, if a person has an imperfect duty to do a kind of action, then he must at least *sometimes* perform an action of that kind when the opportunity arises. For example, Kant maintains that we have an imperfect duty to help others in distress. We should devote at least some of our time to charitable activities, but we are under no obligation to give all of our time to such work.

The perfect/imperfect distinction has been drawn in a variety of ways— none of them entirely clear. Some commentators have said that if a person has a perfect duty to do a certain action, *a*, then there must be someone else who has a corresponding right to demand that *a* be done. This seems to be the case in Kant's second example, but not in his first example. Thus, it isn't clear that we should understand the concept of perfect duty in this way. Although the perfect/imperfect distinction is fairly interesting in itself, it does not play a major role in Kant's theory. Kant introduces the distinction primarily to insure that his examples will illustrate different kinds of duty.

Kant's first example illustrates the application of CI_1 to a case of perfect duty to oneself—the alleged duty to refrain from committing suicide. Kant describes the miserable state of the person contemplating suicide, and tries to show that his categorical imperative entails that the person should not take his own life. In order to simplify our discussion, let us use the abbreviation "a_1" to refer to the act of suicide the man would commit, if he were to commit suicide. According to Kant, every act must have a maxim. Kant tells us the maxim of a_1: "From self-love I make it my principle to shorten my life if its continuance threatens more evil than it promises pleasure."[16] Let us simplify and clarify this maxim, understand-ing it as follows:

$M(a_1)$:   *When continuing to live will bring me more pain than pleasure, I shall commit suicide out of self-love.*

The generalized form of this maxim is as follows:

$GM(a_1)$:   *Whenever continuing to live will bring anyone more pain than pleasure, he will commit suicide out of self-love.*

Since Kant believes that suicide is wrong, he attempts to show that his moral principle, the categorical imperative, entails that a_1 is wrong. To do this, of course, he needs to show that the agent of a_1 cannot consistently will that $GM(a_1)$ be a law of nature. Kant tries to show this in the following passage:

. . . a system of nature by whose law the very same feeling whose function is to stimulate the furtherance of life should actually destroy life would contradict itself and consequently could not subsist as a system of nature. Hence this maxim cannot possibly hold as a universal law of nature and is therefore entirely opposed to the supreme principle of all duty.[17]

The general outline of Kant's argument is clear enough:

SUICIDE EXAMPLE

1. $GM(a_1)$ cannot be a law of nature.

2. If $GM(a_1)$ cannot be a law of nature, then the agent of a_1 cannot consistently will that $GM(a_1)$ be a law of nature.

3. a_1 is morally right if and only if the agent of a_1 can consistently will that $GM(a_1)$ be a law of nature.

4. Therefore, a_1 is not morally right.

In order to determine whether Kant really has shown that this theory entails that a_1 is not right, let us look at this argument more closely. First of all, for our purposes we can agree that the argument is valid. If all the premises are true, then the argument shows that the imagined act of suicide would not be right. CI_1, here being used as premise (3), would thus be shown to imply that a_1 is not right.

Since we are now interested primarily in seeing how Kant makes use of CI_1, we can withhold judgment on the merits of it for the time being.

The second premise seems fairly plausible. For although an irrational person could probably will almost anything, it surely would be difficult for a perfectly rational person to will that something be a law of nature if that thing could not be a law of nature. Let us grant, then, that it would not be possible for the agent to consistently will that $GM(a_1)$ be a law of nature if in fact $GM(a_1)$ could not be a law of nature.

The first premise is the most troublesome, Kant apparently assumes that "self-love" has as its function, the stimulation of the furtherance of life. Given this, he seems to reason that self-love cannot also contribute sometimes to the destruction of life. Perhaps Kant assumes that a given feeling cannot have two "opposite" functions. However, if $GM(a_1)$ were a law of nature, self-love would have to contribute toward self-destruction in some cases. Hence, Kant seems to conclude, $GM(a_1)$ cannot be a law of nature. And so we have our first premise.

If this is Kant's reasoning, it is not very impressive. In the first place, it is not clear why we should suppose that self-love has the function of stimulating the furtherance of life. Indeed, it is not clear why we should suppose that self-love has any function at all! Second, it is hard to see why self-love can't serve two "opposite" functions. Perhaps self-love motivates us to stay alive when continued life would be pleasant, but motivates us to stop living when continued life would be unpleasant. Why should we hold this to be impossible?

So it appears that Kant's first illustration is not entirely success-ful. Before we turn to the second illustration, however, a few further comments may be in order. First, some philosophers would say that it is better that Kant's argument failed here. Many moralists would take the following position: Kant's view about suicide is wrong. The act of suicide out of self-love, a_1, is morally blameless. In certain circum-stances suicide is each person's "own business." Thus, these moralists would say that if the categorical imperative did imply that a_1 is morally wrong, as Kant tries to show, then Kant's theory would be defective. But since Kant was not entirely successful in showing that his theory had this implication, the theory has not been shown to have any incorrect results.

A second point to notice about the suicide example is its scope. It is important to recognize that in this passage Kant has not attempted to show that suicide is always wrong. Perhaps Kant's personal view is that it is never right to commit suicide. However, in the passage in question he attempts to show only that a certain act of suicide, one based on a certain maxim, would be wrong. For all Kant has said here, other acts of suicide, done according to other maxims, might be permitted by the categorical imperative.

Let us turn now to the second illustration. Suppose I find myself hard-pressed financially and I decide that the only way in which I can get some money is by borrowing it from a friend. I realize that I will have to promise to repay the money, even though I won't in fact be able to do so. For I foresee that my financial situation will be even worse later on than it is at present. If I perform this action, a_2, of borrowing money on a false promise, I will perform it on this maxim:

$M(a_2)$:   *When I need money and can get some by borrowing it on a false promise, then I shall borrow the money and promise to repay, even though I know that I won't be able to repay.*

The generalized form of my maxim is this:

$GM(a_2)$:   *Whenever anyone needs money and can get some by borrowing it on a false promise, then he will borrow the money and promise to repay, even though he knows that he won't be able to repay.*

Kant's view is that I cannot consistently will that $GM(a_2)$ be a law of nature. This view emerges clearly in the following passage:

. . . I can by no means will a universal law of lying; for by such a law there could properly be no promises at all, since it would be futile to profess a will for future action to others who would not believe my profession or who, if they did so over-hastily, would pay me back in like coin; and consequently my maxim, as soon as it was made a universal law, would be bound to annul itself.[18]

It is important to be clear about what Kant is saying here. He is not arguing against lying on the grounds that if I lie, others will soon lose confidence in me and eventually won't believe my promises. Nor is he arguing against lying on the grounds that my lie will contribute to a general practice of lying, which in turn will lead to a breakdown of trust and the destruction of the practice of promising. These considerations are basically utilitarian. Kant's point is more subtle. He is saying that there is something covertly self-contradictory about the state of affairs in which, as a law of nature, everyone makes a false promise when in need of a loan. Perhaps Kant's point is this: Such a state of affairs is self-contradictory because, on the one hand, in such a state of affairs everyone in need would borrow money on a false promise, and yet, on the other hand, in that state of affairs no one could borrow money on a false promise—for if promises were always violated, who would be silly enough to loan any money?

Since the state of affairs in which everyone in need borrows money on a false promise is covertly self-contradictory, it is irrational to will it to occur. No one can consistently will that this state of affairs should occur. But for me to will that $GM(a_2)$ be a law of nature is just for me to will that this impossible state of affairs occur. Hence, I cannot consistently will that the generalized form of my maxim be a law of nature. According to CI_1, my act is not right unless I can consistently will that the generalized form of its maxim be a law of nature. Hence, according to CI_1, my act of borrowing the money on the false promise is not morally right.

We can restate the essentials of this argument much more succinctly:

1. $GM(a_2)$ cannot be a law of nature.

2. If $GM(a_2)$ cannot be a law of nature, then I cannot consistently will that $GM(a_2)$ be a law of nature.

3. a_2 is morally right if and only if I can consistently will that $GM(a_2)$ be a law of nature.

4. Therefore, a_2 is not morally right.

The first premise is based upon the view that it would somehow be self-contradictory for it to be a law of nature that everyone in need makes a lying promise. For in that (allegedly impossible) state of affairs there would be promises, since those in need would make them, and there would also not be promises, since no one would believe that anyone was really committing himself to future payment by the use of the words "I promise." So, as Kant says, the generalized form of the maxim "annuls itself." It cannot be a law of nature.

The second premise is just like the second premise in the previous example. It is based on the idea that it is somehow irrational to will that something be the case if in fact it is impossible for it to be the case. So if it really is impossible for $GM(a_2)$ to be a law of nature, then it would be irrational of me to will that it be so. Hence, I cannot consistently will that the generalized form of my maxim be a law of nature. In other words, I cannot consistently will that it be a law of nature that whenever anyone needs money and can get some on a false promise, then he will borrow some and promise to repay, even though he knows that he won't be able to repay.

The third premise of the argument is the categorical imperative. If the rest of the argument is acceptable, then the argument as a whole shows that the categorical imperative, together with these other facts, implies that my lying promise would not be morally right. This would seem to be a reasonable result.

Some readers have apparently taken this example to show that according to Kantianism, it is always wrong to make a false promise. Indeed, Kant himself may have come to this conclusion. Yet if we reflect on the argument for a moment, we will see that the view of these readers is surely not the case. At best, the argument shows only that one specific act of making a false promise would be wrong. That one act is judged to be wrong because its maxim allegedly cannot be universalized. Other acts of making false promises would have to be evaluated independently. Perhaps it will turn out that every act of making a false promise has a maxim that cannot be universalized. If so, CI_1 would imply that they are all wrong. So far, however, we have been given no reason to suppose that this is the case.

Other critics would insist that Kant hasn't even succeeded in showing that a_2 is morally wrong. They would claim that the first premise of the argument is false. Surely it could be a law of nature that everyone will make a false promise when in need of money, they would say. If people borrowed money on false promises rarely enough, and kept their word on other promises, then no contradiction would arise. There would then be no reason to suppose that "no one would believe he was being promised anything, but would laugh at utterances of this kind as empty shams."[19]

Let us turn, then, to the third example. Kant now illustrates the application of the categorical imperative to a case of imperfect duty to oneself. The action in question is the "neglect of natural talents." Kant apparently holds that it is wrong for a person to let all of his natural talents go to waste. Of course, if a person has several natural talents, he is not required to develop all of them. Perhaps Kant considers this to be an imperfect duty partly because a person has the freedom to select which talents he will develop and which he will allow to rust.

Kant imagines the case of someone who is comfortable as he is and who, out of laziness, contemplates performing the act, a_3, of letting all his talents rust. His maxim in doing this would be:

$M(a_3)$:   *When I am comfortable as I am, I shall let my talents rust.*

When generalized, the maxim becomes:

$GM(a_3)$:   *Whenever anyone is comfortable as he is, he will let his talents rust.*

Kant admits that $GM(a_3)$ could be a law of nature. Thus, his argument in this case differs from the arguments he produced in the first two cases. Kant proceeds to outline the reasoning by which the agent would come to see that it would be wrong to perform a_3:

He then sees that a system of nature could indeed always subsist under such a universal law, although (like the South Sea Islanders) every man should let his talents rust and should be bent on devoting his life solely to idleness, indulgence, procreation, and, in a word, to enjoyment. Only he cannot possibly *will* that this should become a universal law of nature or should be implanted in us as such a law by a natural instinct. For as a rational being he necessarily wills that all his powers should be developed, since they serve him, and are given him, for all sorts of possible ends.[20]

Once again, Kant's argument seems to be based on a rather dubious appeal to natural purposes. Allegedly, nature implanted our talents in us for all sorts of purposes. Hence, we necessarily will to develop them. If we also will to let them rust, we are willing both to develop them (as we must) and to refrain from developing them. Anyone who wills both of these things obviously wills inconsistently. Hence, the agent cannot consistently will that his talents rust. This, together with the categorical imperative, implies that it would be wrong to perform the act, a_3, of letting one's talents rust.

The argument can be put as follows:

RUSTING-TALENTS EXAMPLE

1. Everyone necessarily wills that all his talents be developed.

2. If everyone necessarily wills that all his talents be developed, then the agent of a_3 cannot consistently will that $GM(a_3)$ be a law of nature.

3. a_3 is morally right if and only if the agent of a_3 can consistently will that $GM(a_3)$ be a law of nature.

4. Therefore a_3 is not morally right.

This argument seems even less persuasive than the others. In the quoted passage Kant himself presents a counterexample to the first premise. The South Sea Islanders, according to Kant, do not will to develop their talents. This fact, if it is one, is surely inconsistent with the claim that we all necessarily will that all our talents be developed. Even if Kant is wrong about the South Sea Islanders, his first premise is still extremely implausible. Couldn't there be a rational person who, out of idleness, simply does not will to develop his talents? If there could not be such a person, then what is the point of trying to show that we are under some specifically moral obligation to develop all our talents?

Once again, however, some philosophers may feel that Kant would have been worse off if his example had succeeded. These philosophers would hold that we in fact have no moral obligation to develop our talents. If Kant's theory had entailed that we have such an obligation, they would insist, then that would have shown that Kant's theory is defective.

In Kant's fourth illustration the categorical imperative is applied to an imperfect duty to others—the duty to help others who are in distress. Kant describes a man who is flourishing and who contemplates performing the act, a_4, of giving nothing to charity. His maxim is not stated by Kant in this passage, but it can probably be formulated as follows:

$M(a_4)$:   *When I'm flourishing and others are in distress, I shall give nothing to charity.*

When generalized, this maxim becomes:

$GM(a_4)$:   *Whenever anyone is flourishing and others are in distress, he will give nothing to charity.*

As in the other example of imperfect duty, Kant acknowledges that $GM(a_4)$ could be a law of nature. Yet he claims once again that the agent cannot consistently will that it be a law of nature. He explains this by arguing as follows:

For a will which decided in this way would be in conflict with itself, since many a situation might arise in which the man needed love and sympathy from others, and in which, by such a law of nature sprung from his own will, he would rob himself of all hope of the help he wants for himself.[21]

Kant's point here seems to be this: The day may come when the agent is no longer flourishing. He may need charity from others. If that day does come, then he will find that he wills that others give him such aid. However, in willing that $GM(a_4)$ be a law of nature, he has already willed that no one should give charitable aid to anyone. Hence, on that dark day, his will will contradict itself. Thus, he cannot consistently will that $GM(a_4)$ be a law of nature. This being so, the categorical imperative entails that a_4 is not right.

If this is Kant's reasoning, then his reasoning is defective. For we cannot infer from the fact that the person *may* someday want aid from others, that he in fact already is willing inconsistently when he wills today that no one should give aid to anyone. The main reason for this is that that dark day may not come, in which case no conflict will arise. Furthermore, as is pretty obvious upon reflection, even if that dark day does arrive, the agent may steadfastly stick to his general policy. He may say, "I didn't help others when they were in need, and now that I'm in need I don't want any help from them." In this way, he would avoid having inconsistent policies. Unless this attitude is irrational, which it does not seem to be, Kant's fourth example is unsuccessful.

Notes

1. Immanuel Kant (1724–1804) is one of the greatest Continental philosophers. He produced quite a few philosophical works of major importance. The *Critique of Pure Reason* (1781) is perhaps his most famous work.
2. Kant's *Grundlegung zur Metaphysik der Sitten* (1785) has been translated into English many times. All references here are to Immanuel Kant, *Groundwork of the Metaphysic of Morals,* translated and analysed by H. J. Paton (New York: Harper & Row, 1964).
3. Kant, *Groundwork,* p. 70.
4. *Ibid.,* p. 88.
5. *Ibid.,* p. 89.
6. *Ibid.,* p. 91.
7. *Ibid.,* p. 69n.
8. In some unusual cases, it may accidentally happen that the situation to which the maxim applies can occur only once, as, for example, in the case of successful suicide. Nevertheless, the maxim is general in form.
9. Kant, *Groundwork,* p. 65.
10. See, for example, Robert Paul Wolff, *The Autonomy of Reason* (New York: Harper & Row, 1973), p. 163.
11. This is stated especially clearly on p. 107 of the *Groundwork.*
12. For an interesting discussion of various formulations of the golden rule, see Marcus Singer, "The Golden Rule," in *The Encyclopedia of Philosophy,* ed. Paul Edwards (New York: Macmillan; Free Press, 1967), Vol. 3, pp. 365–67.
13. Kant, *Groundwork,* p. 97n.
14. *Ibid.,* pp. 89–91.
15. *Ibid.,* p. 89n.
16. *Ibid.,* p. 89.
17. *Ibid.*
18. *Ibid.,* p. 71.
19. *Ibid.*
20. *Ibid.*
21. *Ibid.,* p. 91.

RESPECT FOR PERSONS
Alan Donagan

Alan Donagan is professor of philosophy at California Institute of Technology and is author of The Theory of Morality *(1977), from which the following selection was taken. After dismissing the Golden Rule ("All things whatsoever ye would that men should do unto you, do ye so to them") as a candidate for a fundamental moral principle, Donagan argues that the injunction, "Love your neighbor as yourself," when appropriately interpreted, can serve as a fundamental moral principle. Donagan claims that this injunction is best understood as equivalent to Kant's second formulation of the categorical imperative, "Act always so that you respect every human being, yourself or another, as being a rational creature." Taking this moral principle as fundamental, Donagan goes on to develop what is often referred to as a "respect for persons" moral theory.*

I

Both Jewish and Christian thinkers have always held that the numerous specific precepts of morality are all derivable from a few substantive general principles, even though the conception of those precepts as binding upon rational creatures as such is compatible with the new intuitionist doctrine that the fundamental principles from which they derive are many. No Jewish or Christian moralist would dispute that the part of morality having to do with duties to God, which lies outside the scope of this investigation, derives from the principle in the Mosaic Shema: that God is one, and is to be loved with one's whole mind and heart (Deut. 6:5). And most of them have held that the part having to do with rational creatures, in their relations with themselves and with one another, also derives from a single first principle. Here, however, tradition has diverged, and two different principles have each won some recognition as fundamental. Some traditional moralists have maintained that the two, despite their obvious differences, coincide at a deeper level. Of these, the most distinguished was Kant, whose first and second formulas of the fundamental principle of morality philosophically restate the two apparently different traditional principles, and who declared that those formulas "are at bottom merely . . . formulations of the very same law."[1]

From Alan Donagan, *The Theory of Morality* (University of Chicago Press). Copyright © 1977 by The University of Chicago. Reprinted by permission of the author and publisher.

The more familiar of the two traditional candidates for recognition as the fundamental principle of morality, with respect to the relations of rational creatures to themselves and to one another, is also the more recent. In Judaism, its authority is talmudic. According to the Babylonian Talmud, a gentile once demanded of Hillel that he be taught the whole Law while he stood on one foot. "Do not do to your fellow what you hate to have done to you," Hillel told him. "This is the whole Law entire; the rest is explanation."[2] A similar saying of Jesus is preserved by Matthew: "All things whatsoever ye would that men should do to you, do ye even so to them."[3] Although one of these formulations is negative and the other positive, they are in fact equivalent; for to forbid an action of a certain kind, and to command one of its contradictory kind, are equivalent. The precept formulated in these two ways has become known as "The Golden Rule."

Two objections are commonly made to receiving the Golden Rule as the fundamental principle of morality. First, it excludes the possibility that it may be right to do anything to another which you would hate to have done to you. Yet, as Kant pointed out, the Hebrew-Christian code calls upon parents, teachers, and judges to do many things to others, for their good or for the common good, which most plain men would hate to have done to them. How many judges would not hate to be sentenced, if they were guilty?[4] Second, the Golden Rule *prima facie* fails to condemn any action which affects the agent alone (as suicide may), or any action between consenting persons, to which there is no other party. Yet common morality as traditionally conceived certainly recognizes the existence of duties to oneself, and hence must forbid actions contributing to violations of those duties when done at the behest of somebody else.

Such objections can be forestalled by appropriate interpretations. For example, with respect to Hillel's formulation, a moralist might distinguish natural hating from unnatural; then, having laid it down that, in the Rule, hating is to be interpreted as natural hating, urge that it is unnatural either to hate getting one's just deserts or not to hate such wrongs to oneself as suicide. By such an interpretation, certain substantive principles of duty are in effect absorbed into the Rule. Other substantive principles can be introduced into it by other interpretations.

That the common objections to it can be forestalled by such interpretations, which are neither dishonest nor arbitrary, points to a characteristic of the Golden Rule which not only exposes its inadequacy as a first principle but also explains its ubiquity. For it is ubiquitous. The earliest known version of it, one very like Hillel's, is credited to Confucius; and others appear in all the major religions. It is proverb in many languages. Nor does the evidence suggest that it was diffused from a single source. The explanation is simple. What a man would or would not have another do to him is in part a function of the mores he has made his own. Hence in cultures whose mores differ radically, what the Golden Rule is taken to require or forbid will differ radically too. And so any system of conduct that can be put forward as rational can include it.

The variability of what, in different cultures, the Golden Rule is taken to require or forbid shows that it is accepted because of its form. It expresses the universality of the precepts of whatever system incorporates it. Its force is therefore, as Sidgwick pointed out, that of a principle of impartiality: in no system that incorporates it can it be permissible for A to treat B in a manner in which it would be impermissible for B to treat A, "merely on the ground that they are two different individuals, and without there being any difference between the natures or the circumstances of the two which can be stated as a reasonable ground for difference of treatment."[5] In its original form, Kant's first formula, "Act only according to that maxim by which you can at the same time will that it should become a universal law,"[6] has the same force. It is a rubric for an act of self-examination by which anybody may verify whether his judgment of how he may treat another has a place in the system of conduct he accepts, or whether it is an exception made in his own interest. But, obviously, no principle of impartiality that is common to different systems of mores can serve as the substantive first principle that distinguishes any one of them from the others.

Although the Golden Rule has always enjoyed popular esteem and has recently been recognized as an adequate substantive principle by so eminent a moralist as R. M. Hare,[7] most traditional moral theologians and philosophers have attached more weight to the second of the two traditional candidates for recognition as the first principle of morality. It is presented in a well-known passage that precedes the parable of the Good Samaritan in Luke's gospel.

And behold, a certain lawyer stood up, and tempted [Jesus], saying, Master, what shall I do to inherit eternal life? He said unto him, What is written in the Law? how readest thou? And he answering said, Thou shalt love the Lord thy God with all thy heart, and with all they soul, and with all thy strength, and with all thy mind; and thy neighbor as thyself. And he said unto him, Thou hast answered right: this do, and thou shalt live (10:25–28).

With the approval of Jesus, the "lawyer" (that is, student of Torah) here offers, as the fundamental principle governing the relations of human beings to themselves and to one another, an injunction from Leviticus, 19:18, *Love your neighbor as yourself*. . . .

In what follows, therefore, I take the fundamental principle of that part of traditional morality which is independent of any theological presupposition to have been expressed in the scriptural commandment, "Thou shalt love thy neighbor as thyself," understanding one's neighbor to be any fellow human being, and love to be a matter, not of feeling, but of acting in ways in which human beings as such can choose to act. The philosophical sense of this commandment was correctly expressed by Kant in his formula that one act so that one treats humanity always as an end and never as a means only. However, Kant was mistaken in thinking this formula to be equivalent to his formula of universal law, in which he captured the philosophical truth underlying the inaccurately stated Golden Rule.

Since treating a human being, in virtue of its rationality, as an end in itself, is the same as respecting it as a rational creature, Kant's formula of the fundamental principle may be restated in a form more like that of the scriptural commandment that is its original: *Act always so that you respect every human being, yourself or another, as being a rational creature*. And, since it will be convenient that the fundamental principle of the system to be developed be formulated in terms of the concept of permissibility analysed in the preceding section, the canonical form in which that principle will hereafter be cited is: *It is impermissible not to respect every human being, oneself or any other, as a rational creature*.

II

The structure of the fundamental principle is itself simple. It contains only one concept peculiar to moral thought, that of (moral) permissibility. And its sense is that no action which falls under the concept of not respecting some human being as a rational creature can fall under the concept of being permissible. The second concept it contains, that of (not) respecting some human being as a rational creature, is not peculiar to moral thinking. It has a place in descriptions of human conduct in anthropology and psychology, and of course in everyday descriptive discourse.

Of those precepts derivable from the first principle which are needed for the solution of serious moral problems, virtually all turn on the concept of respecting a human being as a rational creature, and virtually none on the concept of permissibility. There are, indeed, serious problems about the construction of formal systems in which "it is permissible that" figures as a modal operator, and which are investigated in deontic logic; but their philosophical interest is logical rather than moral. The problems that will occupy us in what follows all have to do with what falls under the concept of respecting a human being as rational, and what does not.

None of these problems can be solved by means of the logical operation of substituting for one expression another that, by definition, is synonymous with it. The concept of respecting a human being as a rational creature is not usefully definable for our purposes. Thus to define it as treating a human being, by virtue of his rationality, as an end in itself, while perhaps clarifying, does not furnish us with a useful substituend. Yet it does not follow that the process of deriving specific precepts from the fundamental principle is arbitrary and unreasoned.

The formal character of such derivations is uncomplicated. Consider the three schemata of specific moral precepts . . . namely,

1. It always permissible to do an action of the kind *K*, as such;

2. It is never permissible to do an action of the kind *K*;

3. It is never morally permissible not to do an action of the kind *K*, if an occasion occurs on which one can be done.

Now let us ask what are the simplest additional premises by which precepts satisfying these schemata can be validly inferred from the fundamental principle

P: It is impermissible not to respect every human being, oneself or any other, as a rational creature,

and a truth about the system of common morality being investigated, namely,

S: The principle (P) is the sole first principle of common morality.

Precepts falling under schema (1) require a proposition derivable from (P) and (S), namely,

1a: No action of a kind which, as such, does not fail to respect any human being as a rational creature, is impermissible as such,

and an additional premise, namely, one satisfying the schema

1b: No action of the kind K, as such, fails to respect any human being as a rational creature.

Precepts satisfying the schemata (2) and (3) are each directly derivable from the fundamental principle (P) together with one additional premise. Thus precepts satisfying (2) follow from (P) and a premise satisfying

2a: All actions of the kind K fail to respect some human being as a rational creature;

and those satisfying (3) follow from (P) and a premise satisfying

3a: If an occasion occurs on which an action of the kind K can be done, not to do it will fail to respect some human being as a rational creature.

Premises satisfying the schemata (1b), (2a), and (3a) may be called "specificatory premises," because they each identify a species of action as falling or not falling under the fundamental generic concept of action in which every human being is respected as a rational creature.

Although simple derivations of these three kinds raise no serious logical questions, the question of how specificatory premises satisfying the schemata (1b), (2a), and 3a) are obtained is both serious and difficult. Nor has it been much studied by philosophers. Of processes analogous to those that are required, perhaps the closest are those by which courts apply legal concepts to new cases. . . .

Legal reasoning, in which a concept is applied to new cases, presupposes that the concept has a content which in part is comprehended by members of the law-abiding community and in part remains to be determined by reflecting on cases to which it and related concepts have been applied. And it further presupposes that the determination of that concept, and its application to new cases, is not arbitrary: that, even though up to a point bad judicial decisions must be allowed to stand, according to the doctrine of *stare decisis*, there is an objective distinction between correct judicial opinions and incorrect ones. The rational processes by which such opinions are arrived at can be pronounced sound or unsound, although they cannot be usefully formalized, because they depend in large measure on weighing likenesses and differences between cases on principles which, although received, are acknowledged to be corrigible. . . .

The respects in which moral reasoning is not analogous to legal, of which the chief are that it is not confined to questions of rights which courts can practically enforce, and of wrongs which they can remedy or punish, and that it is not practically obliged to accord authority even to bad precedents, in no way impair the objectivity with which in moral reasoning general concepts are applied to specific cases. The fundamental concept of respecting every human being as a rational creature is fuzzy at the edges in the superficial sense that its application to this or that species of case can be disputed. But among those who share in the life of a culture in which the Hebrew-Christian moral tradition is accepted, the concept is in large measure understood in itself; and it is connected with numerous applications, as to the different weights of which there is some measure of agreement. This is enough for it to be possible to determine many specificatory premises with virtual certainty and others with a high degree of confidence.

The moral system that may be derived from the fundamental principle in this way may with equal truth be described as a "simple deductive" system according to Robert Nozick's classification,[8] or as an informal analytical one. The structure consisting of fundamental principle, derived precepts, and specificatory premises is strictly deductive; for every derived precept is strictly deduced, by way of some specificatory premise, either from the fundamental principle or from some precept already derived. But that structure is not the whole of the system. For virtually all the philosophical difficulties that are encountered in deriving that structure have to do with establishing the specificatory premises; and that is done by unformalized analytical reasoning in which some concept either in the fundamental principle or in a derived precept is applied to some new species of case. As with the legal reasoning to which it is analogous, many specimens of thinking of this kind are beyond dispute. Others, however, especially those having to do with the more specific and complicated cases, are not. And a further difficulty is that different thinkers sometimes do not agree about what is seriously disputable.

One strategy for indirectly establishing specificatory premises, which will be adopted in a number of the cases that follow, ought to be described in advance. Often direct analysis is not the most effective way to establish a specificatory premise; for the problem is that, while it is evident that certain kinds of action in most cases fall under a certain concept (for example, killing people in most cases is failing to respect them as rational beings), in some cases they do not, or are thought not to (for example, killing in self-defence is not failing to respect the person killed). How is a moralist to determine what the fundamental principle requires with respect to such kinds of action?

A natural approach is to begin by showing that it is impermissible to perform actions of that kind at will, and then to go on to determine the kinds of cases in which it is permissible. Accordingly, with respect to killing human beings, one would begin by establishing that:

K1: To kill another human being merely at will *is not to respect every human being (in particular, the one killed) as a rational creature.*

This would not be denied by any Jewish or Christian moralist. And now an attempt is made to find in what kinds of cases killing another human being is legitimate. For example, it might be argued that:

K2: To kill another human being who is attacking you, and concerning whom you reasonably judge that he may well kill or seriously injure you, and that his attack can only be stopped by killing him, is not to fail in respect to another human being as a rational creature, even to the one killed.

To the extent that it is possible to be assured that a complete list of such cases has been found, it will be possible to infer that:

K3: To kill another human being, except under the circumstances specified in (K2) and the other propositions obtained from the search, is to kill him merely at will.

From (K1) and (K3) it follows that, except under specified circumstances, killing a human being is impermissible. And this conclusion is equivalent, as an appropriate definition will show, to a prohibition of murder.

The chief weakness of this strategy is that it is seldom possible to eliminate all doubts of the completeness of the survey. How can we assure ourselves beyond doubt that no significant case has been overlooked? Nozick goes so far as to state that many who have ceased to assent to "any or very many exceptionless moral principles" although at one time they did so—by which I take him to refer, among others, to the many who have repudiated the traditional morality in which they were brought up—have done so because "more and more complicated cases" forced them into what seemed an interminable process of revision.[9] And he ventures the suggestion that such a history would be common among lawyers, who know by experience how difficult it is to devise, in advance, rules adequate to "all the bizarre, unexpected, arcane, and complicated cases which actually arise."[10]

This misplaces the difficulty by comparing a moralist's task to that of a legislative draftsman, to which its resemblance, despite Hare, is slight. The task of legislative draftsmen is seldom to formulate specific precepts derived from a fundamental legal principle: almost always it is to contrive a set of regulations to further the complex and politically determined objects of public policy. Thus they attempt to solve such problems as how to frame legislation by which the rich will not be able to escape income tax, but also by which municipalities may continue to raise money by selling bonds at low interest, given that the established method, exempting such interest from income tax, enables the rich to avoid income tax. Moralists and judges do not have tasks of this kind. Their business is not to contrive ways of furthering a variety of ends, many of them hard to reconcile, and all of them subject to change; they have only to work out what rationally justifiable moral and legal principles really do require, however disconcerting the result may be.

The difficulties that arise for moralists in any tradition mostly consist of discrepancies between precepts derived by established methods from their first principle or principles, and what seem to be intuitively evident applications of those first principles to cases falling under those precepts. To invert the example given above: it is an established doctrine in the Hebrew-Christian tradition that it is permissible to kill another human being in self-defence; but to some, for example Quakers, killing another human being seems to be quite evidently incompatible with respecting his humanity. Such problems have arisen, as a matter of history, far less often from "bizarre, unexpected, arcane, and complicated cases," than from deeper reflection on cases already considered in what is now a very long tradition. And that is why Nozick seems to have exaggerated as well as misplaced the difficulty of surveying all the possible kinds of circumstances in which an action, impermissible if done merely at will, is permissible. Unusual and unexpected cases are unlikely to make much difference. The chief source of doubt is the suspicion of having overlooked the significance of some feature of a case already known.

Notes

1. Kant, *Grundlegung*, p. 79 (p. 436).
2. *Babylonian Talmud*, Shabbat, p. 31a.
3. Matt. 7 : 12.
4. Cf. Kant, *Grundlegung*, p. 68 n. (p. 430).
5. Sidgwick, *Methods of Ethics*, 7th ed. (London: Routledge, 1963), p. 380.
6. Kant, *Grundlegung*, p. 52 (p. 421), tr. Beck.
7. Hare, *Freedom and Reason* (Oxford: Clarendon Press, 1963), pp. 86–111, 157–85.
8. Cf. Nozick, *Anarchy, State, and Utopia* (New York: Basic Books, 1968), pp. 4–7.
9. Ibid., p. 5.
10. Ibid., p. 5.

THE ETHICS OF RESPECT FOR PERSONS
William Frankena

William Frankena, professor emeritus at the University of Michigan, is widely published in the area of ethics. He is critical of respect-for-persons moral theories and, in the selection below, raises objections against Donagan's theory. Frankena is doubtful that there is a clear and unambiguous concept of respect that can be used to distinguish right from wrong action. Thus, according to Frankena, Donagan's respect-for-persons theory suffers from being indeterminate.

The idea of respect has been getting much respect lately both in our current moral debates and in moral philosophy, e.g. in talk of respect for life and respect for the environment or biotic community, not to mention talk of respect for authority, law, or property. Moral use of the term respect is not new, of course, being found, for example, in Shakespeare's line,

Is there no respect of place, person, nor time in you?[1]

but it has had a decided revival in our day. Respect for something is *a* vocal part at least of many people's ethics or moral value systems, and in some of them it is *the* focal point, especially in those I am calling ethics of respect for persons. By an ethics here I mean a philosophical theory held by some person, and more specifically a normative moral theory, not a meta-ethical one; and by an ethics of respect for persons (ERP), I mean roughly normative moral theories like those of Kant and a number of recent writers such as Downie and Telfer, Gauthier, and Donagan. There can, of course, also be a morality of respect for persons in practice in the life of a people, which could be called an ERP (some would say that Christian morality is an ERP), but I shall have philosophical ERPs primarily in mind, though much of what I say will apply to corresponding practicing moralities too, since these can be thought of as involving implicit normative theories or quasi-theories. . . .

I

I shall now define an ERP of the sort I mainly want to discuss as one that asserts three propositions. The first is proposition

From William Frankena, "The Ethics of Respect for Persons," *Philosophical Topics* 14 (1986): pp. 149–167. Reprinted by permission of the author and publisher.

A: All persons and only persons are moral agents.
   Or: X is a moral agent if and only if X is a person.

That is, persons and persons alone are subjects (or objects) of moral judgments for their actions, intentions, motives, traits of character, etc.; or, alternatively, persons and only persons have moral duties, rights, or virtues. Of course, actions, etc., can be said to be morally right, wrong, virtuous, etc., but then they are thought of as the actions, traits, etc., of persons. This proposition is the main part of an ERP's *theory of moral agency*, though of course this will include a good deal more. It is a proposition that would be accepted by most, if not all, moralists, and is not peculiar to ERPs. Also, it leaves open the question what beings are persons and therefore moral agents; some views equate persons, moral agents, and human beings, but some regard certain non-human beings as persons and moral agents, e.g., God or certain animals.
   The second proposition in an ERP is

B: All persons and only persons are moral patients.
   Or: X is a moral patient if and only if X is a person.

This says that persons and persons alone are morally considerable or relevant, directly or as such, i.e., that persons and persons alone need to be taken into consideration by an agent in determining what he or she morally should do or be, or that how one relates to non-persons is morally indifferent except insofar as it affects persons indirectly. Of course, an ERP will allow that we may have moral duties about animals (even if they are not persons), property, and the environment, but it will insist that we do not have moral duties to such beings directly or as such. This proposition, B, is the main part of an ERP's *theory of moral patiency*, but, again, it can he held by opponents of an ERP, though it would be less commonly held than A. It too leaves open the question what beings, human or not human, are persons. Some people would express B in terms of rights, i.e., as saying that all persons and only persons have moral rights. But an ERP need not recognize the notion of rights at all, or, if it does, may regard rights as secondary to duties or virtues.
   Any ethics that is personalistic in the sense of being person-centered will subscribe to Propositions A and B. But A and B do nothing to tell us what duties, rights, or virtues are or should be involved in the relations of moral agents to moral patients, or of persons to persons. For this something more substantive is needed, and for an ERP this must be a principle of *respect* for persons, e.g., that all persons and only persons are to be respected, which may be variously put by saying that respect for persons

is a duty, a right, or a virtue. But an ERP must hold more than this; it must also assert that respect for persons is basically the only duty, right, or virtue in morality. It must therefore maintain something like proposition

C: *Persons and their dispositions are morally good or virtuous, and their actions morally right, if and only if, and because they embody* respect *for persons as such.*

This provides an ERP with its *theory (normative) of moral rightness and/or goodness*, which says, in effect, that the principle of respect for persons is the supreme principle of morality. As Donagan puts it, the fundamental principle of morality is: "*Act always so that you respect every human being, yourself or another, as being a rational creature.*"[2] On this hangeth, for an ERP, the whole law and the prophets, as far as morality is concerned. . . .

I do not find in Kant any very clear concept of respect or of treating persons as ends and not as means—any concept that shows us just how RP [Respect for Persons] entails not committing suicide, etc. I like his second form better than his first or third; it has an attraction and intuitive plausibility for me, but when I try to get his concept and his derivation clear, I am at a loss.[3] Anyway, I shall content myself by looking instead at Donagan's ERP, partly because it is the fullest and best recent one, and partly because I have much the same troubles with it that I have with Kant's.

After some discussion of the Golden Rule, the Law of Love, and Kant's first two forms of the Categorical Imperative, Donagan arrives at the Principle of Respect for Persons quoted earlier, restating it as follows:

It is impermissible not to respect every human being, oneself or any other, as a rational creature,[4]

and adding that it is the sole first principle of the system of common morality. His view is that the rest of the system, consisting of more specific precepts, can be *inferentially* derived from this principle taken as a premise with the help of other or "specificatory" premises, according to the schema:

1. the above principle used as a first premise,

2. a specificatory second premise like: actions of kind K (e.g., killing another human being merely at will) are a way of not respecting human beings as rational creatures (or are a way of respecting them),

3. a conclusion that therefore actions of kind K are impermissible (or permissible).

Thus his view nicely illustrates ERPs as I have described them. . . .
    . . . In particular it assumes that we can know the premises in (1) and (2) independently of each other and antecedently to knowing the conclusion in (3). In any case, it clearly requires (a) an account of what respecting a person as a rational being is, and (b) an account of the way in which we can know the specificatory premises in (2). About what respect is, Donagan has disappointingly little to say. He identifies it as an unloaded concept in my sense, saying that it is not a specifically moral or normative concept, as impermissibility is (about which he also says rather little), but has a place in the descriptive discourse of anthropology, psychology, and everyday life. However, he makes no such attempt to define it. . . .
    He writes only,

The concept of respecting a human being as a rational creature is not usefully definable for our purposes. Thus to define it as treating a human being, by virtue of his rationality, as an end in itself, while perhaps clarifying, does not furnish us with a useful substituend.

I agree with the second sentence, I think, but the first sentence is surely neither clarifying nor otherwise useful. It leaves one unclear that the concept of respect as Donagan uses it in what follows is actually unloaded and descriptive . . . It also gives us no definition of the respect involved here that enables us to see, say, just how killing another person at will is a way of not respecting persons. It is, of course, plausible to say it is, but one wants a clearer ground for saying this. What Donagan says does not even explain why hating a person is not a way of respecting him or her. . . . It certainly gives us no way of seeing how to distinguish the killing that is said to be inconsistent with respect from that which is not, e.g., killing in self-defense, or of seeing how to settle the debate between the Quakers and the non-pacifists, or of seeing whether utilitarianism is or is not compatible with respect for persons. Later Donagan claims that, "if a man respects other men as rational creatures, not only will he not injure them, he will necessarily also take satisfaction in their achieving the well-being they seek, and will further their efforts as far as he prudently can."[5] But how can we see that respecting persons involves all this? Why does respecting involve more than not injuring, telling the truth, keeping promises, etc.? And how can we see that, if we do not do more than we prudently can, we are still respecting others? Having an account of what respect is that enables us to answer such questions seems to me not only useful but essential, and to say it is not even useful strikes me as incredible. Or maybe it is a kind of recognition of the difficulty of finding a clear concept of a kind of respect that will do just what an ERP needs it to do.

Coming to (b), Donagan claims it does not follow from the little he says about what respect is "that the process of deriving specific precepts from the fundamental principle is arbitrary and unreasoned." Perhaps not, but it does follow that its logic is vague and questionable. He defends himself in part by an appeal to E. H. Levi's theory of legal reasoning, especially as it appears in the application of a concept like that of a wheeled vehicle to new cases like that of roller skates. But I find the same vagueness and uncertainty in the legal reasoning involved in such cases that I find in the business of finding specificatory premises for applying his ethical first principle, and so am not helped by this legal analogy, especially since there are disanalogies as well. Referring to these Donagan writes,

The fundamental concept of respecting every human being as a rational creature is fuzzy at the edges in the superficial sense that its application to this or that species of case can be disputed. But among those who share in the life of a culture in which the Hebrew-Christian tradition is accepted, the concept is in large measure understood in itself; and it is connected with numerous applications, as to the different weights of which there is some measure of agreement. This is enough for it to be possible to determine many specificatory premises with virtual certainty and others with a high degree of confidence.

This does not convince me, however, that such a culture has a viable concept of respecting persons that can be used to determine specificatory premises; it may only be that it has a great deal of agreement about what is right or wrong in the first place.

Going on, Donagan seems to distinguish two ways of determining specificatory premises. One is by "direct analysis" of the concept of respecting persons as rational beings. But can one do it in this way if the concept is taken as Donagan takes it, as undefined and intuitively grasped? He does not himself show by direct analysis that the concept of respect excludes killing persons at will; he only says this "would not be denied by any Jewish or Christian moralist," which is not the same thing. The other method is more indirect, and Donagan does not make it very clear; it may just be a series of applications of the first method. At any rate, it is necessary for showing in what kinds of cases killing a person is permissible, and especially for showing that, except under such and such circumstances, killing a person is always wrong. It involves the difficulty of being sure that a complete review has been made of all the circumstances, and Donagan is concerned to show, as against Nozick, that this is not a serious matter, but he does not do so very convincingly. In the course of doing this he remarks that a more serious difficulty consists of conflict between precepts derived from first principles "by established methods" and "what seem to be intuitively evident applications of those first principles to cases falling under those precepts," e.g., the conflict, referred to earlier, between those who regard it as permissible to kill in self-defense and the Quakers who do not. He does not seem, however, to see how grave a difficulty *this* is for his project, or to ask just how it can be resolved by specifications of the basic principle, direct or indirect.

I cannot help but doubt, as a result of this look at Donagan, that there is a clear, unambiguous, and unloaded concept of respect that can be identified and distinguished from similar attitudes, and is such that there is a visibly objective way in which one can see that certain kinds of action are and others are not ways of respecting persons in the required sense, i.e., such that specificatory premises can be established by reference to it. I have the same doubt about Kant's concept of respect of persons as treating them as ends and not as means. I further conclude, therefore, that, as far as Proposition C is concerned, the project of an ERP is a dubious one, i.e., the project of taking C as a *premise* from which to derive less basic and more specific precepts *deductively*, the main difficulty being to exhibit the kinds of conduct regarded as right or wrong as specifications of a clearly and independently identified concept of respect.

Notes

1. *Twelfth Night*, Act II, Scene 3.
2. Alan Donagan, *The Theory of Morality*, Chicago: University of Chicago Press, 1977, 65. [p. 153 of this text.]
3. I do not object to regarding persons as ends, as some do. My question is about what doing this is, and my suggestion is that it is just believing that there are right and wrong ways of treating persons as such, i.e., having consideration respect for them.
4. *Op. cit.*, 66. [p. 153 of this text.]
5. *Op. cit.*, 85.

CHAPTER 7

Utilitarianism

THE PRINCIPLE OF UTILITY
Jeremy Bentham

Jeremy Bentham (1748–1832) is often called the father of modern utilitarianism. In this selection from his classic, The Principles of Morals and Legislation *(1789), Bentham presents and defends a hedonistic version of utilitarianism. According to the principle of utility, the morality of an individual action depends on how much utility that action would produce, where utility is measured in amounts of pleasure and pain. Because the focus is on the effects of* concrete *actions, this view is often called "act utilitarianism."*

After defending the claim that the principle of utility is the basic principle of right conduct, Bentham proceeds to set forth his famous "hedonic calculus"—a list of seven considerations to be used in calculating the utility of actions.

The principle of utility is the foundation of the present work: it will be proper therefore at the outset to give an explicit and determinate account of what is meant by it. By the principle of utility is meant that principle which approves or disapproves of every action whatsoever, according to the tendency which it appears to have to augment or diminish the happiness of the party whose interest is in question: or, what is the same thing in other words, to promote or to oppose that happiness. I say of every action whatsoever; and therefore not only of every action of a private individual, but of every measure of government.

By utility is meant that property in any object, whereby it tends to produce benefit, advantage, pleasure, good, or happiness, (all this in the present case comes to the same thing) or (what comes again to the same thing) to prevent the happening of mischief, pain, evil, or unhappiness to the party whose interest is considered: if that party be the community in general, then the happiness of the community: if a particular individual, then the happiness of that individual.

The interest of the community is one of the most general expressions that can occur in the phraseology of morals: no wonder that the meaning of it is often lost. When it has a meaning, it is this. The community is a fictitious *body*, composed of the individual persons who are considered as constituting as it were its *members*. The interest of the community then is, what?—the sum of the interests of the several members who compose it.

It is in vain to talk of the interest of the community, without understanding what is the interest of the individual. A thing is said to promote the interest, or to be *for* the interest, of an individual, when it tends to add to the sum total of his pleasures: or, what comes to the same thing, to diminish the sum total of his pains.

An action then may be said to be conformable to the principle of utility, or, for shortness sake, to utility, (meaning with respect to the community at large) when the tendency it has to augment the happiness of the community is greater than any it has to diminish it.

A measure of government (which is but a particular kind of action, performed by a particular person or persons) may be said to be conformable to or dictated by the principle of utility, when in like manner the tendency which it has to augment the happiness of the community is greater than any which it has to diminish it.

When an action, or in particular a measure of government, is supposed by a man to be conformable to the principle of utility, it may be convenient, for the purposes of discourse, to imagine a kind of law or dictate, called a law or dictate of utility: and to speak of the action in question, as being conformable to such law or dictate.

A man may be said to be a partizan of the principle of utility, when the approbation or disapprobation he annexes to any action, or to any measure, is determined by and proportioned to the tendency which he conceives it to have to augment or to diminish the happiness of the community: or in other words, to its conformity or unconformity to the laws or dictates of utility.

Of an action that is conformable to the principle of utility one may always say either that it is one that ought to be done, or at least that it is not one that ought not to be done. One may say also, that it is right it should be done; at least that it is not wrong it should be done: that it is a right action; at least that it is not a wrong action. When thus interpreted, the words *ought*, and *right* and *wrong*, and others of that stamp, have a meaning: when otherwise, they have none.

Has the rectitude of this principle been ever formally contested? It should seem that it had, by those who have not known what they have been meaning. Is it susceptible of any direct proof? it should seem not: for that which is used to prove every thing else, cannot itself be proved: a chain of proofs must have their commencement somewhere. To give such proof is as impossible as it is needless.

Not that there is or ever has been that human creature breathing, however stupid or perverse, who has not on many, perhaps on most occasions of his life, deferred to it. By the natural constitution of the human frame, on most occasions of their lives men in general embrace this principle, without thinking of it: if not for the ordering of their own actions, yet for the trying of their own actions, as well as of those of other men. There have been, at the same time, not many, perhaps, even of the most intelligent, who have been disposed to embrace it purely and without reserve. There are even few who have not taken some occasion or other to quarrel with it, either on account of their not understanding always how to apply it, or on account of some prejudice or other which they were afraid to examine into, or could not bear to part with. For such is the stuff that man is made of: in principle and in practice, in a right track and in a wrong one, the rarest of all human qualities is consistency.

When a man attempts to combat the principle of utility, it is with reasons drawn, without his being aware of it, from that very principle itself. His arguments, if they prove any thing, prove not that the principle is *wrong*, but that, according to the applications he supposes to be made of it, it is *misapplied*. Is it possible for a man to move the earth? Yes; but he must first find out another earth to stand upon.

To disprove the propriety of it by arguments is impossible; but, from the causes that have been mentioned, or from some confused or partial view of it, a man may happen to be disposed not to relish it. Where this is the case, if he thinks the settling of his opinions on such a subject worth the trouble, let him take the following steps, and at length, perhaps, he may come to reconcile himself to it.

Let him settle with himself, whether he would wish to discard this principle altogether; if so, let him consider what it is that all his reasonings (in matters of politics especially) can amount to?

If he would, let him settle with himself, whether he would judge and act without any principle, or whether there is any other he would judge and act by?

If there be, let him examine and satisfy himself whether the principle he thinks he has found is really any separate intelligible principle; or whether it be not a mere principle in words, a kind of phrase, which at bottom expresses neither more nor less than the mere averment of his own unfounded sentiments; that is, what in another person he might be apt to call caprice?

If he is inclined to think that his own approbation or disapprobation, annexed to the idea of an act, without any regard to its consequences, is a sufficient foundation for him to judge and act upon, let him ask himself whether his sentiment is to be a standard of right and wrong, with respect to every other man, or whether every man's sentiment has the same privilege of being a standard to itself?

In the first case, let him ask himself whether his principle is not despotical, and hostile to all the rest of human race?

In the second case, whether it is not anarchial, and whether at this rate there are not as many different standards of right and wrong as there are men? and whether even to the same man, the same thing, which is right to-day, may not (without the least change in its nature) be wrong to-morrow? and whether the same thing is not right and wrong in the same place at the same time? and in either case, whether all argument is not at an end? and whether, when two men have said, 'I like this,' and 'I don't like it,' they can (upon such a principle) have any thing more to say?

If he should have said to himself, No: for that the sentiment which he proposes as a standard must be grounded on reflection, let him say on what particulars the reflection is to turn? if on particulars having relation to the utility of the act, then let him say whether this is not deserting his own principle, and borrowing assistance from that very one in opposition to which he sets it up: or if not on those particulars, on what other particulars?

If he should be for compounding the matter, and adopting his own principle in part, and the principle of utility in part, let him say how far he will adopt it?

When he has settled with himself where he will stop, then let him ask himself how he justifies to himself the adopting it so far? and why he will not adopt it any farther?

Admitting any other principle than the principle of utility to be a right principle, a principle that it is right for a man to pursue; admitting (what is not true) that the word *right* can have a meaning without reference to utility, let him say whether there is any such thing as a *motive* that a man can have to pursue the dictates of it: if there is, let him say what that motive is, and how it is to be distinguished from those which enforce the dictates of utility: if not, then lastly let him say what it is this other principle can be good for? . . .

Pleasures then, and the avoidance of pains, are the *ends* which the legislator has in view: it behoves him therefore to understand their *value*.

Pleasures and pains are the *instruments* he has to work with: it behoves him therefore to understand their force, which is again, in other words, their value.

To a person considered *by himself*, the value of a pleasure or pain considered *by itself*, will be greater or less, according to the four following circumstances:

1. Its *intensity*.

2. Its *duration*.

3. Its *certainty* or *uncertainty*.

4. Its *propinquity* or *remoteness*.

These are the circumstances which are to be considered in estimating a pleasure or a pain considered each of them by itself. But when the value of any pleasure or pain is considered for the purpose of estimating the tendency of any *act* by which it is produced, there are two other circumstances to be taken into the account; these are,

5. Its *fecundity*, or the chance it has of being followed by sensations of the *same* kind: that is, pleasures, if it be a pleasure: pains, if it be a pain.

6. Its *purity*, or the chance it has of *not* being followed by sensations of the *opposite* kind: that is, pains, if it be a pleasure: pleasures, if it be a pain.

These two last, however, are in strictness scarcely to be deemed properties of the pleasure or the pain itself; they are not, therefore, in strictness to be taken into the account of the value of that pleasure or that pain. They are in strictness to be deemed properties only of the act, or other event, by which such pleasure or pain has been produced; and accordingly are only to be taken into the account of the tendency of such act or such event.

To a *number* of persons, with reference to each of whom the value of a pleasure or a pain is considered, it will be greater or less, according to seven circumstances: to wit, the six preceding ones; *viz*.

1. Its *intensity*.

2. Its *duration*.

3. Its *certainty* or *uncertainty*.

4. Its *propinquity* or *remoteness*.

5. Its *fecundity*.

6. Its *purity*.

And one other; to wit:

7. Its *extent;* that is, the number of persons to whom it *extends;* or (in other words) who are affected by it.

To take an exact account then of the general tendency of any act, by which the interests of a community are affected, proceed as follows. Begin with any one person of those whose interests seem most immediately to be affected by it: and take an account,

1. Of the value of each distinguishable *pleasure* which appears to be produced by it in the *first* instance.

2. Of the value of each *pain* which appears to be produced by it in the *first* instance.

3. Of the value of each pleasure which appears to be produced by it *after* the first. This constitutes the *fecundity* of the first *pleasure* and the *impurity* of the first *pain*.

4. Of the value of each *pain* which appears to be produced by it after the first. This constitutes the *fecundity* of the first *pain*, and the *impurity* of the first pleasure.

5. Sum up all the values of all the *pleasures* on the one side, and those of all the pains on the other. The balance, if it be on the side of pleasure, will give the *good* tendency of the act upon the whole, with respect to the interests of that *individual* person; if on the side of pain, the *bad* tendency of it upon the whole.

6. Take an account of the *number* of persons whose interests appear to be concerned; and repeat the above process with respect to each. *Sum up* the numbers expressive of the degrees of *good* tendency, which the act has, with respect to each individual, in regard to whom the tendency of it is *good* upon the whole: do this again with respect to each individual, in regard to whom the tendency of it is *good* upon the whole: do this again with respect to each individual, in regard to whom the tendency of it is *bad* upon the whole. Take the *balance;* which, if on the side of *pleasure,* will give the general

good tendency of the act, with respect to the total number or community of individuals concerned; if on the side of pain, the general *evil tendency*, with respect to the same community.

It is not to be expected that this process should be strictly pursued previously to every moral judgment, or to every legislative or judicial operation. It may, however, be always kept in view: and as near as the process actually pursued on these occasions approaches to it, so near will such process approach to the character of an exact one.

The same process is alike applicable to pleasure and pain, in whatever shape they appear: and by whatever denomination they are distinguished: to pleasure, whether it be called *good* (which is properly the cause or instrument of pleasure) or *profit* (which is distant pleasure, or the cause or instrument of distant pleasure,) or *convenience*, or *advantage, benefit, emolument, happiness*, and so forth: to pain, whether it be called *evil*, (which corresponds to *good*) or *mischief*, or *inconvenience*, or *disadvantage*, or *loss*, or *unhappiness*, and so forth.

Nor is this a novel and unwarranted, any more than it is a useless theory. In all this there is nothing but what the practice of mankind, wheresoever they have a clear view of their own interest, is perfectly conformable to. An article of property, an estate in land, for instance, is valuable, on what account? On account of the pleasures of all kinds which it enables a man to produce, and what comes to the same thing the pains of all kinds which it enables him to avert. But the value of such an article of property is universally understood to rise or fall according to the length of shortness of the time which a man has in it: the certainty or uncertainty of its coming into possession: and the nearness or remoteness of the time at which, if at all, it is to come into possession. As to the *intensity* of the pleasures which a man may derive from it, this is never thought of, because it depends upon the use which each particular person may come to make of it; which cannot be estimated till the particular pleasures he may come to derive from it, or the particular pains he may come to exclude by means of it, are brought to view. For the same reason, neither does he think of the *fecundity* or *purity* of those pleasures. . . .

IN DEFENSE OF UTILITARIANISM
J. S. Mill

John Stuart Mill (1806–1873), a British philosopher, was a leading intellectual of the nineteenth century. In the following excerpt from his book, Utilitarianism *(1863), Mill considers three objections to the utilitarian theory. First, some opponents charge that the emphasis on the pursuit of pleasure makes utilitarianism "a doctrine worthy of swine." Mill responds by distinguishing higher from lower pleasures. Because utilitarianism considers pursuit of higher, distinctively human pleasures (such as enjoying great literature) as especially important, it is, Mill asserts, a doctrine worthy of human beings. Second, some argue that utilitarian moral theory sets standards that are "too high for humanity." Third, still others object that in ordinary circumstances calling for a moral decision, we lack the time needed for calculating the utility of actions. Mill argues that these latter two objections are based on misunderstandings of the utilitarian theory. After answering these objections, Mill offers what he calls an "indirect proof" of the principle of utility.*

T he creed which accepts as the foundation of morals, Utility, or the Greatest Happiness Principle, holds that actions are right in proportion as they tend to promote happiness, wrong as they tend to produce the reverse of happiness. By happiness is intended pleasure, and the absence of pain; by unhappiness, pain, and the privation of pleasure. To give a clear view of the moral standard set up by the theory, much more requires to be said; in particular, what things it includes in the ideas of pain and pleasure; and to what extent this is left an open question. But these supplementary explanations do not affect the theory of life on which this theory of morality is grounded—namely, that pleasure, and freedom from pain, are the only things desirable as ends; and that all desirable things (which are as numerous in the utilitarian as in any other scheme) are desirable either for the pleasure inherent in themselves, or as means to the promotion of pleasure and the prevention of pain.

Now, such a theory of life excites in many minds, and among them in some of the most estimable in feeling and purpose, inveterate dislike. To suppose that life has (as they express it) no higher end than pleasure—no better and nobler object of desire and pursuit—they designate as utterly

Reprinted from *Utilitarianism* (1863).

mean and grovelling; as a doctrine worthy only of swine, to whom the followers of Epicurus were, at a very early period, contemptuously likened; and modern holders of the doctrine are occasionally made the subject of equally polite comparisons by its German, French, and English assailants.

When thus attacked, the Epicureans have always answered, that it is not they, but their accusers, who represent human nature in a degrading light; since the accusation supposes human beings to be capable of no pleasures except those of which swine are capable. If this supposition were true, the charge could not be gainsaid, but would then be no longer an imputation; for if the sources of pleasure were precisely the same to human beings and to swine, the rule of life which is good enough for the one would be good enough for the other. The comparison of the Epicurean life to that of beasts is felt as degrading, precisely because a beast's pleasures do not satisfy a human being's conceptions of happiness. Human beings have faculties more elevated than the animal appetites, and when once made conscious of them, do not regard anything as happiness which does not include their gratification. I do not, indeed, consider the Epicureans to have been by any means faultless in drawing out their scheme of consequences from the utilitarian principle. To do this in any sufficient manner, many Stoic, as well as Christian elements require to be included. But there is no known Epicurean theory of life which does not assign to the pleasures of the intellect, of the feelings and imagination, and of the moral sentiments, a much higher value as pleasures than to those of mere sensation. It must be admitted, however, that utilitarian writers in general have placed the superiority of mental over bodily pleasures chiefly in the greater permanency, safety, uncostliness, &c., of the former—that is, in their circumstantial advantages rather than in their intrinsic nature. And on all these points utilitarians have fully proved their case; but they might have taken the other, and, as it may be called, higher ground, with entire consistency. It is quite compatible with the principle of utility to recognise the fact, that some *kinds* of pleasure are more desirable and more valuable than others. It would be absurd that while, in estimating all other things, quality is considered as well as quantity, the estimation of pleasures should be supposed to depend on quantity alone.

If I am asked, what I mean by difference of quality in pleasures, or what makes one pleasure more valuable than another, merely as a pleasure, except its being greater in amount, there is but one possible answer. Of two pleasures, if there be one to which all or almost all who have experience of both give a decided preference, irrespective of any feeling of moral obligation to prefer it, that is the more desirable pleasure. If one of the two is, by those who are competently acquainted with both, placed so far above the other that they prefer it, even though knowing it to be attended with a greater amount of discontent, and would not resign it for any quantity of the other pleasure which their nature is capable of, we are justified in ascribing to the preferred enjoyment a superiority in quality, so far outweighing quantity as to render it, in comparison, of small account.

Now it is an unquestionable fact that those who are equally acquainted with, and equally capable of appreciating and enjoying, both, do give a most marked preference to the manner of existence which employs their higher faculties. Few human creatures would consent to be changed into any of the lower animals, for a promise of the fullest allowance of a beast's pleasures; no intelligent human being would consent to be a fool, no instructed person would be an ignoramus, no person of feeling and conscience would be selfish and base, even though they should be persuaded that the fool, the dunce, or the rascal is better satisfied with his lot than they are with theirs. They would not resign what they possess more than he for the most complete satisfaction of all the desires which they have in common with him. If they ever fancy they would, it is only in cases of unhappiness so extreme, that to escape from it they would exchange their lot for almost any other, however undesirable in their own eyes. A being of higher faculties requires more to make him happy, is capable probably of more acute suffering, and is certainly accessible to it at more points, than one of an inferior type; but in spite of these liabilities, he can never really wish to sink into what he feels to be a lower grade of existence. We may give what explanation we please of this unwillingness; we may attribute it to pride, a name which is given indiscriminately to some of the most and to some of the least estimable feelings of which mankind are capable; we may refer it to the love of liberty and personal independence, an appeal to which was with the Stoics one of the most effective means for the inculcation of it; to the love of power, or to the love of excitement, both of which do really enter into and contribute to it: but its most appropriate appellation is a sense of dignity, which all human beings possess in one form or other, and in some, though by no means in exact, proportion to their higher faculties, and which is so essential a part of the happiness of those in whom it is strong, that nothing which conflicts with it could be, otherwise than momentarily, an object of desire to them. Whoever supposes that this preference takes place at a sacrifice of happiness—that the superior being, in anything like the equal circumstances, is not happier than the inferior—confounds the two very different ideas, of happiness, and content. It is indisputable that the being whose capacities of enjoyment are low, has the greatest chance of having them fully satisfied; and a highly-endowed being will always feel that any happiness which he can look for, as the world is constituted, is imperfect. But he can learn to bear its imperfections, if they are at all bearable; and they will not make him envy the being who is indeed unconscious of the imperfections, but only because he feels not at all the good which those imperfections qualify. It is better to be a human being dissatisfied than a pig satisfied; better to be Socrates dissatisfied than a fool satisfied. And if the fool, or the pig, is of a different opinion, it is because they only know their own side of the question. The other party to the comparison knows both sides. . . .

. . . The objectors to utilitarianism cannot always be charged with representing it in a discreditable light. On the contrary, those among them who entertain anything like a just idea of its disinterested character, sometimes find fault with its standard as being too high for humanity. They say it is exacting too much to require that people shall always act from the inducement of promoting the general interests of society. But this is to mistake the very meaning of a standard of morals, and to confound the rule of action with the motive of it. It is the business of ethics to tell us what are our duties, or by what test we may know them; but no system of ethics requires that the sole motive of all we do shall be a feeling of duty; on the contrary, ninety-nine hundredths of all our actions are done from other motives, and rightly so done, if the rule of duty does not condemn them. It is the more unjust to utilitarianism that this particular misapprehension should be made a ground of objection to it, inasmuch as utilitarian moralists have gone beyond almost all others in affirming that the motive has nothing to do with the morality of the action, though much with the worth of the agent. He who saves a fellow creature from drowning does what is morally right, whether his motive be duty, or the hope of being paid for his trouble: he who betrays the friend that trusts him, is guilty of a crime, even if his object be to serve another friend to whom he is under greater obligations. But to speak only of actions done from the motive of duty, and in direct obedience to principle: it is a misapprehension of the utilitarian mode of thought, to conceive it as implying that people should fix their minds upon so wide a generality as the world, or society at large. The great majority of good actions are intended, not for the benefit of the world, but for that of individuals, of which the good of the world is made up; and the thoughts of the most virtuous man need not on these occasions travel beyond the particular persons concerned, except so far as is necessary to assure himself that in benefiting them he is not violating the rights—that is, the legitimate and authorized expectations—of any one else. The multiplication of happiness is, according to the utilitarian ethics, the object of virtue: the occasions on which any person (except one in a thousand) has it in his power to do this on an extended scale, in other words, to be a public benefactor, are but exceptional; and on these occasions alone is he called on to consider public utility; in every other case, private utility, the interest or happiness of some few persons, is all he has to attend to. Those alone the influence of whose actions extends to society in general, need concern themselves habitually about so large an object. In the case of abstinences indeed—of things which people forbear to do, from moral considerations, though the consequences in the particular case might be beneficial—it would be unworthy of an intelligent agent not to be consciously aware that the action is of a class which, if practised generally, would be generally injurious, and that this is the ground of the obligation to abstain from it. The amount of regard for the public interest implied in this recognition, is no greater than is demanded by every system of morals; for they all enjoin to abstain from whatever is manifestly pernicious to society. . . .

. . . Again, defenders of utility often find themselves called upon to reply to such objections as this—that there is not time, previous to action, for calculating and weighing the effects of any line of conduct on the general happiness. This is exactly as if any one were to say that it is impossible to guide our conduct by Christianity, because there is not time, on every occasion on which anything has to be done, to read through the Old and New Testaments. The answer to the objection is, that there has been ample time, namely, the whole past duration of the human species. During all that time mankind have been learning by experience the tendencies of actions; on which experience all the prudence, as well as all the morality of life, is dependent. People talk as if the commencement of this course of experience had hitherto been put off, and as if, at the moment when some man feels tempted to meddle with the property or life of another, he had to begin considering for the first time whether murder and theft are injurious to human happiness. Even then I do not think that he would find the question very puzzling; but, at all events, the matter is now done to his hand. It is truly a whimsical supposition that if mankind were agreed in considering utility to be the test of morality, they would remain without any agreement as to what *is* useful, and would take no measures for having their notions on the subject taught to the young, and enforced by law and opinion. There is no difficulty in proving any ethical standard whatever to work ill, if we suppose universal idiocy to be conjoined with it, but on any hypothesis short of that, mankind must by this time have acquired positive beliefs as to the effects of some actions on their happiness; and the beliefs which have thus come down are the rules of morality for the multitude, and for the philosopher until he has succeeded in finding better. That philosophers might easily do this, even now, on many subjects; that the received code of ethics is by no means of divine right; and that mankind have still much to learn as to the effects of actions on the general happiness, I admit, or rather, earnestly maintain. The corollaries from the principle of utility, like the precepts of every practical art, admit of indefinite improvement, and, in a progressive state of the human mind, their improvement is perpetually going on. But to consider the rules of morality as improvable, is one thing; to pass over the intermediate generalizations entirely, and endeavour to test each individual action directly by the first principle, is another. It is a strange notion that the acknowledgment of a first principle is inconsistent with the admission of secondary ones. To inform a traveller respecting the place of his ultimate destination, is not to forbid the use of landmarks and direction-posts on the way. The proposition that happiness is the end and aim of morality, does not mean that no road ought to be laid down to that goal, or that persons going thither should not be advised to take one direction rather than another. Men really ought to leave off talking a kind of nonsense on this subject, which they would neither talk nor listen to in other matters of practical concernment. Nobody argues that the art of navigation is not founded on astronomy, because sailors cannot wait to calculate the Nautical Almanack. Being rational creatures, they go to sea with it ready calculated; and all rational creatures go out upon the sea of life with their minds made up on the common questions of right and wrong, as well as on many of the far more difficult questions of wise and foolish. And this, as long as foresight is a human quality, is to be presumed they will continue to do. Whatever we adopt as the fundamental principle of morality, we require subordinate principles to apply it by: the impossibility of doing without them, being common to all systems, can afford no argument against any one in particular: but gravely to argue as if no such secondary principles could be had, and as if mankind had remained till now, and always must remain, without drawing any general conclusion from the experience of human life, is as high a pitch, I think, as absurdity has ever reached in philosophical controversy. . . .

Of What Sort of Proof
the Principle of Utility Is Susceptible

It has already been remarked, that questions of ultimate ends do not admit of proof, in the ordinary acceptation of the term. To be incapable of proof by reasoning is common to all first principles; to the first premises of our knowledge, as well as to those of our conduct. But the former, being matters of fact, may be the subject of a direct appeal to the faculties which judge of fact—namely, our senses, and our internal consciousness. Can an appeal be made to the same faculties on questions of practical ends? Or by what other faculty is cognizance taken of them?

Questions about ends are, in other words, questions what things are desirable. The utilitarian doctrine is, that happiness is desirable, and the only thing desirable, as an end; all other things being only desirable as means to that end. What ought to be required of this doctrine—what conditions is it requisite that the doctrine should fulfil—to make good its claim to be believed?

The only proof capable of being given that an object is visible, is that people actually see it. The only proof that a sound is audible, is that people hear it: and so of the other sources of our experience. In like manner, I apprehend, the sole evidence it is possible to produce that anything is desirable, is that people do actually desire it. If the end which the utilitarian doctrine proposes to itself were not, in theory and in practice, acknowledged to be an end, nothing could ever convince any person that it was so. No reason can be given why the general happiness is desirable, except that each person, so far as he believes it to be attainable, desires his own happiness. This, however, being a fact, we have not only all the proof which the case admits of, but all which it is possible to require, that happiness is a good: that each person's happiness is a good to that person, and the general happiness, therefore, a good to the aggregate of all persons. Happiness has made out its title as *one* of the ends of conduct, and consequently one of the criteria of morality.

But it has not, by this alone, proved itself to be the sole criterion. To do that, it would seem, by the same rule, necessary to show, not only that people desire happiness, but that they never desire anything else. Now it is palpable that they do desire things which, in common language, are decidedly distinguished from happiness. They desire, for example, virtue, and the absence of vice, no less really than pleasure and the absence of pain. The desire of virtue is not as universal, but it is as authentic a fact, as the desire of happiness. And hence the opponents of the utilitarian standard deem that they have a right to infer that there are other ends of human action besides happiness, and that happiness is not the standard of approbation and disapprobation.

But does the utilitarian doctrine deny that people desire virtue, or maintain that virtue is not a thing to be desired? The very reverse. It maintains not only that virtue is to be desired, but that it is to be desired disinterestedly, for itself. Whatever may be the opinion of utilitarian moralists as to the original conditions by which virtue is made virtue; however they may believe (as they do) that actions and dispositions are only virtuous because they promote another end than virtue; yet this being granted, and it having been decided, from considerations of this description, what *is* virtuous, they not only place virtue at the very head of the things which are good as means to the ultimate end, but they also recognise as a psychological fact the possibility of its being, to the individual, a good in itself, without looking to any end beyond it; and hold, that the mind is not in a right state, not in a state conformable to Utility, not in the state most conducive to the general happiness, unless it does love virtue in this manner—as a thing desirable in itself, even although, in the individual instance, it should not produce those other desirable consequences which it tends to produce, and on account of which it is held to be virtue. This opinion is not, in the smallest degree, a departure from the Happiness principle. The ingredients of happiness are very various, and each of them is desirable in itself, and not merely when considered as swelling an aggregate. The principle of utility does not mean that any given pleasure, as music, for instance, or any given exemption from pain, as for example health, are to be looked upon as a means to a collective something termed happiness, and to be desired on that account. They are desired and desirable in and for themselves; besides being means, they are a part of the end. Virtue, according to the utilitarian doctrine, is not naturally and originally part of the end, but it is capable of becoming so; and in those who love it disinterestedly it has become so, and is desired and cherished, not as a means to happiness, but as a part of their happiness. . . .

ACT UTILITARIANISM
J. L. Mackie

J. L. Mackie (1917–1982) was a fellow in philosophy at University College, Oxford. Against act utilitarianism, Mackie raises two objections. First, he argues that, despite the seeming simplicity and unity of the theory, it suffers from indeterminacy. That is, it leaves unanswered such questions as how we are to measure utility and whether the utilities of lower animals and future generations should be factored into our moral calculations. Second, Mackie objects that utilitarianism is not livable or "practicable." That is, the theory requires too much of us and so could not function as a livable moral code. (Mackie's second argument here should be compared with the second objection Mill considers in his defense of utilitarianism in the preceding selection.)

A morality in the broad sense would be a general, all-inclusive theory of conduct: the morality to which someone subscribed would be whatever body of principles he allowed ultimately to guide or determine his choices of action. In the narrow sense, a morality is a system of a particular sort of constraints on conduct—ones whose central task is to protect the interests of persons other than the agent and which present themselves to an agent as checks on his natural inclinations or spontaneous tendencies to act. In this narrow sense, moral considerations would be considerations from some limited range, and would not necessarily include everything that a man allowed to determine what he did. In this second sense, someone could say quite deliberately, 'I admit that morality requires that I should do such-and-such, but I don't intend to: for me other considerations here overrule the moral ones.' And he need not be putting 'morality' here into either visible or invisible inverted commas. It may well be his morality of which he is speaking, the moral constraints that he himself in general accepts and endorses as such. But because in this narrow sense moral considerations are only some considerations among others which he also endorses, not an inclusive system which incorporates and, where necessary, weighs against one another all the reasons that this man accepts as reasons for or against doing anything, it is possible that in some particular situation moral considerations should be overruled. But no-one could, in his choices of action, deliberately overrule what was his morality in the broad sense, though he might diverge from it through 'weakness of will'.

There is no point in discussing whether the broad or the narrow sense of 'morality' is the more correct. Both are used, and both have important roots and connections in our thought. But it is essential not to confuse them, not to think that what we recognize as (in the narrow sense) peculiarly moral considerations are (jumping to the broad sense) necessarily finally authoritative with regard to our actions. We should not suppose that any general system of principles of choice which we can on reflection accept must be constructed wholly of materials that we would call moral in the narrow sense. . . .

'Morality in the narrow sense' was roughly distinguished as a particular sort of constraints on conduct, and the remainder of that chapter discussed why such constraints were needed for the flourishing of human

life. The view sketched there of morality in the narrow sense was therefore utilitarian in the very broad sense that it took general human well-
being as in some way the foundation of morality. However, it is not very
illuminating to use the term 'utilitarianism' as broadly as this; it is better
to restrict it, or qualified variants of it, to more specific views about the
way in which moral conclusions are to be derived from or founded upon
human happiness, to specific methods of determining the content of the
first order moral system.

One such view is extreme or act utilitarianism. This holds that where
an agent has a choice between courses of action (or inaction) the right act
is that which will produce the most happiness, not just for the agent
himself but for all who are in any way affected. The greatest possible total
happiness or 'utility'—or, as it is sometimes rather misleadingly put, 'The
greatest happiness of the greatest number'—is proposed as the criterion
of right action, and happiness is usually interpreted hedonistically as a
balance of pleasure over pain. The suggestion is that for each alternative
course of action it is possible in principle to measure all the amounts of
pleasure it produces for different persons and to add these up, similarly to
measure and add up all the amounts of pain or distress it produces, and
subtract the sum of pain from the sum of pleasure; then the right action is
that for which there is the greatest positive or the least negative balance of
pleasure over pain; presumably if for two or more actions the balances are
equal, but better than the balances for all others, each of them is *a* right
action.

This proposal has several obvious merits. It seems reasonable that
morality, if it is to guide conduct, should have something to do with
happiness. It seems natural to seek pleasure and to avoid pain and
distress, but it also seems sensible to balance these against each other, to
put up with a certain amount of pain in order to achieve a quantity of
pleasure that outweighs it. In taking the *general* happiness as the standard of right action this proposal seems to satisfy at once the pre-
sumptions that moral actions should be unselfish and that moral principles should be fair. It seems to provide a coherent system of conduct; all
decisions about what is right or wrong would flow directly from a single
source, whereas in other proposed first order moral systems we find a
multiplicity of independent rules and principles, perhaps arbitrarily
thrown together, possibly conflicting with one another in certain circumstances. Also it has been argued, particularly by Sidgwick, that if we
confront utilitarianism with common-sense or intuitionist morality,
utilitarianism can swallow up its rival. We can explain many of the
common-sense or intuitive rules as being in general justified by their
tendency to promote the general happiness, but where two common-

sense rules come into conflict we need to appeal directly to utility to decide what to do. Common-sense morality can be seen as a practically convenient approximation to utilitarianism, but not, therefore, something whose requirements can resist those of utility in the rare cases where there is an open conflict between them.

Closer examination, however, reveals cracks in this apparently unitary structure. There are difficulties for and indeterminacies in utilitarianism. What are we to include in 'all who are in any way affected'? Does this mean 'all human beings' or 'all sentient beings'? Are non-human animals included? A theory that equates good with pleasure and evil with pain would appear to have no non-arbitrary reason for excluding from consideration any creatures that are capable of feeling either pleasure or pain. Does it include only those who are now alive, or also future generations; and if so, only those who will exist or also those who might exist? We may have to compare alternative courses of action one of which would lead to there being a large population each of whose members was only moderately happy, and another of which would lead to there being a smaller population each of whose members was very happy; in the former there will be more total utility or happiness, in the latter a higher average utility or happiness. For a fixed population, the maxima of total utility and of average utility must coincide, but if the size of the population is itself variable they can fall apart. Which of the two, then, is it whose maximization is to be the criterion of right action? Again, is it really possible to measure quantities of pleasure and pain even for the same person at different times and in different sorts of experience? Is pleasure even sufficiently of the same category as pain to be measurable on the same scale and so to allow a quantity of one to balance a quantity of the other? Interpersonal measurement presents even greater difficulties, and the problem becomes still more acute if the pleasures and pains of non-human animals are to be taken into account. It can be argued that utilitarianism only appears to avoid the arbitrariness of some rival methods of ethics. It only pretends to provide a unitary decision procedure, and arbitrariness breaks out within any serious attempt to implement it, in whatever decisions are made in answer to some of these questions and in estimates of the comparative amounts of pleasure and pain that various courses of action will produce.

Again it can be asked whether the proposed criterion is simply the greatest total happiness (or perhaps average happiness), or whether it matters how happiness is distributed. Is a state of affairs in which one person is supremely happy and nine are miserable better than one in which all ten are equally happy, provided only that the total balance of happiness is greater? Are we to interpret utilitarianism as being founded on an aggregative principle alone, or as including a distributive principle as well—and if so, what distributive principle: should happiness be distributed equally or in proportion to some kind of merit? Bentham's remark that 'everybody [is] to count for one, nobody for more than one' has been taken as a distributive thesis; but it offers no clear principle of distribution, and is more naturally taken simply as an instruction that there is to be no unequal weighting, that the happiness of an aristocrat is not more important than that of a peasant, which would, however, leave us with only the aggregative requirement that total utility so calculated should be maximized.

There is even a problem about the distribution of happiness within the life of one person. A period of misery followed by one of happiness seems preferable to a period of happiness followed by one of misery, even if the quantities of misery and happiness are respectively equal. However, it could be argued that order as such is indifferent; what makes the difference here is that when one is unhappy the anticipation of future happiness is itself pleasant, whereas the recollection of past happiness is not (but is even, according to Tennyson and Dante, 'sorrow's crown of sorrow') while the reverse holds for the anticipation and recollection of misery when one is happy. One can enjoy troubles when they are over. When we take into account these joys and sorrows of anticipation and recollection, the aggregate of happiness is greater when the order is right, even if the quantities of misery and happiness were *otherwise* equal.

The utilitarian might try to deal analogously with problems of interpersonal distribution. Thus the familiar rule that happiness should be proportionate to merit is merely an incentive device for increasing the aggregate of happiness, merit being measured by a person's contribution to the happiness of others. Material goods have a diminishing marginal utility, so a more equal distribution of whatever goods there are is (apart from the just-mentioned incentive requirement) likely to produce a greater aggregate utility. Less plausibly, the utilitarian might say that it is not possible for a less equal distribution (even of happiness as opposed to material goods) to yield a higher aggregate (still apart from incentive effects) on the ground that (starting from a position of equality) one person's happiness cannot be pushed up much by any procedure that essentially involves reducing the happiness of others. A case, though not, I think, in the end a very convincing case, could thus be made out for a utilitarianism based on an aggregative principle only, without any independent principle of distribution.

All these difficulties and indeterminacies tell, in the first place, only against the claim that utilitarianism offers a peculiarly unitary and systematic basis for morality. A utilitarian can simply decide which of the various options to take up, and he can plausibly argue that rival views are subject to similar indeterminacies. In particular, many thinkers would give some weight to utility, even though they differ from utilitarians in that they recognize other moral requirements as well; such thinkers will obviously have the same problems about how to calculate the utility of which they propose to take account.

The Ethics of Fantasy

However, even if all the difficulties and indeterminacies mentioned in the last section were resolved, by argument or by decision, there would still be a fatal objection to the resulting act utilitarian system. It would be wholly impracticable. The system can, indeed, be looked at in several different ways, but this charge can be sustained against each interpretation in turn. Suppose, first, that it is considered as a morality in the broad sense, as an all-inclusive theory of conduct. Then, when utility or the general happiness is proposed as the immediate criterion of right action, is it intended that each agent should take the happiness of all as his goal? This, surely, is too much to expect. Mill himself conceded this, and replied to this objection by saying that it confuses the rule of action with the motive of it. 'The great majority of good actions,' he said, 'are intended not for the benefit of the world, but for that of individuals . . . and the thoughts of the most virtuous man need not . . . travel beyond the particular persons concerned, except as far as is necessary to assure himself that in benefiting them he is not violating the rights, that is, the legitimate and authorized expectations, of any one else.' But even if we accept this clarification, and take utilitarianism to be supplying not the motive but only a test of right actions, the charge of impracticality still stands. We cannot require that the actions of people generally should even pass the test of being such as to maximize the happiness of all, whether or not this is their motive. Even within a small village or commune it is too much to expect that the efforts of all members should be wholly directed towards the promoting of the well-being of all. And such total cooperation is out of the question on the scale of a nation state, let alone where the 'all' are to be the whole human race, including its future or possible future members, and perhaps all other sentient beings as well. The question, which moral philosophers sometimes discuss, 'What would happen if there were a society of pure act utilitarians?' is purely academic. We can indeed work out an answer, though only with difficulty, because this hypothesis is so far removed from anything within our experience that it is difficult to envisage it consistently and thoroughly. But the answer would have no direct bearing on any policies of practical importance. All real societies, and all those which it is of direct practical use to consider, are ones whose members have to a great extent divergent and conflicting purposes. And we must expect that their actions will consist largely of the pursuit of these divergent and conflicting purposes, and consequently will not only not be motivated by a desire for the general happiness but also will commonly fail the proposed test of being such as to maximize the general happiness.

Act utilitarianism is by no means the only moral theory that displays this extreme of impracticality. The biblical commandment 'Thou shalt love thy neighbour as thyself,' though it has its roots in a mistranslation of a much more realistic rule, is often taken as prescribing a universal and equal concern for all men. So interpreted, it is, as Mill says, effectively equivalent to the utilitarian principle. And it is similarly impracticable. People simply are not going to put the interests of all their 'neighbours' on an equal footing with their own interests and specific purposes and with the interests of those who are literally near to them. Such universal concern will not be the actual motive of their choices, nor will they act as if it were. . . .

But why have moralists and preachers thought it worthwhile to propound rules that obviously have so little chance of being followed? They must surely have thought that by setting up such admittedly unattainable ideals they might induce at least some movement towards them, that if men were told to let universal beneficence guide all their conduct, they would not indeed do this, but would allow some small admixture of universal beneficence to help to direct their actions.

This would amount to proposing utilitarianism (or the doctrine of neighbourly love) no longer as a morality in the broad sense but indirectly and in effect as one in the narrow sense: not as an overriding guide to conduct in general, but as a check or corrective on conduct which was very largely otherwise motivated and otherwise directed. I shall discuss utilitarianism, explicitly so presented, in the next section. Here I would remark only that if this is what is intended, it would be much better if it were explicitly so presented. To put forward as a morality in the broad sense something which, even if it were admirable, would be an utterly impossible ideal is likely to do, and surely has in fact done, more harm than good. It encourages the treatment of moral principles not as guides to action but as a fantasy which accompanies actions with which it is quite incompatible. It is a commonplace that religious morality often has little effect on the lives of believers. It is equally true, though not so frequently pointed out, that utilitarian morality is often treated as a topic of purely academic discussion, and is not taken any more seriously as a practical guide. In both cases the mistake is the same. To identify morality with something that certainly will not be followed is a sure way of bringing it into contempt—practical contempt, which combines all too readily with theoretical respect.

But why, it may be asked, are such moralities of universal concern impracticable? Primarily because a large element of selfishness—or, in an older terminology, self-love—is a quite ineradicable part of human nature. Equally, if we distinguish as Butler did the particular passions and affections from self-love, we must admit that they are inevitably the major part of human motivation, and the actions which express and realize them cannot be expected in general to tend towards the *general* happiness. Even what we recognize as unselfishness or benevolence is equally incompatible with *universal* concern. It takes the form of what Broad called self-referential altruism—concern for others, but for others who have some special connection with oneself; children, parents, friends, workmates, neighbours in the literal, not the metaphorically extended, sense. Wider affections than these usually centre upon devotion to some special cause—religious, political, revolutionary, nationalist—not upon the welfare of human beings, let alone sentient beings, in general. It is much easier, and commoner, to display a self-sacrificing love for some of one's fellow men if one can combine this with hostility to others. It is quite implausible for Mill to argue that such an array of limited motives can express themselves in actions which will conform to the utilitarian standard, provided only that the agent assures himself that he is not violating the rights of anyone else. As a proposed general pattern of conduct, there is indeed much to be said for the pursuit of some such array of special and limited goals within bounds set by respect for some 'rights' of others. But it is misleading to present such a pattern as a consequence of the act utilitarian standard of right action, and to suggest that each choice that is a component in such a pattern could be validated as that which, out of the options available to that agent at that time, would contribute more than any other to the happiness of all men or of all sentient things.

But could not human nature be changed? I do not know. Of course, given the techniques of mass persuasion adolescents can be turned into Red Guards or Hitler Youth or pop fans, but in each of these we have only fairly superficial redirection of what are basically the same motives. It is far more doubtful whether any agency could effect the far more fundamental changes that would be needed to make practicable a morality of universal concern. Certainly no ordinary processes of education can bring them about.

Besides, if such changes could be effected, they might well prove self-defeating. Thus Bernard Williams has argued that in becoming capable of acting out of universal concern, people would have to be stripped of the motives on which most of what is of value in human life is based—close affections, private pursuits, and many kinds of competition and struggle. Even if our ultimate goal were the utilitarian one of maximizing the general happiness, the cultivation of such changes in human nature as would make an act utilitarian morality practicable might not be the most sensible way of pursuing it. But in any case this is at most a remote possibility, and has little relevance to our present choice of a first order moral system. For the present our terms of reference can be summed up in words close to those of Rousseau: we are to take men as they are and moral laws as they might be.

It may be objected that if we trim down moral demands to fit present human capacity, we bring morality into contempt in another way. But I do not mean that moral demands are to be so minimal that they are likely to be fulfilled by most people pretty well at once. We may well advocate moral principles that are in conflict with established habits of thought and behaviour, that prescribe a degree of respect for the claims of others— and of distant others—which can flourish only by overcoming ingrained selfishness and limitations of generosity that are authorized by the existing law and the real conventional morality (as contrasted with the fantasy moralities of utilitarianism and neighbourly love). All I am insisting upon is that we should advocate practicable reforms, that we should look for rules or principles of conduct that can fit in with the relatively permanent tendencies of human motives and thought.

Morality in the Narrow Sense

Act utilitarianism, then, is not viable as a morality in the broad sense—an all-inclusive theory of conduct—nor is it wise to propound it as such in the hope that it will then operate as a morality in the narrow sense, as a counterpoise to selfishness or excessively narrow sympathies. But this leaves open the possibility of supporting it explicitly as a morality in the narrow sense. Could it not be one factor among others which we allow to influence choices, but the factor which has the special function of countering the bad effects of limited sympathies? Warnock states, before going on to criticize, this suggestion:

The essential evil to be remedied . . . is the propensity of people to be concerned in practice, if not exclusively with their own, yet with some restricted range of, interests and ends; and surely the *direct* way to counter, or to limit, the evils liable to result from this propensity to counter it *itself*—to inculcate . . . a directly remedial propensity to be concerned with, and in practice to take into account, the welfare, needs, wants, interests of *all*.

Plausible though this suggestion is, I would agree with Warnock in rejecting it, though for reasons other than the ones on which he chiefly relies. My main reason is that such a propensity is too indeterminate to do the trick. It is not now being proposed that an agent should either take the general happiness as his overiding aim or act as if he were doing so, but only that he should give it some weight against the more special interests to which he is primarily attached. But how much weight? When should the one consideration override the other? The utilitarian principle now gives no answer. The function we are now assigning it is to set a boundary to the pursuit of selfish or special or narrowly altruistic aims. Now a boundary may be blurred, uncertain, disputed, wavering, and yet still fulfil to some extent its function as a boundary; but it must be at least roughly indicated, at least dimly visible. The utilitarian principle sets up no visible boundary at all. . . .

CLASSICAL UTILITARIANISM
John Rawls

John Rawls is professor of philosophy at Harvard University and author of the highly influential book, A Theory of Justice *(1971). In the excerpt below, taken from that book, Rawls argues that classical utilitarianism of the sort defended by Bentham and Mill fails to mesh with the idea that individual people are, in some deep and interesting sense, separate.*

There are many forms of utilitarianism, and the development of the theory has continued in recent years. I shall not survey these forms here, nor take account of the numerous refinements found in contemporary discussions. My aim is to work out a theory of justice that represents an alternative to utilitarian thought generally and so to all of these different versions of it. I believe that the contrast between the contract view and utilitarianism remains essentially the same in all these cases. Therefore I shall compare justice as fairness with familiar variants of intuitionism, perfectionism, and utilitarianism in order to bring out the underlying differences in the simplest way. With this end in mind, the kind of utilitarianism I shall describe here is the strict classical doctrine which receives perhaps its clearest and most accessible formulation in Sidgwick. The main idea is that society is rightly ordered, and therefore just, when its major institutions are arranged so as to achieve the greatest net balance of satisfaction summed over all the individuals belonging to it.

We may note first that there is, indeed, a way of thinking of society which makes it easy to suppose that the most rational conception of justice is utilitarian. For consider: each man in realizing his own interests is certainly free to balance his own losses against his own gains. We may impose a sacrifice on ourselves now for the sake of a greater advantage later. A person quite properly acts, at least when others are not affected, to achieve his own greatest good, to advance his rational ends as far as possible. Now why should not a society act on precisely the same principle applied to the group and therefore regard that which is rational for one man as right for an association of men? Just as the well-being of a person is constructed from the series of satisfactions that are experienced at different moments in the course of his life, so in very much the same way the well-being of society is to be constructed from the fulfillment of the systems of desires of the many individuals who belong to it. Since the principle for an individual is to advance as far as possible his own welfare, his own system of desires, the principle for society is to advance as far as possible the welfare of the group, to realize to the greatest extent the comprehensive system of desire arrived at from the desires of its members. Just as an individual balances present and future gains against present and future losses, so a society may balance satisfactions and dissatisfactions between different individuals. And so by these reflections one reaches the principle of utility in a natural way: a society is properly arranged when its institutions maximize the net balance of satisfaction. The principle of choice for an association of men is interpreted as an extension of the principle of choice for one man. Social justice is the principle of rational prudence applied to an aggregative conception of the welfare of the group.

This idea is made all the more attractive by a further consideration. The two main concepts of ethics are those of the right and the good; the concept of a morally worthy person is, I believe, derived from them. The structure of an ethical theory is, then, largely determined by how it defines and connects these two basic notions. Now it seems that the simplest way of relating them is taken by teleological theories: the good is defined independently from the right, and then the right is defined as that which maximizes the good.[1] More precisely, those institutions and acts are right which of the available alternatives produce the most good, or at least as much good as any of the other institutions and acts open as real possibilities (a rider needed when the maximal class is not a single-ton). Teleological theories have a deep intuitive appeal since they seem to embody the idea of rationality. It is natural to think that rationality is maximizing something and that in morals it must be maximizing the good. Indeed, it is tempting to suppose that it is self-evident that things should be arranged so as to lead to the most good.

It is essential to keep in mind that in a teleological theory the good is defined independently from the right. This means two things. First, the theory accounts for our considered judgments as to which things are good (our judgments of value) as a separate class of judgments intuitively distinguishable by common sense, and then proposes the hypothesis that the right is maximizing the good as already specified. Second, the theory enables one to judge the goodness of things without referring to what is right. For example, if pleasure is said to be the sole good, then presum-ably pleasures can be recognized and ranked in value by criteria that do not presuppose any standards of right, or what we would normally think of as such. Whereas if the distribution of goods is also counted as a good, perhaps a higher order one, and the theory directs us to produce the most good (including the good of distribution among others), we no longer have a teleological view in the classical sense. The problem of distribution falls under the concept of right as one intuitively understands it, and so the theory lacks an independent definition of the good. The clarity and simplicity of classical teleological theories derives largely from the fact that they factor our moral judgments into two classes, the one being characterized separately while the other is then connected with it by a maximizing principle.

Teleological doctrines differ, pretty clearly, according to how the conception of the good is specified. If it is taken as the realization of human excellence in the various forms of culture, we have what may be called perfectionism. This notion is found in Aristotle and Nietzsche, among others. If the good is defined as pleasure, we have hedonism; if as happiness, eudaimonism, and so on. I shall understand the principle of utility in its classical form as defining the good as the satisfaction of desire, or perhaps better, as the satisfaction of rational desire. This accords with the view in all essentials and provides, I believe, a fair interpretation of it. The appropriate terms of social cooperation are settled by whatever in the circumstances will achieve the greatest sum of satisfaction of the rational desires of individuals. It is impossible to deny the initial plausibility and attractiveness of this conception.

The striking feature of the utilitarian view of justice is that it does not matter, except indirectly, how this sum of satisfactions is distributed among individuals any more than it matters, except indirectly, how one man distributes his satisfactions over time. The correct distribution in either case is that which yields the maximum fulfillment. Society must allocate its means of satisfaction whatever these are, rights and duties, opportunities and privileges, and various forms of wealth, so as to achieve this maximum if it can. But in itself no distribution of satisfaction is better than another except that the more equal distribution is to be preferred to break ties. It is true that certain common sense precepts of justice, particularly those which concern the protection of liberties and rights, or which express the claims of desert, seem to contradict this contention. But from a utilitarian standpoint the explanation of these precepts and of their seemingly stringent character is that they are those precepts which experience shows should be strictly respected and departed from only under exceptional circumstances if the sum of advantages is to be maximized. Yet, as with all other precepts, those of justice are derivative from the one end of attaining the greatest balance of satisfaction. Thus there is no reason in principle why the greater gains of some should not compensate for the lesser losses of others; or more importantly, why the violation of the liberty of a few might not be made right by the greater good shared by many. It simply happens that under most conditions, at least in a reasonably advanced stage of civilization, the greatest sum of advantages is not attained in this way. No doubt the strictness of common sense precepts of justice has a certain usefulness in limiting men's propensities to injustice and to socially injurious actions, but the utilitarian believes that to affirm this strictness as a first principle of morals is a mistake. For just as it is rational for one man to maximize the fulfillment of his system of desires, it is right for a society to maximize the net balance of satisfaction taken over all of its members.

The most natural way, then, of arriving at utilitarianism (although not, of course, the only way of doing so) is to adopt for society as a whole the principle of rational choice for one man. Once this is recognized, the place of the impartial spectator and the emphasis on sympathy in the history of utilitarian thought is readily understood. For it is by the conception of the impartial spectator and the use of sympathetic identification in guiding our imagination that the principle for one man is applied to society. It is this spectator who is conceived as carrying out the required organization of the desires of all persons into one coherent system of desire; it is by this construction that many persons are fused into one. Endowed with ideal powers of sympathy and imagination, the impartial spectator is the perfectly rational individual who identifies with and experiences the desires of others as if these desires were his own. In this way he ascertains the intensity of these desires and assigns them their appropriate weight in the one system of desire the satisfaction of which the ideal legislator then tries to maximize by adjusting the rules of the social system. On this conception of society separate individuals are thought of as so many different lines along which rights and duties are to be assigned and scarce means of satisfaction allocated in accordance with rules so as to give the greatest fulfillment of wants. The nature of the decision made by the ideal legislator is not, therefore, materially different from that of an entrepreneur deciding how to maximize his profit by producing this or that commodity, or that of a consumer deciding how to maximize his satisfaction by the purchase of this or that collection of goods. In each case there is a single person whose system of desires determines the best allocation of limited means. The correct decision is essentially a question of efficient administration. This view of social cooperation is the consequence of extending to society the principle of choice for one man, and then, to make this extension work, conflating all persons into one through the imaginative acts of the impartial sympathetic spectator. Utilitarianism does not take seriously the distinction between persons.

Note

1.   Here I adopt W. K. Frankena's definition of teleological theories in *Ethics* (Englewood Cliffs, N.J., Prentice Hall, Inc., 1963), p. 13.

RULE UTILITARIANISM
John Hospers

John Hospers is currently director of the School of Philosophy at the University of California at Los Angeles. The following selection is from his Human Conduct: An Introduction to the Problems of Ethics. *A common objection to act utilitarianism is that it fails to cohere with certain of our core moral beliefs about the morality of actions. It is often pointed out that some individual actions are right even though they would not maximize utility, and that some individual actions would be wrong even though they would maximize utility. Some philosophers sympathetic to the utilitarian outlook on morality, but wanting to avoid problems with act utilitarianism, have embraced rule utilitarianism. According to this theory, all actions fall under rules, and we judge the morality of an action by judging the utility of adopting the associated rule. After explaining how rule utilitarianism apparently avoids the coherence problems besetting act utilitarianism, Hospers goes on to explain which rules, from among the many rules associated with each action, are relevant for judging the morality of actions.*

1. In order to receive a high enough grade average to be admitted to medical school, a certain student must receive either an A or a B in one of my courses. After his final examination is in, I find, on averaging his grades, that his grade for the course comes out to a C. The student comes into my office and begs me to change the grade, on the ground that I have not read his paper carefully enough. So I reread his final exam paper, as well as some of the other papers in the class in order to get a better sense of comparison; the rechecking convinces me that his grade should be no higher than the one I have given him—if anything, it should be lower. I inform him of my opinion and he still pleads with me to change the grade, but for a different reason. "I know I didn't deserve more than a C, but I appeal to you as a human being to change my grade, because without it I can't get into medical school, which naturally means a great deal to me." I inform him that grades are supposed to be based on achievement in the course, not on intentions or need or the worthiness of one's plans. But he pleads: "I know it's unethical to change a grade when the student doesn't deserve a higher one, but can't you please make an exception to the rule just this once?" And before I can reply, he sharpens his plea: "I appeal to you as a utilitarian. Your goal is the greatest happiness of everyone concerned, isn't it? If you give me only the grade I deserve, who will be happier? Not, I, that's sure. Perhaps you will for a little while, but you have hundreds of students and you'll soon forget about it; and I will be ever so much happier for being admitted into a school that will train me for the profession I have always desired. It's true that I didn't work as hard in your course as I should have, but I realize my mistake and I wouldn't waste so much time if I had it to do over again. Anyway, you should be forward-looking rather than backward-looking in your moral judgments, and there is no doubt whatever that much more happiness

will be caused (and unhappiness prevented) by your giving me the higher grade even though I fully admit that I don't deserve it."

After pondering the matter, I persist in believing that it would not be right to change the grade under these circumstances. Perhaps you agree with my decision and perhaps you don't, but *if* you agree that I should not have changed the grade, and *if* you are also a utilitarian, how are you going to reconcile such a decision with utilitarianism? *Ex hypothesi*, the greatest amount of happiness will be brought about by my changing the grade, so why shouldn't I change it?

Of course, if I changed the grade and went around telling people about it, my action would tend to have an adverse effect on the whole system of grading—and this system is useful to graduate schools and future employers to give some indication of the student's achievement in his various courses. But of course if I tell no one, nobody will know, and my action cannot set a bad example to others. This in turn raises an interesting question: If it is wrong for me to do the act publicly, is it any the less wrong for me to do it secretly?

2.   A man is guilty of petty theft and is sentenced to a year in prison. Suppose he can prove to the judge's satisfaction that he would be happier out of jail, that his wife and family would too (they depend on his support), that the state wouldn't have the expense of his upkeep if he were freed, and that people won't hear about it because his case didn't hit the papers and nobody even knows that he was arrested—in short, everyone concerned would be happier and nobody would be harmed by his release. And yet, we feel, or at least many people would, that to release him would be a mistake. The sentence imposed on him is the minimum permitted by law for his offense, and he should serve out his term in accordance with the law.

3.   A district attorney who has prosecuted a man for robbery chances upon information which shows conclusively that the man he has prosecuted is innocent of the crime for which he has just been sentenced. The man is a wastrel who, if permitted to go free, would almost certainly commit other crimes. Moreover, the district attorney has fairly conclusive evidence of the man's guilt in prior crimes, for which, however, the jury has failed to convict him. Should he, therefore, "sit on the evidence" and let the conviction go through in this case, in which he knows the man to be innocent? We may not be able to articulate exactly *why*, but we feel strongly that the district attorney should not sit on the evidence but that he should reveal every scrap of evidence he knows, even though the revelation means releasing the prisoner (now known to be innocent) to do more crimes and be convicted for them later.

x. It seems to me that some acts are right or wrong, not *regardless* of the consequences they produce, but *over and above* the consequences they produce. We would all agree, I suppose, that you should break a promise to save a life but not that you should break it whenever you considered it probable (even with good reason) that more good effects will come about through breaking it. Suppose you had promised someone you would do something and you didn't do it. When asked why, you replied, "Because I thought breaking it would have better results." Wouldn't the promisee condemn you for your action, and rightly? This example is quite analogous, I think, to the example of the district attorney; the district attorney might argue that more total good will be produced by keeping the prisoner's innocence secret. Besides, if he is released, people may read about it in the newspaper and say, "You see, you can get by with anything these days" and may be encouraged to violate the law themselves as a result. Still, even though it would do more total good if the man were to remain convicted, wouldn't it be wrong to do so in view of the fact that he is definitely innocent of *this* crime? The law punishes a man, not necessarily because the most good will be achieved that way, but because he has committed a crime; if we don't approve of the law, we can do our best to have it changed, but meanwhile aren't we bound to follow it? Those who execute the law are sworn to obey it; they are *not* sworn to produce certain consequences.

Y. Yes, but remember that the facts *might* always come out after their concealment and that we can never be sure they won't. If they do, keeping the man in prison will be far worse than letting the man go; it will result in a great public distrust for the law itself; nothing is more demoralizing than corruption of the law by its own supposed enforcers. Better let a hundred human derelicts go free than risk that! You see, *one* of the consequences you always have to consider is the effect of *this* action on the *general practice* of law-breaking itself; and when you bring in *this* consequence, it will surely weigh the balance in favor of divulging the information that will release the innocent man. So utilitarianism will still account quite satisfactorily for this case. I agree that the man should be released, but I do so on utilitarian grounds; I needn't abandon my utilitarianism at all to take care of this case.

x. But your view is open to one fatal objection. You say that one never can be sure that the news *won't* leak out. Perhaps so. But suppose that in a given case one *could* be sure; would that really make any difference? Suppose you are the only person that knows and you destroy the only existing evidence. Since you are not going to talk, there is simply no chance that the news will leak out, with consequent damage to public morale. Then is it all right to withhold the information? You see, I hold that if it's wrong not to reveal the truth when others might find out, then it's equally wrong not to reveal it when *nobody* will find out. You utilitarians are involved in the fatal error of making the rightness or wrongness of an act depend on whether performing it will ever be publicized. And I hold that it is immoral even to consider this condition; the district attorney should reveal the truth regardless of whether his concealing it would ever be known.

Y. But surely you aren't saying that one should *never* conceal the truth? not even if your country is at war against a totalitarian enemy and revealing truths to the people would also mean revealing them to the enemy?

X. Of course I'm not saying that—don't change the subject. I am saying that *if* in situation S it is wrong to convict an innocent man, then it is equally wrong whether or not the public knows that it is wrong; the public's knowledge will certainly have bad consequences, but the conviction would be wrong anyway even *without* these bad consequences; so you can't appeal to the consequences of the conviction's becoming public as grounds for saying that the conviction is wrong. I think that you utilitarians are really stuck here. For you, the consideration "but nobody is ever going to know about it anyway" is a relevant consideration. It has to be; for the rightness of an act (according to you) is estimated in terms of its total consequences, and its total consequences, of course, include its effects (or lack of effects) on other acts of the same kind, and there won't be any such effects if the act is kept absolutely secret. You have to consider *all* the consequences relevant; the matter of keeping the thing quiet is one consequence; so you have to consider this one relevant too. Yet I submit to you that it isn't relevant; the suggestion "but nobody is going to know about it anyway" is not one that will help make the act permissible if it wasn't before. If anything, it's the other way round: something bad that's done publicly and openly is not as bad as if it's done secretly so as to escape detection; secret sins are the worst. . . .

Y. I deny what you say. It seems to me worse to betray a trust in public, where it may set an example to others, than to do so in secret, where it can have no bad effects on others.

X. And I submit that you would never say that if you weren't already committed to the utilitarian position. Here is a situation where you and practically everyone else would not hesitate to say that an act done in secret is no less wrong than when done in public, were it not that it flies in the face of a doctrine to which you have already committed yourself on the basis of quite different examples.

4.   Here is a still different kind of example. We consider it our duty in a democracy to vote and to do so wisely and intelligently as possible, for only if we vote wisely can a democracy work successfully. But in a national election my vote is only one out of millions, and it is more and more improbable that *my* vote will have any effect upon the outcome. Nor is my failure to vote going to affect other people much, if at all. Couldn't a utilitarian argue this way: "My vote will have no effect at all—at least far, far less than other things I could be doing instead. Therefore, I shall not vote." Each and every would-be voter could argue in exactly the same way. The result would be that nobody would vote, and the entire democratic process would be destroyed.

What conclusion emerges from these examples? If the examples point at all in the right direction, they indicate that there are some acts which it is right to perform, even though by themselves they will not have good consequences (such as my voting), and that there are some acts which it is wrong to perform, even though by themselves they would have good consequences (such as sitting on the evidence). But this conclusion is opposed to utilitarianism as we have considered it thus far. . . .

Rule-Utilitarianism and Objections to It

The batter swings, the ball flies past, the umpire yells "Strike three!" The disappointed batter pleads with the umpire, "Can't I have four strikes just this once?" We all recognize the absurdity of this example. Even if the batter could prove to the umpire's satisfaction that he would be happier for having four strikes this time, that the spectators would be happier for it (since most of the spectators are on his side), that there would be little dissatisfaction on the side of the opposition (who might have the game clinched anyway), and that there would be no effect on future baseball games, we would still consider his plea absurd. We might think, "Perhaps baseball would be a better game—i.e., contribute to the greatest total enjoyment of all concerned—if four strikes were permitted. If so, we should change the rules of the game. But until that time, we must play baseball according to the rules which are now the accepted rules of the game."

This example, though only an analogy, gives us a clue to the kind of view we are about to consider—let us call it *rule-utilitarianism*. Briefly stated (we shall amplify it gradually), rule-utilitarianism comes to this: Each act, in the moral life, falls under a *rule*; and we are to judge the rightness or wrongness of the act, not by *its* consequences, but by the consequences of its universalization—that is, by the consequences of the adoption of the *rule* under which this act falls. This . . . interpretation of Kant's categorical imperative . . . differs from Kant in being concerned with consequences, but retains the main feature which Kant introduced, that of universalizability.

Thus: The district attorney may do more good in a particular case by sitting on the evidence, but even if this case has no consequences for future cases because nobody ever finds out, still, the general policy or *practice* of doing this kind of thing is a very bad one; it uproots one of the basic premises of our legal system, namely that an innocent person should not be condemned. Our persistent conviction that it would be wrong for him to conceal the evidence in this case comes *not* from the conviction that concealing the evidence will produce less good—we may be satisfied that it will produce more good in this case—but from the conviction that the *practice* of doing this kind of thing will have very bad consequences. In other words, "Conceal the evidence when you think that it will produce more happiness" would be a bad rule to follow, and it is because this *rule* (if adopted) would have bad consequences, not because *this* act itself has bad consequences, that we condemn the act.

The same applies in other situations: . . . perhaps I can achieve more good, in this instance, by changing the student's grade, but the consequences of the general practice of changing students' grades for such reasons as these would be very bad indeed; a graduate school or a future employer would no longer have reason to believe that the grade-transcript of the student had any reference to his real achievement in his courses; he would wonder how many of the high grades resulted from personal factors like pity, need, and irrelevant appeals by the student to the teacher. The same considerations apply also to the voting example: if Mr. Smith can reason that his vote won't make any difference to the outcome, so can Mr. Jones and Mr. Robinson and every other would-be voter; but if everyone reasoned in this way, no one would vote, and this *would* have bad effects. It is considered one's duty to vote, not because the consequences of one's not doing so are bad, but because the consequences of the general practice of not doing so are bad. To put it in Kantian language, the maxim of the action, if universalized, would have bad consequences. But the individual act of *your* not voting on a specific occasion—or of any *one* person's not voting, as long as *others* continued to vote—would probably have no bad consequences.

There are many other examples of the same kind of thing. If during a water shortage there is a regulation that water should not be used to take baths every day or to water gardens, there will be virtually no bad consequences if only *I* violate the rule. Since there will be no discernible difference to the city water supply and since my plants will remain green and fresh and pleasant to look at, why shouldn't I water my plants? But if everyone watered his plants, there would not be enough water left to drink. My act is judged wrong, not because of *its* consequences, but because the consequences of everyone doing so would be bad. If I walk on the grass where the sign says, "Do not walk on the grass," there will be no ill effects; but if everyone did so it would destory the grass. There are some kinds of act which have little or no effect if any one person (or two, or three) does them but which have very considerable effects if everyone (or even just a large number) does them. Rule-utilitarianism is designed to take care of just such situations.

Rule-utilitarianism also takes care of situations which are puzzling in traditional utilitarianism, . . . namely, the secrecy with which an act is performed. "But no one will ever know, so my act won't have any consequences for future acts of the same kind," the utilitarian argued; and we felt that he was being somehow irrelevant, even immoral: that if something is wrong when people know about it, it is just as wrong when done in secret. Yet this condition *is* relevant according to traditional utilitarianism, for if some act with bad consequences is never known to anyone, this ignorance does mitigate the bad consequences, for it undeniably keeps the act from setting an example (except, of course, that it may start a habit in the agent himself). Rule-utilitarianism solves this difficulty. If I change the student's grade in secret, my act is wrong, in spite of its having almost no consequences (and never being known to anyone else), because if I change the grade and don't tell anyone, how do I know how many other teachers are changing their students' grades without telling anybody? It is the result of the *practice* which is bad, not the result of my single action. The result of the practice is bad whether the act is done in secret or not: the result of the practice of changing grades in secret is just as bad as the results of the practice done in full knowledge of everyone; it would be equally deleterious to the grading system, equally a bad index of a student's actual achievement. In fact, if changing grades is done in secret, this in one way is worse; for prospective employers will not know, as they surely ought to know in evaluating their prospective employees, that their grades are not based on achievement but on other factors such as poverty, extra-curricular work load, and persuasive appeal.

Rule-utilitarianism is a distinctively twentieth-century amendment of the utilitarianism of Bentham and Mill, often called *act-utilitarianism*. . . . Since this pair of labels is brief and indicates clearly the contents of the theories referred to, we prefer these terms to a second pair of labels, which are sometimes used for the same theories: *restricted utilitarianism* as opposed to *unrestricted* (or extreme, or *traditional*) *utilitarianism*. (Whether or not Mill's theory is strictly act-utilitarianism is a matter of dispute. Mill never made the distinction between act-utilitarianism and rule-utilitarianism. . . . Some of Mill's examples, however, have to do not with individual acts but with general principles and rules of conduct. Mill and Bentham were both legislators, interested in amending the laws of England into greater conformity to the utilitarian principle; and to the extent that Mill was interested in providing a criterion of judging rules of conduct rather than individual acts, he may be said to have been a rule-utilitarian.)

Much more must be said before the full nature of the rule-utilitarian theory becomes clear. To understand it better, we shall consider some possible questions, comments, and objections that can be put to the theory as thus far stated.

1.   Doesn't the . . . problem arise here . . . of *what* precisely we are to universalize? Every act can be put into a vast variety of classes of acts; or, in our present terminology, every act can be made to fall under many different general rules. Which rule among this vast variety are we to select? We can pose our problem by means of an imaginary dialogue referring back to Kant's ethics and connecting it with rule-utilitarianism:

A. Whatever may be said for Kant's ethics in general, there is one principle of fundamental importance which must be an indispensable part of every ethics—the principle of universalizability. If some act is right for me to do, it would be right for all rational beings to do it; and if it is wrong for them to do it, it would be wrong for me too.

B. If this principle simply means that nobody should make an exception in his own favor, the principle is undoubtedly true and is psychologically important in view of the fact that people constantly do make exceptions in their own favor. But as it stands I can't follow you in agreeing with Kant's principle. Do you mean that if it is wrong for Smith to get a divorce, it is also wrong for Jones to do so? But this isn't so. Smith may be hopelessly incompatible with his wife, and they may be far better off apart, whereas Jones may be reconcilable with his wife (with some mutual effort) and a divorce in his case would be a mistake. Each case must be judged on its own merits.

A. The principle doesn't mean that if it's right for one person, A, to do it, it is therefore right for B and C and D to do it. It means that if it's right for one person to do it, it is right for anyone *in those circumstances* to do it. And Jones isn't in the same circumstances as Smith. Smith and his wife would be better off apart, and Jones and his wife would be better off together.

B. I see. Do you mean *exactly* the same circumstances or *roughly* the same (similar) circumstances?

A. I think I would have to mean exactly the same circumstances for if the circumstances were not quite alike, that little difference might make the difference between a right act (done by Smith) and a wrong act (done by Jones). For instance, if in Smith's case there are no children and in Jones' case there are, this fact may make a difference.

B. Right. But I must urge you to go even further. Two men might be in exactly the same *external* circumstances, but owing to their *internal constitution* what would be right for one of them wouldn't be for the other. Jones may have the ability to be patient, impartial, and approach problems rationally, and Smith may not have this ability; here again is a relevant difference between them, although not a difference in their external circumstances. Or: Smith, after he reaches a certain point of fatigue, would do well to go fishing for a few days—this would refresh and relax him as nothing else could. But Jones dislikes fishing; it tries and irritates and bores him; so even if he were equally tired and had an equally responsible position, he would not be well advised to go fishing. Or again: handling explosives might be all right for a trained intelligent person, but not for an ignorant blunderbuss. In the light of such examples as these, you see that under the "same circumstances" you'll have to include not only the external circumstances in which they find themselves but their own internal character.

A. I grant this. So what?

B. But now your universalizability principle becomes useless. For two people never *are* in exactly the same circumstances. Nor can they be: if Smith were in exactly the same circumstances as Jones, including all his traits of character, his idiosyncracies, and his brain cells, he would *be* Jones. You see, your universalizability principle is inapplicable. It would become applicable only under conditions (two people being the same person) which are self-contradictory,—and even if not self-contradictory, you'll have to admit that two exactly identical situations never occur; so once again the rule is inapplicable.

A. I see your point; but I don't think I need go along with your conclusion. Smith and Jones should do the same thing only if their situation or circumstances are the same in certain *relevant respects*. The fact that Jones is wearing a white shirt and Smith a blue one, is a difference of circumstances, but, surely, an *irrelevant* difference, a difference that for moral purposes can be ignored. But the fact that Smith and his wife are emotionally irreconcilable while Jones and his wife could work things out, would be a morally relevant circumstance.

B. Possibly. But how are you going to determine which differences are relevant and which are not?

Kant . . . never solved this problem. He assumed that "telling a lie" was morally relevant but that "telling a lie to save a life" was not; but he gave no reason for making this distinction. The rule-utilitarian has an answer.

Suppose that a red-headed man with one eye and a wart on his right cheek tells a lie on a Tuesday. What rule are we to derive from this event? Red-headed men should not tell lies? People shouldn't lie on Tuesdays? Men with warts on their cheeks shouldn't tell lies on Tuesdays? These rules seem absurd, for it seems so obvious that whether it's Tuesday or not, whether the man has a wart on his cheek or not, has nothing whatever to do with the rightness of his action—these circumstances are just *irrelevant*. But this is the problem: how are we going to establish this irrelevance? What is to be our criterion?

The criterion we tried to apply . . . was to make the rule more *specific:* instead of saying, "This is a lie and is therefore wrong," . . . we made it more specific and said, "This is a lie told to save a life and is therefore right." We could make the rule more specific still, involving the precise circumstances in which this lie is told, other than the fact that it is told to save a life. But, now it seems, the use of greater specificity will not always work: instead of "Don't tell lies," suppose we say, "Don't tell lies on Tuesdays." The second is certainly more specific than the first, but is it a better rule? It seems plain that it is not—that its being a Tuesday is, in fact, wholly irrelevant. Why?

"Because," says the rule-utilitarian, "there is no difference between the effects of lies told on Tuesdays and the effects of lies told on any other day. This is simply an empirical fact, and because of this empirical fact, bringing in Tuesday is irrelevant. If lies told on Tuesdays always had good consequences and lies told on other days were disastrous, then a lie's being told on a Tuesday would be relevant to the moral estimation of the act; but in fact this is not true. Thus there is no advantage in specifying the subclass of lies, 'lies told on Tuesdays.' The same is true of 'lies told by redheads' and 'lies told by persons with warts on their cheeks.' The class of lies can be made more specific—that is no problem—but not more *relevantly* specific, at least not in the direction of Tuesdays and redheads. (However, the class can be made more relevantly specific considering certain other aspects of the situation, such as whether the lie was told to produce a good result that could not have been brought about otherwise.)"

Consider by contrast a situation in which the class of acts can easily be made relevantly more specific. A pacifist might argue as follows: "I should never use physical violence in any form against another human being, since if everyone refrained from violence, we would have a warless world." There are aspects of this example that we cannot discuss now, but our present concern with it is as follows. We can break down violence into more specific types such as violence which is unprovoked, violence in defense of one's life against attack by another, violence by a policeman in catching a lawbreaker, violence by a drunkard in response to an imaginary affront. The effects of these subclasses of violence do differ greatly in their effects upon society. Violence used by a policeman in apprehending a lawbreaker (at least under some circumstances, which could be spelled out) and violence used in preventing a would be murderer from killing you, do on the whole have good effects; but the unprovoked violence of an aggressor or a drunkard does not. Since these subclasses do have different effects, therefore, it *is* relevant to consider them. Indeed, it is imperative to do so: the pacifist who condemns *all* violence would probably, if he thought about it, not wish to condemn the policeman who uses violent means to prevent an armed madman from killing a dozen people. In any event, the effects of the two subclasses of acts are vastly different; and, the rule-utilitarian would say, it is accordingly very important for us to consider them—to break down the general class of violent acts into more specific classes and consider separately the effects of each one until we have arrived at subclasses which cannot *relevantly* be made more specific.

How specific shall we be? Won't we get down to "acts of violence to prevent aggression, performed on Tuesdays at 11:30 P.M. in hot weather" and subclasses of that sort? And aren't these again plainly irrelevant? Of course they are, and the reason has already been given: acts of violence performed on Tuesdays, or at 11:30 P.M., or by people with blue suits, are no different in their effects from acts-of-violence-to-prevent-aggression done in circumstances other than these; and therefore these circumstances, though more specific, are not relevantly more specific. When the consequences of these more specific classes of acts differ from the consequences of the more general class, it is this specific class which should be considered; but when the consequences of the specific class are not different from those of the more general class, the greater specificity is irrelevant and can be ignored.

The rule, then, is this: we should consider the consequences of the general performance of certain classes of actions only if that class contains within itself no subclasses, the consequences of the general practice of which would be either better or worse than the consequences of the class itself.

Let us take an actual example of how this rule applies. Many people, including Kant, have taken the principle "Thou shalt not kill" as admitting of no exceptions. But as we have just seen, such principles can be relevantly made more specific. Killing for fun is one thing, killing in self-defense another. Suppose, then, that we try to arrive at a general rule on which to base our actions in this regard. We shall try to arrive at that rule the general following of which will have the best results. Not to kill an armed bandit who is about to shoot you if you don't shoot him first, would appear to be a bad rule by utilitarian standards; for it would tend to eliminate the good people and preserve the bad ones; moreover, if nobody resisted aggressors, the aggressors, knowing this, would go hog-wild and commit indiscriminate murder, rape, and plunder. Therefore, "Don't kill except in self-defense" (though we might improve this rule too) would be a better rule than "Never kill." But "Don't kill unless you feel angry at the victim" would be a bad rule, because the adoption of this rule would lead to no end of indiscriminate killing for no good reason. The trick is to arrive at the rule which, if adopted, would have the very best possible consequences (which includes, of course, the absolute minimum of bad consequences). Usually no simple or easily statable rule will do this, the world being as complex as it is. There will usually be subclasses of classes-of-acts which are relevantly more specific than the simple, general class with which we began. And even when we think we have arrived at a satisfactory rule, there always remains the possibility that it can relevantly be made more specific, and thus amended, with an increase in accuracy but a consequent decrease in simplicity.

To a considerable extent most people recognize this complexity. Very few people would accept the rule against killing without some qualifications. However much they may preach and invoke the rule "Thou shall not kill" in situations where it happens to suit them, they would never recommend its adoption in all circumstances: when one is defending himself against an armed killer, almost everyone would agree that killing is permissible, although he may not have formulated any theory from which this exception follows as a logical consequence. Our practical rule against killing contains within itself (often not explicitly stated) certain *classes of exceptions:* "Don't kill *except* in self-defense, in war against an aggressor nation, in carrying out the verdict of a jury recommending capital punishment." This would be a far better rule—judged by its consequences—than any simple one-line rule on the subject. Each of the classes of exceptions could be argued pro and con, of course. But such arguments would be empirical ones, hinging on whether or not the adoption of such classes of exceptions into the rule would have the maximum results in intrinsic good. (Many would argue, for example, that capital punishment achieves no good effects; on the other hand, few would contend that the man who pulls the switch at Sing Sing is committing a crime in carrying out the orders of the legal representatives of the state.) And there may always be other kinds of situations that we have not previously thought of, situations which, if incorporated into the rule, would improve the rule—that is, make it have better consequences; and thus the rule remains always open, always subject to further qualification if the addition of such qualification would improve the rule.

These qualifications of the rule are not, strictly speaking, *exceptions to* the rule. According to rule-utilitarianism, the rule, once fully stated, admits of no exceptions; but there may be, and indeed there usually are, numerous classes of exceptions *built into* the rule; a simple rule becomes through qualification a more complex rule. Thus, if a man kills someone in self-defense and we do not consider his act wrong, we are not making him an exception to the rule. Rather, his act *falls under* the rule—the rule that includes killing in self-defense as one of the classes of acts which is permissible (or, if you prefer, the rule that includes self-defense as one of the circumstances in which the rule against killing does not apply). Similarly, if a man parks in a prohibited area and the judge does not fine him because he is a physician making a professional call, the judge is not extending any favoritism to the physician; he is not making the physician an exception to the rule; rather, the rule (though it may not always be written out in black and white) includes within itself this recognized class of exceptions—or, more accurately still, the rule includes within itself a reference to just this kind of situation, so that the action of the judge in exonerating the physician is just as much an application of the rule (not an exception to it) as another act of the same judge in imposing a fine on someone else for the same offense.

We can now see how our previous remarks about acts committed in secret fit into the rule-utilitarian scheme. On the one hand, the rule "Don't break a promise except (1) under extreme duress and (2) to promote some very great good" is admittedly somewhat vague, and perhaps it could be improved by still further qualification; but at least it is much better than the simple rule "Never break promises." On the other hand, the rule "Don't break a promise except when nobody will know about it" is a bad rule: there are many situations in which keeping promises is important . . . situations in which promises could not be relied on if this rule were adopted. That is why, among the circumstances which excuse you from keeping your word, the fact that it was broken in secret is not one of them—and for a very good reason: if this class of exceptions were incorporated into the rule, the rule's adoption would have far worse effects than if it did not contain such a clause. . . .

. . . Rule-utilitarianism and act-utilitarianism are alike with regard to relativism. They are *not* relativistic in that they have one standard, one "rule of rules," one supreme norm, applicable to all times and situations: "Perform that act which will produce the most intrinsic good" (act-utilitarianism), "Act according to the rule whose adoption will produce the most intrinsic good" (rule-utilitarianism). But within the scope of that one standard, the recommended rules of conduct may well vary greatly from place to place. . . . In a desert area the act of wasting water will cause much harm and is therefore wrong, but it is not wrong in a region where water is plentiful. In a society where men and women are approximately equal in number, it will be best for a husband to have only one wife; but in a society in which there is great numerical disparity between the two, this arrangement may no longer be wise. So much for act-utilitarianism; the same goes for rule-utilitarianism. The rule "Never waste water" is a good rule, indeed an indispensable rule, in a desert region but not in a well-watered region. Monogamy seems to be the best possible marital system in our society but not necessarily in all societies—it depends on the conditions. What are the best acts and the best rules at a given time and place, then, depends on the special circumstances of that time and place. Some conditions, of course, are so general that the rules will be much the same everywhere: a rule against killing (at least within the society) is an indispensable condition of security and survival and therefore must be preserved in all societies.

The situation, then, is this: Rule or Act A is right in circumstances C_1, and Rule or Act B is right in circumstances C_2. In X-land circumstances C_1 prevail, so A is right; and in Y-land circumstances C_2 prevail, so B is right. Perhaps this is all the relativism that ethical relativists will demand.

4.   Can't there be, in rule-utilitarianism, a conflict of rules? Suppose you have to choose between breaking a promise and allowing a human life to be lost. . . . What would the rule-utilitarian say? Which rule are we to go by?

No rule-utilitarian would hold such a rule as "Never break a promise" or "Never take a human life." Following such rigid, unqualified rules would certainly not lead to the best consequences—for example, taking Hitler's life would have had better consequences than sparing him. Since such simple rules would never be incorporated into rule-utilitarian ethics to begin with, there would be no conflict between these rules. The rule-utilitarian's rule on taking human life would be of the form, "Do not take human life except in circumstances of types A, B, C . . ." and these circumstances would be those in which taking human life *would* have the best consequences. And the same with breaking promises. Thus, when the rules in question are fully spelled out, there would be no conflict.

In any event, if there were a conflict between rules, there would have to be a second-order rule to tell us which first-order rule to adopt in cases of conflict. Only with such a rule would our rule-utilitarian ethics be *complete*, i.e., made to cover every situation that might arise. But again such a second-order rule would seldom be simple. It would not say, "In cases of conflict between preserving a life and keeping a promise, always preserve the life." For there might always be kinds of cases in which this policy would not produce the best consequences: a president who has promised something to a whole nation or who has signed a treaty with other nations which depend on that treaty being kept and base their own national policies upon it, would not be well advised to say simply, "In cases of conflict, always break your word rather than lose one human life." In cases of this kind, keeping the promise would probably produce the best results, though the particular instance would have to be decided empirically. We would have to go through a detailed empirical examination to discover which rule, among all the rules we might adopt on the matter, would have the best consequences if adopted.

5.   Well then, why not just make the whole thing simple and say, "Always keep your promises except when breaking them will produce the most good," "Always conserve human life except when taking it will produce the most good"? In other words, "In every case do what will have the best consequences"—why not make this the Rule of Rules? To do so is to have act-utilitarianism with us once again; but why not? Is there anything more obvious in ethics than that we should always try to produce the most good possible?

"No," says the rule-utilitarian, "not if this rule means that we should always do the individual *act* that produces the most good possible. We must clearly distinguish rules from acts. 'Adopt the rule which will have the best consequences' is different from 'Do the act which will have the best consequences.' (When you say, 'Always do the most good,' this is ambiguous—it could mean either one.)" The rule-utilitarian, of course, recommends the former in preference to the latter; for if everyone were to do acts which (taken individually) had the best consequences, the result would *not* in every case be a policy having the best consequences. For example, my not voting but doing something else instead may produce better consequences than my voting (my voting may have no effect at all); your not voting will do the same; and so on for every individual, as long as most *other* people vote. But the results would be very bad, for if each individual adopted the policy of not voting, nobody would vote. In other words, the rule "Vote, except in situations where not voting will do more good" is a rule which, if followed, would *not* produce the best consequences.

Another example: The rule "Don't kill except where killing will do the most good"—which the act-utilitarian would accept—is not, the rule-utilitarian would say, as good a rule to follow as "Don't kill except in self-defense . . ." (and other classes of acts which we discussed earlier).

That is, the rule to prohibit killing except under special kinds of conditions specified in advance would do more good, if followed, than the rule simply to refrain except when not refraining will do more good. The former is better, not just because people will rationalize themselves into believing that what they want to do will produce the most good in a particular situation (though this is very important), but also because when there are certain standard classes of exceptions built into the rule, there will be a greater *predictability* of the results of such actions; the criminal will know what will happen if he is caught. If the law said, "Killing is prohibited except when it will do the most good," what could you expect? Every would-be killer would think it would do the most good in his specific situation. And would you, a potential victim, feel more secure or less secure, if such a law were enacted? Every criminal would think that he would be exonerated even if he were caught, and every victim (or would-be victim) would fear that this would be so. The effects of having such a rule, then, would be far worse than the effects of having a general rule prohibiting killing, with certain classes of qualifications built into the rule.

There is, then, it would seem, a considerable difference between act-utilitarianism and rule-utilitarianism.

CHAPTER 8

Virtue and the Ethics of Perfectionism

VIRTUE AND CHARACTER
Aristotle

Aristotle (384–322 B.C.) is one of the most important philosophers ever to have lived. The son of a physician, he was a student of Plato and served as tutor to Alexander the Great. He contributed important works on logic, the sciences, and virtually every area of philosophy.

In the following selection from his Nicomachean Ethics, *Aristotle begins by arguing that a happy or good life essentially involves a life of activity in accordance with virtue. He then goes on to define virtue as a disposition to avoid extremes in feeling and action. For example, in matters relating to money, the virtue of generosity stands between the extremes of extravagance and stinginess.*

Characteristics of the Good

1. The good is the end of action.

But let us return once again to the good we are looking for, and consider just what it could be, since it is apparently one thing in one action or craft, and another thing in another; for it is one thing in medicine, another in generalship, and so on for the rest.

What, then, is the good in each of these cases? Surely it is that for the sake of which the other things are done; and in medicine this is health, in generalship victory, in house-building a house, in another case something else, but in every action and decision it is the end, since it is for the sake of the end that everyone does the other things.

And so, if there is some end of everything that is pursued in action, this will be the good pursued in action; and if there are more ends than one, these will be the goods pursued in action.

Our argument has progressed, then, to the same conclusion [as before, that the highest end is the good]; but we must try to clarify this still more.

2.   The good is complete.

Though apparently there are many ends, we choose some of them, e.g. wealth, flutes and, in general, instruments, because of something else; hence it is clear that not all ends are complete. But the best good is apparently something complete. Hence, if only one end is complete, this will be what we are looking for; and if more than one are complete, the most complete of these will be what we are looking for.

CRITERIA FOR COMPLETENESS

An end pursued in itself, we say, is more complete than an end pursued because of something else; and an end that is never choiceworthy because of something else is more complete than ends that are choiceworthy both in themselves and because of this end; and hence an end that is always [choiceworthy, and also] choiceworthy in itself, never because of something else, is unconditionally complete.

3.   Happiness meets the criteria for completeness, but other goods do not.

Now happiness more than anything else seems unconditionally complete, since we always [choose it, and also] choose it because of itself, never because of something else.

Honour, pleasure, understanding and every virtue we certainly choose because of themselves, since we would choose each of them even if it had no further result, but we also choose them for the sake of happiness, supposing that through them we shall be happy. Happiness, by contrast, no one ever chooses for their sake, or for the sake of anything else at all.

4.   The good is self-sufficient; so is happiness.

The same conclusion [that happiness is complete] also appears to follow from self-sufficiency, since the complete good seems to be self-sufficient.

Now what we count as self-sufficient is not what suffices for a solitary person by himself, living an isolated life, but what suffices also for parents, children, wife and in general for friends and fellow-citizens, since a human being is a naturally political [animal]. Here, however, we must impose some limit; for if we extend the good to parents' parents and children's children and to friends of friends, we shall go on without limit; but we must examine this another time.

Anyhow, we regard something as self-sufficient when all by itself it makes a life choiceworthy and lacking nothing; and that is what we think happiness does.

5. The good is most choiceworthy; so is happiness.

Moreover, [the complete good is most choiceworthy, and] we think happiness is most choiceworthy of all goods, since it is not counted as one good among many. If it were counted as one among many, then, clearly, we think that the addition of the smallest of goods would make it more choiceworthy; for [the smallest good] that is added becomes an extra quantity of goods [so creating a good larger than the original good], and the larger of two goods is always more choiceworthy. [But we do not think any addition can make happiness more choiceworthy; hence it is most choiceworthy.]

Happiness, then, is apparently something complete and self-sufficient, since it is the end of the things pursued in action.

A clearer account of the good: the human soul's activity expressing virtue.

But presumably the remark that the best good is happiness is apparently something [generally] agreed, and what we miss is a clearer statement of what the best good is.

1. If something has a function, its good depends on its function.

Well, perhaps we shall find the best good if we first find the function of a human being. For just as the good, i.e. [doing] well, for a flautist, a sculptor, and every craftsman, and, in general, for whatever has a function and [characteristic] action, seems to depend on its function, the same seems to be true for a human being, if a human being has some function.

2. What sorts of things have functions?

Then do the carpenter and the leatherworker have their functions and actions, while a human being has none, and is by nature idle, without any function? Or, just as eye, hand, foot and, in general, every [bodily] part apparently has its functions, may we likewise ascribe to a human being some function besides all of theirs?

3.   *The human function.*

What, then, could this be? For living is apparently shared with plants, but what we are looking for is the special function of a human being; hence we should set aside the life of nutrition and growth. The life next in order is some sort of life of sense-perception; but this too is apparently shared, with horse, ox and every animal. The remaining possibility, then, is some sort of life of action of the [part of the soul] that has reason.

Clarification of 'has reason' and 'life.'

Now this [part has two parts, which have reason in different ways], one as obeying the reason [in the other part], the other as itself having reason and thinking. [We intend both.] Moreover, life is also spoken of in two ways [as capacity and as activity], and we must take [a human being's special function to be] life as activity, since this seems to be called life to a fuller extent.

4.   *The human good is activity expressing virtue.*

(a) We have found, then, that the human function is the soul's activity that expresses reason [as itself having reason] or requires reason [as obeying reason]. (b) Now the function of F, e.g. of a harpist, is the same in kind, so we say, as the function of an excellent F, e.g. an excellent harpist. (c) The same is true unconditionally in every case, when we add to the function the superior achievement that expresses the virtue; for a harpist's function, e.g. is to play the harp, and a good harpist's is to do it well. (d) Now we take the human function to be a certain kind of life, and take this life to be the soul's activity and actions that express reason. (e) [Hence by (c) and (d)] the excellent man's function is to do this finely and well. (f) Each function is completed well when its completion expresses the proper virtue. (g) Therefore [by (d), (e) and (f)] the human good turns out to be the soul's activity that expresses virtue.

5.   *The good must also be complete.*

And if there are more virtues than one, the good will express the best and most complete virtue. Moreover, it will be in a complete life. For one swallow does not make a spring, nor does one day; nor, similarly, does one day or a short time make us blessed and happy. . . .

Virtues of Character in General

HOW A VIRTUE OF CHARACTER IS ACQUIRED

Virtue, then, is of two sorts, virtue of thought and virtue of character. Virtue of thought arises and grows mostly from teaching, and hence needs experience and time. Virtue of character [i.e. of *ēthos*] results from habit [*ethos*]; hence its name 'ethical', slightly varied from '*ethos*'.

Virtue comes about, not by a process of nature, but by habituation.

Hence it is also clear that none of the virtues of character arises in us naturally.

1. What is natural cannot be changed by habituation.

For if something is by nature [in one condition], habituation cannot bring it into another condition. A stone, e.g., by nature moves downwards, and habituation could not make it move upwards, not even if you threw it up ten thousand times to habituate it; nor could habituation make fire move downwards, or bring anything that is by nature in one condition into another condition.

Thus the virtues arise in us neither by nature nor against nature, but we are by nature able to acquire them, and reach our complete perfection through habit.

2. Natural capacities are not acquired by habituation.

Further, if something arises in us by nature, we first have the capacity for it, and later display the activity. This is clear in the case of the senses; for we did not acquire them by frequent seeing or hearing, but already had them when we exercised them, and did not get them by exercising them.

Virtues, by contrast, we acquire, just as we acquire crafts, by having previously activated them. For we learn a craft by producing the same product that we must produce when we have learned it, becoming builders, e.g., by building and harpists by playing the harp; so also, then, we become just by doing just actions, temperate by doing temperate actions, brave by doing brave actions.

3. Legislators concentrate on habituation.

What goes on in cities is evidence for this also. For the legislator makes the citizens good by habituating them, and this is the wish of every legislator; if he fails to do it well he misses his goal. [The right] habituation is what makes the difference between a good political system and a bad one.

4. Virtue and vice are formed by good and bad actions.

Further, just as in the case of a craft, the sources and means that develop each virtue also ruin it. For playing the harp makes both good and bad harpists, and it is analogous in the case of builders and all the rest; for building well makes good builders, building badly, bad ones. If it were not so, no teacher would be needed, but everyone would be born a good or a bad craftsman.

It is the same, then, with the virtues. For actions in dealings with [other] human beings make some people just, some unjust; actions in terrifying situations and the acquired habit of fear or confidence make some brave and others cowardly. The same is true of situations involving appetites and anger; for one or another sort of conduct in these situations makes some people temperate and gentle, others intemperate and irascible.

Conclusion: The importance of habituation.

To sum up, then, in a single account: A state [of character] arises from [the repetition of] similar activities. Hence we must display the right activities, since differences in these imply corresponding differences in the states. It is not unimportant, then, to acquire one sort of habit or another, right from our youth; rather, it is very important, indeed all-important. . . .

But our claims about habituation raise a puzzle: How can we become good without being good already?

However, someone might raise this puzzle: 'What do you mean by saying that to become just we must first do just actions and to become temperate we must first do temperate actions? For if we do what is grammatical or musical, we must already be grammarians or musicians. In the same way, then, if we do what is just or temperate, we must already be just or temperate.'

First reply: Conformity versus understanding.

But surely this is not so even with the crafts, for it is possible to produce something grammatical by chance or by following someone else's instructions. To be a grammarian, then, we must both produce something grammatical and produce it in the way in which the grammarian produces it, i.e. expressing grammatical knowledge that is in us.

Second Reply: Crafts versus virtues.

Moreover, in any case what is true of crafts is not true of virtues. For the products of a craft determine by their own character whether they have been produced well; and so it suffices that they are in the right state when they have been produced. But for actions expressing virtue to be done temperately or justly [and hence well] it does not suffice that they are themselves in the right state. Rather, the agent must also be in the right state when he does them. First, he must know [that he is doing virtuous actions]; second, he must decide on them, and decide on them for themselves; and, third, he must also do them from a firm and unchanging state.

As conditions for having a craft these three do not count, except for the knowing itself. As a condition for having a virtue, however, the knowing counts for nothing, or [rather] for only a little, whereas the other two conditions are very important, indeed all-important. And these other two conditions are achieved by the frequent doing of just and temperate actions.

Hence actions are called just or temperate when they are the sort that a just or temperate person would do. But the just and temperate person is not the one who [merely] does these actions, but the one who also does them in the way in which just or temperate people do them.

It is right, then, to say that a person comes to be just from doing just actions and temperate from doing temperate actions; for no one has even a prospect of becoming good from failing to do them.

Virtue requires habituation, and therefore requires practice, not just theory.

The many, however, do not do these actions but take refuge in arguments, thinking that they are doing philosophy, and that this is the way to become excellent people. In this they are like a sick person who listens attentively to the doctor, but acts on none of his instructions. Such a course of treatment will not improve the state of his body; any more than will the many's way of doing philosophy improve the state of their souls.

A *Virtue of Character is a State Intermediate between Two Extremes, and Involving Decision*

THE GENUS

Feelings, capacities, states.   Next we must examine what virtue is. Since there are three conditions arising in the soul—feelings, capacities and states—virtue must be one of these.

By feelings I mean appetite, anger, fear, confidence, envy, joy, love, hate, longing, jealousy, pity, in general whatever implies pleasure or pain.

By capacities I mean what we have when we are said to be capable of these feelings—capable of, e.g., being angry or afraid or feeling pity.

By states I mean what we have when we are well or badly off in relation to feelings. If, e.g., our feeling is too intense or slack, we are badly off in relation to anger, but if it is intermediate, we are well off; and the same is true in the other cases.

Virtue is not a feeling . . .

First, then, neither virtues nor vices are feelings. (a) For we are called excellent or base in so far as we have virtues or vices, not in so far as we have feelings. (b) We are neither praised nor blamed in so far as we have feelings; for we do not praise the angry or the frightened person, and do not blame the person who is simply angry, but only the person who is angry in a particular way. But we are praised or blamed in so far as we have virtues or vices. (c) We are angry and afraid without decision; but the virtues are decisions of some kind, or [rather] require decision. (d) Besides, in so far as we have feelings, we are said to be moved; but in so far as we have virtues or vices, we are said to be in some condition rather than moved.

Or a capacity . . .

For these reasons the virtues are not capacities either; for we are neither called good nor called bad in so far as we are simply capable of feelings. Further, while we have capacities by nature, we do not become good or bad by nature; we have discussed this before.

But a state

If, then, the virtues are neither feelings nor capacities, the remaining possibility is that they are states. And so we have said what the genus of virtue is.

But we must say not only, as we already have, that it is a state, but also what sort of state it is.

Virtue and the human function. It should be said, then, that every virtue causes its possessors to be in a good state and to perform their functions well; the virtue of eyes, e.g., makes the eyes and their functioning excellent, because it makes us see well; and similarly, the virtue of a horse makes the horse excellent, and thereby good at galloping, at carrying its rider and at standing steady in the face of the enemy. If this is true in every case, then the virtue of a human being will likewise be the state that makes a human being good and makes him perform his function well. . . .

The numerical mean and the mean relative to us. In everything continuous and divisible we can take more, less and equal, and each of them either in the object itself or relative to us; and the equal is some intermediate between excess and deficiency.

By the intermediate in the object I mean what is equidistant from each extremity; this is one and the same for everyone. But relative to us the intermediate is what is neither superfluous nor deficient; this is not one, and is not the same for everyone.

If, e.g., ten are many and two are few, we take six as intermediate in the object, since it exceeds [two] and is exceeded [by ten] by an equal amount, [four]; this is what is intermediate by numerical proportion. But that is not how we must take the intermediate that is relative to us. For if, e.g., ten pounds [of food] are a lot for someone to eat, and two pounds a little, it does not follow that the trainer will prescribe six, since this might also be either a little or a lot for the person who is to take it—for Milo [the athlete] a little, but for the beginner in gymnastics a lot; and the same is true for running and wrestling. In this way every scientific expert avoids excess and deficiency and seeks and chooses what is intermediate—but intermediate relative to us, not in the object.

Virtue seeks the mean relative to us: Argument from craft to virtue.

This, then, is how each science produces its product well, by focusing on what is intermediate and making the product conform to that. This, indeed, is why people regularly comment on well-made products that nothing could be added or subtracted, since they assume that excess or deficiency ruins a good [result] while the mean preserves it. Good craftsmen also, we say, focus on what is intermediate when they produce their product. And since virtue, like nature, is better and more exact than any craft, it will also aim at what is intermediate.

Arguments from the nature of virtue of character.   By virtue I mean virtue of character; for this [pursues the mean because] it is concerned with feelings and actions, and these admit of excess, deficiency and an intermediate condition. We can be afraid, e.g., or be confident, or have appetites, or get angry, or feel pity, in general have pleasure or pain, both too much and too little, and in both ways not well; but [having these feelings] at the right times, about the right things, towards the right people, for the right end, and in the right way, is the intermediate and best condition, and this is proper to virtue. Similarly, actions also admit of excess, deficiency and the intermediate condition.

Now virtue is concerned with feelings and actions, in which excess and deficiency are in error and incur blame, while the intermediate condition is correct and wins praise, which are both proper features of virtue. Virtue, then, is a mean, in so far as it aims at what is intermediate.

Moreover, there are many ways to be in error, since badness is proper to what is unlimited, as the Pythagoreans pictured it, and good to what is limited; but there is only one way to be correct. That is why error is easy and correctness hard, since it is easy to miss the target and hard to hit it. And so for this reason also excess and deficiency are proper to vice, the mean to virtue; 'for we are noble in only one way, but bad in all sorts of ways.'

Definition of virtue.   Virtue, then, is (a) a state that decides, (b) [consisting] in a mean, (c) the mean relative to us, (d) which is defined by reference to reason, (e) i.e., to the reason by reference to which the intelligent person would define it. It is a mean between two vices, one of excess and one of deficiency.

It is a mean for this reason also: Some vices miss what is right because they are deficient, others because they are excessive, in feelings or in actions, while virtue finds and chooses what is intermediate.

Hence, as far as its substance and the account stating its essence are concerned, virtue is a mean; but as far as the best [condition] and the good [result] are concerned, it is an extremity.

The definition must not be misapplied to cases in which there is no mean.

But not every action or feeling admits of the mean. For the names of some automatically include baseness, e.g. spite, shamelessness, envy [among feelings], and adultery, theft, murder, among actions. All of these and similar things are called by these names because they themselves, not their excesses or deficiencies, are base.

Hence in doing these things we can never be correct, but must invariably be in error. We cannot do them well or not well—e.g. by committing adultery with the right woman at the right time in the right way; on the contrary, it is true unconditionally that to do any of them is to be in error.

[To think these admit of a mean], therefore, is like thinking that unjust or cowardly or intemperate action also admits of a mean, an excess and a deficiency. For then there would be a mean of excess, a mean of deficiency, an excess of excess and a deficiency of deficiency.

Rather, just as there is no excess or deficiency of temperance or of bravery, since the intermediate is a sort of extreme [in achieving the good], so also there is no mean of these [vicious actions] either, but whatever way anyone does them, he is in error. For in general there is no mean of excess or of deficiency, and no excess or deficiency of a mean.

The Definition of Virtue as a Mean
Applies to the Individual Virtues

However, we must not only state this general account but also apply it to the particular cases. For among accounts concerning actions, though the general ones are common to more cases, the specific ones are truer, since actions are about particular cases, and our account must accord with these. Let us, then, find these from the chart.

CLASSIFICATION OF VIRTUES OF CHARACTER

Virtues concerned with feelings. 1. First, in feelings of fear and confidence the mean is bravery. The excessively fearless person is nameless (and in fact many cases are nameless), while the one who is excessively confident is rash; the one who is excessively afraid and deficient in confidence is cowardly.

2. In pleasures and pains, though not in all types, and in pains less than in pleasures, the mean is temperance and the excess intemperance. People deficient in pleasure are not often found, which is why they also lack even a name; let us call them insensible.

Virtues concerned with external goods. 3. In giving and taking money the mean is generosity, the excess wastefulness and the deficiency ungenerosity. Here the vicious people have contrary excesses and defects; for the wasteful person spends to excess and is deficient in taking, whereas the ungenerous person takes to excess and is deficient in spending. At the moment we are speaking in outline and summary. . . .

4. In questions of money there are also other conditions. Another mean is magnificence; for the magnificent person differs from the generous by being concerned with large matters, while the generous person is concerned with small. The excess is ostentation and vulgarity, and the

deficiency niggardliness, and these differ from the vices related to generosity. . . .

5. In honour and dishonour the mean is magnanimity, the excess something called a sort of vanity, and the deficiency pusillanimity.

6. And just as we said that generosity differs from magnificence in its concern with small matters, similarly there is a virtue concerned with small honours, differing in the same way from magnanimity, which is concerned with great honours. For honour can be desired either in the right way or more or less than is right. If someone desires it to excess, he is called an honour-lover, and if his desire is deficient he is called indifferent to honour, but if he is intermediate he has no name. The corresponding conditions have no name either, except the condition of the honour-lover, which is called honour-loving.

This is why people at the extremes claim the intermediate area. Indeed, we also sometimes call the intermediate person an honour-lover, and sometimes call him indifferent to honour; and sometimes we praise the honour-lover, sometimes the person indifferent to honour. . . .

Virtues concerned with social life. 7. Anger also admits of an excess, deficiency and mean. These are all practically nameless; but since we call the intermediate person mild, let us call the mean mildness. Among the extreme people let the excessive person be irascible, and the vice be irascibility, and let the deficient person be a sort of inirascible person, and the deficiency be inirascibility.

There are three other means, somewhat similar to one another, but different. For they are all concerned with association in conversations and actions, but differ in so far as one is concerned with truth-telling in these areas, the other two with sources of pleasure, some of which are found in amusement, and the others in daily life in general. Hence we should also discuss these states, so that we can better observe that in every case the mean is praiseworthy, while the extremes are neither praiseworthy nor correct, but blameworthy. Most of these cases are also nameless, and we must try, as in the other cases also, to make names ourselves, to make things clear and easy to follow.

8. In truth-telling, then, let us call the intermediate person truthful, and the mean truthfulness; pretence that overstates will be boastfulness, and the person who has it boastful; pretence that understates will be self-deprecation, and the person who has it self-deprecating.

9. In sources of pleasure in amusements let us call the intermediate person witty, and the condition wit; the excess buffoonery and the person who has it a buffoon; and the deficient person a sort of boor and the state boorishness.

10. In the other sources of pleasure, those in daily life, let us call the person who is pleasant in the right way friendly, and the mean state friendliness. If someone goes to excess with no [further] aim he will be ingratiating; if he does it for his own advantage, a flatterer. The deficient person, unpleasant in everything, will be a sort of quarrelsome and ill-tempered person.

Mean states that are not virtues. 11. There are also means in feelings and concerned with feelings: shame, e.g., is not a virtue, but the person prone to shame as well as the virtuous person we have described receives praise. For here also one person is called intermediate, and another—the person excessively prone to shame, who is ashamed about everything—is called excessive; the person who is deficient in shame or never feels shame at all is said to have no sense of disgrace; and the intermediate one is called prone to shame.

12. Proper indignation is the mean between envy and spite; these conditions are concerned with pleasure and pain at what happens to our neighbours. For the properly indignant person feels pain when someone does well undeservedly; the envious person exceeds him by feeling pain when anyone does well, while the spiteful person is so deficient in feeling pain that he actually enjoys [other people's misfortunes].

VIRTUE AND MORAL THEORY
Bernard Mayo

Bernard Mayo is author of Ethics and the Moral Life *(1958). In the following selection from that book, he contrasts moral theories that are concerned primarily with questions of* what to do *with those whose main focus is on* how to be. *Mayo contends that theories of the latter sort, which we find in the writings of Plato and Aristotle, can provide us with what he calls a "unity of character." Thus, instead of providing principles and rules telling us what to do, moral theories such as Aristotle's tell us to be a person of a certain sort, and Mayo offers the lives of such figures as St. Francis and Buddha as models.*

From Bernard Mayo, *Ethics and Moral Life* (London: Macmillan, 1958). Reprinted by permission of Bernard Mayo.

The philosophy of moral principles, which is characteristic of Kant and the post-Kantian era, is something of which hardly a trace exists in Plato. . . . Plato says nothing about rules or principles or laws, except when he is talking politics. Instead he talks about virtues and vices, and about certain types of human character. The key word in Platonic ethics is Virtue; the key word in Kantian ethics is Duty. And modern ethics is a set of footnotes, not to Plato, but to Kant. . . .

Attention to the novelists can be a welcome correction to a tendency of philosophical ethics of the last generation or two to lose contact with the ordinary life of man which is just what the novelists, in their own way, are concerned with. Of course there are writers who can be called in to illustrate problems about Duty (Graham Greene is a good example). But there are more who perhaps never mention the words duty, obligation or principle. Yet they are all concerned—Jane Austen, for instance, entirely and absolutely—with the moral qualities or defects of their heroes and heroines and other characters. This points to a radical one-sidedness in the philosophers' account of morality in terms of principles: it takes little or no account of qualities, of what people *are*. It is just here that the old-fashioned word Virtue used to have a place; and it is just here that the work of Plato and Aristotle can be instructive. Justice, for Plato, though it is closely connected with acting according to law, does not *mean* acting according to law: it is a quality of character, and a just action is one such as a just man would do. Telling the truth, for Aristotle, is not, as it was for Kant, fulfilling an obligation; again it is a quality of character, or, rather, a whole range of qualities of character, some of which may actually be defects, such as tactlessness, boastfulness, and so on—a point which can be brought out, in terms of principles, only with the greatest complexity and artificiality, but quite simply and naturally in terms of character.

If we wish to enquire about Aristotle's moral views, it is no use looking for a set of principles. Of course we can find *some* principles to which he must have subscribed—for instance, that one ought not to commit adultery. But what we find much more prominently is a set of character-traits, a list of certain types of person—the courageous man, the niggardly man, the boaster, the lavish spender and so on. The basic moral question, for Aristotle, is not, What shall I do? but, What shall I be?

These contrasts between doing and being, negative and positive, and modern as against Greek morality were noted by John Stuart Mill; I quote from the *Essay on Liberty:*

Christian morality (so-called) has all the characters of a reaction; it is, in great part, a protest against Paganism. Its ideal is negative rather than positive, passive rather than active; Innocence rather than Nobleness; Abstinence from Evil, rather than energetic Pursuit of the Good; in its precepts (as has been well said) "Thou shalt not" predominates unduly over "Thou shalt . . ." Whatever exists of magnanimity, highmindedness, personal dignity, even the sense of honour, is derived from the purely human, not the religious part of our education, and never could have grown out of a standard of ethics in which the only worth, professedly recognised, is that of obedience.

Of course, there are connections between being and doing. It is obvious that a man cannot just *be;* he can only be what he is by doing what he does; his moral qualities are ascribed to him because of his actions, which are said to manifest those qualities. But the point is that an ethics of Being must include this obvious fact, that Being involves Doing; whereas an ethics of Doing, such as I have been examining, may easily overlook it. As I have suggested, a morality of principles is concerned only with what people do or fail to do, since that is what rules are for. And as far as this sort of ethics goes, people might well have no moral qualities at all except the possession of principles and the will (and capacity) to act accordingly.

When we speak of a moral quality such as courage, and say that a certain action was courageous, we are not merely saying something about the action. We are referring, not so much to what is done, as to the kind of person by whom we take it to have been done. We connect, by means of imputed motives and intentions, with the character of the agent as courageous. This explains, incidentally, why both Kantians and Utilitarians encounter, in their different ways, such difficulties in dealing with motives, which their principles, on the face of it, have no room for. A Utilitarian, for example, can only praise a courageous action in some such way as this: the action is of a sort such as a person of courage is likely to perform, and courage is a quality of character the cultivation of which is likely to increase rather than diminish the sum total of human happiness. But Aristotelians have no need of such circumlocution. For them a courageous action just is one which proceeds from and manifests a certain type of character, and is praised because such a character trait is good, or better than others, or is a virtue. An evaluative criterion is sufficient: there is no need to look for an imperative criterion as well, or rather instead, according to which it is not the character which is good, but the cultivation of the character which is right. . . .

No doubt the fundamental moral question is just "What ought I to do?" And according to the philosophy of moral principles, the answer (which must be an imperative "Do this") must be derived from a conjunction of premises consisting (in the simplest case) firstly of a rule, or universal imperative, enjoining (or forbidding) all actions of a certain type in situations of a certain type, and, secondly, a statement to the effect that this is a situation of that type, falling under that rule. In practice the emphasis may be on supplying only one of these premises, the other being assumed or taken for granted: one may answer the question "What ought I to do?" either by quoting a rule which I am to adopt, or by showing that my case is legislated for by a rule which I do adopt. To take a previous example of moral perplexity, if I am in doubt whether to tell the truth about his condition to a dying man, my doubt may be resolved by showing that the case comes under a rule about the avoidance of un- necessary suffering, which I am assumed to accept. But if the case is without precedent in my moral career, my problem may be soluble only by adopting a new principle about what I am to do now and in the future about cases of this kind.

This second possibility offers a connection with moral ideas. Suppose my perplexity is not merely an unprecedented situation which I could cope with by adopting a new rule. Suppose the new rule is thoroughly inconsistent with my existing moral code. This may happen, for instance, if the moral code is one to which I only pay lip-service; if . . . its authority is not yet internalised, or if it has ceased to be so; it is ready for rejection, but its final rejection awaits a moral crisis such as we are assuming to occur. What I now need is not a rule for deciding how to act in this situation and others of its kind. I need a whole set of rules, a complete morality, new principles to live by.

Now according to the philosophy of moral character, there is another way of answering the fundamental question "What ought I to do?" Instead of quoting a rule, we quote a quality of character, a virtue: we say "Be brave," or "Be patient" or "Be lenient." We may even say "Be a man": if I am in doubt, say, whether to take a risk, and someone says "Be a man," meaning a morally sound man, in this case a man of sufficient courage. (Compare the very different ideal invoked in "Be a gentleman." I shall not discuss whether this is a *moral* ideal.) Here, too, we have the extreme cases, where a man's moral perplexity extends not merely to a particular situation but to his whole way of living. And now the question "What ought I to do?" turns into the question "What ought I to be?"—as, indeed, it was treated in the first place. ("Be brave.") It is answered, not by quoting a rule or a set of rules, but by describing a quality of character or a type of person. And here the ethics of character gains a practical simplic- ity which offsets the greater logical simplicity of the ethics of principles. We do not have to give a list of characteristics or virtues, as we might list a set of principles. We can give a unity to our answer.

Of course we can in theory give a unity to our principles: this is implied by speaking of a *set* of principles. But if such a set is to be a system and not merely aggregate, the unity we are looking for is a logical one, namely the possibility that some principles are deductible from others, and ultimately from one. But the attempt to construct a deductive moral system is notoriously difficult, and in any case ill-founded. Why should we expect that all rules of conduct should be ultimately reducible to a few?

Saints and Heroes

But when we are asked "What shall I be?" we can readily give a unity to our answer, though not a logical unity. It is the unity of character. A person's character is not merely a list of dispositions; it has the organic unity of something that is more than the sum of its parts. And we can say, in answer to our morally perplexed questioner, not only "Be this" and "Be that," but also "Be like So-and-So"—where So-and-So is either an ideal type of character, or else an actual person taken as representative of the ideal, an exemplar. Examples of the first are Plato's "just man" in the Republic; Aristotle's man of practical wisdom, in the Nicomachean Ethics; Augustine's citizen of the City of God; the good Communist; the American way of life (which is a collective expression for a type of character). Examples of the second kind, the exemplar, are Socrates, Christ, Buddha, St. Francis, the heroes of epic writers and of novelists. Indeed the idea of the Hero, as well as the idea of the Saint, are very much the expression of this attitude to morality. Heroes and saints are not merely people who did things. They are people whom we are expected, and expect ourselves, to imitate. And imitating them means not merely doing what they did; it means being like them. Their status is not in the least like that of legislators whose laws we admire; for the character of a legislator is irrelevant to our judgment about his legislation. The heroes and saints did not merely give us principles to live by (though some of them did that as well): they gave us examples to follow.

Kant, as we should expect, emphatically rejects this attitude as "fatal to morality." According to him, examples serve only to render *visible* an instance of the moral principle, and thereby to demonstrate its practical feasibility. But every exemplar, such as Christ himself, must be judged by the independent criterion of the moral law, before we are entitled to recognize him as worthy of imitation. I am not suggesting that the subordination of exemplars to principles is incorrect, but that it is one-sided and fails to do justice to a large area of moral experience.

Imitation can be more or less successful. And this suggests another defect of the ethics of principles. It has no room for ideals, except the ideal of a perfect set of principles (which, as a matter of fact, is intelligible only in terms of an ideal character or way of life), and the ideal of perfect conscientiousness (which is itself a character-trait). This results, of course, from the "black-or-white" nature of moral verdicts based on rules. There

are no degrees by which we approach or recede from the attainment of a
certain quality or virtue; if there were not, the word "ideal" would have
no meaning. Heroes and saints are not people whom we try to be *just*
like, since we know that is impossible. It is precisely because it is
impossible for ordinary human beings to achieve the same qualities as the
saints, and in the same degree, that we do set them apart from the rest of
humanity. It is enough if we try to be a little like them. . . .

A DEFENSE OF PERFECTIONISM
Edmund L. Pincoffs

*Edmund L. Pincoffs is professor of philosophy at the University of Texas
at Austin. In the following selection from his book,* Quandaries and
Virtues *(1986), he presents and defends a perfectionistic moral theory.
According to moral perfectionism, the moral permissibility of an action
depends on the extent to which the action accords with standards of
excellence. On Pincoffs's theory, considerations of virtue serve as the
standards of excellence governing the morality of action. After presenting
his theory, Pincoffs argues that it should be distinguished from various
mistaken forms of perfectionism—what he calls Brittle Perfectionism.
Arbitrary Perfectionism, and Spiritual Egotism.*

In what follows, I will defend a form of virtue-oriented ethics against
criticisms that it is, in some damaging sense, a kind of perfectionism. The
thesis I want to defend is that in talk and thought about what ought to be
done, there is a certain kind of consideration that governs moral acceptability—a kind that has to do with the virtues and vices. Whether this
thesis, more fully made out below, is one that is defensible, all things
considered, I do not know and certainly do not try to show here. My
objective is merely to show that, although it is perfectionistic in a sense
that I will explain, it is a morally defensible form of perfectionism.

From Edmund Pincoffs, *Quandaries and Virtues: Against Reductionism in Ethics* (Lawrence, Kans.:
University Press of Kansas, 1986). Copyright © 1986 by the University Press of Kansas. Reprinted by
permission of the University Press of Kansas.

Ethical theorists have tended not to pay much attention to a range of considerations that often play a crucial role in reflection, debate, and justification. Quite often, a particular course of action or a policy is characterized as unkind, cowardly, cruel, dishonest, vindictive, unjust, disloyal, or selfish. These terms, plus a few more, and their positive counterparts—kind, honest, and so on—form a class, the size of which is indefinitely, but not very, large. Let us call this class the class of virtue and vice considerations. Each such consideration points to a particular quality of an act or policy, a quality that makes the doing of (or the agreeing to) it morally desirable or morally questionable. The introduction of a virtue consideration (for short) has a tendency to give shape to the subsequent discussion, since it introduces rules of relevance. Thus, to say of a proposal to sell sophisticated arms to Taiwan that it would be disloyal to Mainland China is to introduce a line of discussion that will focus on rather different, primarily historical, considerations than would have been relevant if the contention had been that the policy was dishonest. That discussion, in turn, would be a different one from the discussion of whether selling arms to Taiwan would be an unfair policy with respect to Mainland China or that it would be a cowardly policy or a merely selfish one. The discussion of whether an action or a policy is morally acceptable or unacceptable often turns on such considerations. These considerations have claim, at the least, to being weighty ones in moral discourse, as can be seen by reflecting on their relation to ones having to do with rights and duties.

Suppose it is contended that Mainland China has a right that we not sell arms to Taiwan. This contention appeals either to a supposed or to an actual network of rights and duties that result from agreed upon or understood rules or principles that govern relations between us and Mainland China or between nations generally. But in addition to the question of whether a right would be violated, there is the question of what the moral import would be of violating the right. This is a question that turns back on the agent, so to speak, and critically probes his motives. To violate the right of Mainland China might be morally more acceptable if at the same time the policy is what loyalty to Taiwan requires or if the policy is motivated by concern for the well-being of Taiwan, supposing that Taiwan is under a threat of invasion. To admit to violating a right is to concede that one has the burden of moral proof in adopting the course of action in question; but the admission does not dispose of the problem of what to do. It does not dispose of the problem because what is still at issue is what morally follows, if we do what it is proposed that we should do. We do not want to do what is cruel, unjust, cowardly, disloyal, and so forth. But if, on the other hand, none of this were to follow, if no virtue considerations could be brought to bear adversely on the course of action, then, even though a right is being violated, the course of action is morally permissible. Rights talk, in short, must be qualified by the sort of talk we engage in when we make use of virtue considerations.

It is possible, then, to hold a weak thesis to the effect that virtue considerations have weight, that they cannot be ignored, or that they qualify in some way the moral acceptability of a proposed action or policy. Or a stronger thesis can be maintained to the effect that they govern moral acceptability. I will defend the stronger thesis against 'perfectionist' criticisms. To say that virtue considerations govern acceptability is to say that it is a necessary and sufficient condition of the moral acceptability of an action or a course of action that it not violate the requirements of the relevant set of virtue considerations. The 'not violating' of those requirements is a relative matter. It may be that some balancing of the considerations must be done: some may have to give way, more or less, to others. In the happy circumstances when there is no conflict between virtue considerations with respect to a course of action, we may say that the course of action or the policy is the one that is fully acceptable. Thus, to show that it is morally fully acceptable that we sell sophisticated arms to Taiwan, we would have to show that there are no relevant virtue considerations that oppose it and that the relevant considerations approve it. Needless to say, it is difficult to show that a course of action is fully acceptable, and we may more typically have to settle for trying to show that it is acceptable—that, for example, even though the policy is arguably a bit unfair to the People's Republic of China, it is required by loyalty to Taiwan and by the sense that not to supply Taiwan with what would prevent its being invaded would be callous and, given the history of our relationships, ungrateful.

In what sense is the thesis that virtue considerations govern the moral acceptability of actions or policies ('the Thesis' for short) a perfectionistic one? Perfectionistic theories cover a very wide range. They differ on the criteria of perfection, on who or what is to be perfected, on who is to do the perfecting, and on how the perfecting is to be accomplished. Not only may the criteria of excellence in which perfection is thought to exist differ, but the height of the standards of excellence may vary. The legendary honesty of Lincoln may set a higher standard of honest behavior than that set by the average professor of philosophy. Perfectionistic doctrines may have primarily or exclusively to do with the perfection of the agent or of some group or of everyone in general. The agent of perfection may be a person or a group or everyone or God. And perfection may be brought about in a variety of ways.

I will take it that moral perfectionism, in its most general form, as it bears on actions and policies, is the doctrine that the overall acceptability or unacceptability of an action or policy is to be determined by the extent to which the action or policy accords with standards of excellence. That is a sufficiently general understanding to incorporate the differences in criteria, objects, agents, and means of perfection that I have mentioned. To say that virtue considerations govern moral acceptability is, then, a perfectionistic position. It may not be the most general perfectionistic position, since other criteria are imaginable; but it is very wide and open. It does not insist that any particular moral criterion—for example, justice—has sole claim to relevance when the question is what ought to be done. And it posits no hierarchical relations between the criteria, or considerations, whose relevance it maintains.

No ethical theory that I know of rules out virtue considerations as being relevant to moral decision or justification; but they may be systematically relegated to the periphery of moral thought. This may happen by making them conceptually vacuous, as deriving all of their force from 'more fundamental' conceptions: rules, principles, rights, and duties. Or it may happen by promoting virtue considerations to the region of the supererogatory, a region that has to do, not with what is morally most significant, but with what is a kind of moral luxury: the admirable-if-it-occurs. A reason for relegating virtue considerations to the periphery may be the justified suspicion that they are perfectionistic, combined with the unjustified notion that perfectionistic considerations should not have a place at the center of moral concern. They should yield that place to sterner matters, matters that have to do, not with what would be more or less perfect, but with what is required of us, as morally mandatory. Achieving excellence, it might be thought, is fine enough, but we may pursue it with a clear conscience only after we have attended to our duties and met our obligations. What those are is the first and fundamental question. Let me sketch an alternative way of thinking about the weight of moral considerations.

As a preliminary, let me remark that in thinking about excellence, we must also think about the absence of excellence and the various ways in which we can be far from excellence. We can say that an act is a courageous or loyal thing to do only against a background understanding of what it is for an act to be cowardly or disloyal, so that we can think of courageous acts as having a preferred place on a continuum that leads all the way from 'cowardly' to 'indifferent' to 'courageous'. So we must not think that a consideration's being perfectionistic amounts only to its being concerned with the attainment of the high end of the scale. It may also have to do with the low end—with not doing what is morally to be avoided. Perfectionistic considerations should not, then, be regarded as being concerned only with moral luxuries, with pictures of ideal behavior, or with the emulation of ideal moral models. This is not at all to rule out the relevance to moral deliberation and justification of such notions; but it is to say that if the objection to perfectionism is that it is only concerned with this end of the continuum, then the objection is misconceived; it fails to find the mark.

One way to assess the weight of moral considerations is to think not so much in terms merely of what I ought to do simpliciter, what my rights and duties are, but of what I would be by doing or agreeing to a given thing. What has weight with me is what I think of myself as being. This is the side of moral deliberation that tends to be overlooked or under-played by contemporary ethical theories. If I do not care what I am or am becoming, whether I am fair or unfair, cruel or kind, honest or dishonest, then moral talk will have little significance for me. To what-ever extent I have moral standards or ideals, to whatever extent I have aversions to selves that I could become, I will find virtue considera-tions weighty.

Virtue considerations are sometimes thought of as moral principles. . . . But the way in which they function as principles must be set off rather carefully from the way in which some other sorts of principles operate. The point to notice is that these principles are substantive, in the sense that living by them is conceptually tied to being a certain sort of person, where the sort in question is morally significant. It will be helpful to contrast the principle that one should do what is required by a virtue consideration with the principle that one should so act as to maximize happiness and minimize misery. The latter principle can be adopted out of a variety of motives. A person may hope to gain glory by increasing the general happiness or power or the love of the populace. He will be nonetheless an effective advocate of the principle for any of that. The principle that one should act in this happiness-maximizing way should be distinguished from the principle that one should be benevolent toward others. Aside from the points that the happiness-maximizing principle is understood and advocated as the sole principle that ought to govern action and that the benevolence principle generally is not, there is the less-often-noted point that benevolence has to do with a particular kind of motive and happiness maximizing does not.

The argument has often been offered against utilitarianism that if the public happiness is taken as the sole end, a variety of morally question-able means could be used to achieve it: for example, the enslavement of a minority, the punishment of the innocent, or sub-rosa coercion. What should also be apparent is that being a good utilitarian is consistent with being a morally undesirable sort of person. It is not necessarily the case that the person who wants and strives for the general happiness is therefore benevolent. He could even be misanthropic and, in some Kafka-like scenario, think that by increasing the general average happiness, he will at the same time be contributing to the general decline of humanity and to its disappearance from the face of the earth.

A parallel point can be made about being a formalist, the sort of Kantian who insists on the first formulation of the categorical imperative and forgets the second. The first formulation, which has to do solely with the consistency of self-legislated universal rules, can be adhered to by a person of vile moral character who happens at the same time to be consistent—consistently vile. The second formulation, on the other hand, comes close to being a virtue consideration. It would be so if it told us to be respectful of other people, to be concerned about them. Perhaps that is what Kant means. I think that it is. But he says to treat everyone, including ourselves, as ends in themselves and never merely as means. While it may require a stretch of the imagination, it is still conceivable that even this principle could be obeyed for the wrong motives and by a person whose moral character is far from desirable. A person might treat others and himself as ends in themselves without any deeper concern for them or for himself than that he thought that was what was required of him by God (or perhaps by the ghost of Kant). He could even think that the treating of persons as ends in themselves was commanded by Satan, whom he worships and feels bound to obey, but who has malevolent intentions toward the human race. He could treat people as ends in themselves out of a sort of moral ennui in which he picks up that principle as no more tiring than the others that are offered to him.

But let us return to the question of whether the contention that virtue considerations govern moral acceptability (the Thesis) is a defensible form of moral perfectionism. In pursuing that question, I will take up three forms, or varieties, of perfectionism, corresponding to the chief objections to an undifferentiated 'perfectionism': Brittle Perfectionism, Arbitrary Perfectionism, and Spiritual Egotism. These are, respectively, theories that require the attainment of an impossible ideal of perfection, theories that arbitrarily impose standards of perfection on persons who have a right to choose their own standards, and theories that emphasize a kind of psyche polishing that can rightly be regarded as a form of egotism. My conclusion will be not only that the Thesis has no necessary connection with theories of these kinds but also that it is a mistake to confuse the Thesis with any of these forms of perfectionism. The Thesis is, just the same, a perfectionistic one.

The advocate of the Thesis is not, of course, committed to the view that we must, on pain of some kind of moral failing, attain *perfect* honesty, justice, courage, or loyalty. It is nevertheless worth exploring Brittle Perfectionism a little so as to point up the ease with which one could come to think of the Thesis as a form of Brittle Perfectionism. To begin with, we should notice that it is not really clear what kind of impossibility is in question when it is said that it is impossible to attain perfect honesty or justice. Why is it *impossible* to attain perfect honesty, say? Is the impossibility in question an empirical one, a conceptual one, or some other kind? Is it so *difficult* to attain perfect honesty that we can never quite manage it, or is 'perfect honesty' an incoherent notion, so that we don't know what it would mean to attain it? With respect to empirical impossibility, trying to be honest *does* seem to be like trying to overcome 'real', not conceptual, difficulties. We can recognize that it is not enough to tell the truth in everyday contexts, not to filch from the cash register, or not to cheat at poker. We could pass these tests and still not be honest. But why is this so? Why is it hard, perhaps impossible, to be *completely* honest? It seems that no matter what we do or don't do, the question can still be asked whether we could not be more honest than we are.

The answer might be given that honesty is an open-textured concept: no formula will provide, in the end, all of the requirements for being honest. If we say that being honest is being open and undeceptive, then the problem descends to the question of what it is to be open and undeceptive. And if we offer formulae for those notions, the terms used in the formulae will be found to be open-textured too. We cannot find the end of that road. But is not our problem a general one? Very many of the terms in natural language are open-textured. Questions can be raised about what really is a mountain or a desk, as well as about what really is justice or honesty. If our problem is a special case of the general problem that many of the terms of natural language are open-textured, then it is not a problem that should disturb us. For just as we have no problem in deciding that the Rockies are mountains, we have no trouble in deciding that Lincoln was honest. Honest people are people who behave honestly, and we can "go on from there." By pointing to the open texture of virtue terms, we have not explained just why or in what sense it is very hard to fulfill the requirements of justice, honesty, or courage.

It is not a problem of open texture, but of 'high redefinition' that makes perfect honesty impossible to attain. No matter what even an Abe Lincoln does in trying to be honest, he can still ask himself whether he is being truly honest. This is so because no matter what standards he attains, the standards can always be cranked up another notch, so that he can never reach *the* highest standard. Jones's maximal honesty—paying debts and telling the truth—may be Smith's minimal honesty, and Smith's minimal standard may fall below Green's minimal standard. The open question, then, is a question of the relative height of standards. If, in principle, the standard can always be set higher than 'the top' standard, perfection can never be attained. Brittle Perfectionism thus requires the attainment of what it is impossible to attain. Since, however, the advocate of the Thesis need not also be engaged in the business of meeting the requirements of an ever-receding top standard, the Thesis is not a form of Brittle Perfectionism.

The second theory-defining objection, which defines Arbitrary Perfectionism, is that the standard of perfection is set by fiat, without regard for reasoned objections. Arbitrary Perfectionism would, presumably, attempt to regiment everyone under the banners of some improvement campaign to which people in a free society need not agree: a puritanical community, say, or a community of stoics or one of saints.

The question is whether the Thesis, by insisting that virtue considerations govern, becomes or in some way invites Arbitrary Perfectionism. This raises, in turn, the question of whether appeals to honesty, justice, and so forth, invoke arbitrary standards, standards that can then only be imposed on everyone by fiat. In approaching the issue, it is useful to bear in mind a distinction. The Thesis does not hold that any particular act or policy is morally acceptable or unacceptable. It holds, rather, that to justify choice or rejection, one must show that the choice or rejection accords with the requirements of the virtue considerations. Therefore the Thesis is perfectionistic at the level of criteria of justification, rather than at the level of choice or decision. It is, thus, not an objection to the Thesis that it would or would not approve of this or that choice. . . .

An example of Arbitrary Perfectionism is the theory that speaks of the 'real nature' of human beings as something that we must strive toward. This is to introduce a supposed standard under which it is possible to list just those qualities that the writer or speaker approves as virtues. The notion may be, as in Saint Thomas, that we have a God-given nature that we must do our best to attain. It may be that we are urged, as by Epictetus, to "follow our natures." Or it may be that, in some inverted sense of moral perfection, following our natures becomes, as for Freud, the attainment of an ideal of mental health. Self-realizational ethics, too, may provide us with examples of Arbitrary Perfectionism, since the choice between possible selves to be realized may be an arbitrary one.

It could be argued that arbitrariness is inevitable in insisting that virtue considerations govern the acceptability of actions and policies, since that insistence amounts to saying that the action or policy that is worthy of choice is the one that approximates most closely to a certain arbitrarily chosen *ideal*. The ideal is, so it might be thought, a certain pattern of virtues in action or policy. It must be an arbitrarily chosen pattern, since there is no general agreement on which pattern is most desirable. Whichever pattern we choose is, thus, chosen arbitrarily and becomes the ideal against which we measure the moral acceptability or un-acceptability of the act or policy. However, this argument presupposes, falsely, that to say of an action or policy that it is the alternative most favored by the virtue considerations is to appeal tacitly to some ideal pattern of virtues. It does not follow from the admission of multiple criteria of assessment—the virtue considerations—that there is some preferred pattern, an ideal, that must be exemplified by that which is chosen. It is possible to honor virtue in the absence of a picture of some ideal model of action toward which we must move. One need not have any such ideal in order to assess actions and policies along the different parameters of justice, loyalty, noncruelty, and so on.

I turn now to the third theory-defining objection to perfectionism: that it is what John Dewey calls 'spiritual egotism'. "Some," Dewey says, "are preoccupied with the state of their character, concerned for the purity of their motives and the goodness of their souls. The exultation of conceit which sometimes accompanies this absorption can produce a corrosive inhumanity which exceeds the possibilities of any other known form of selfishness."[1]

One kind of spiritual egotist, Dewey might agree, is the 'moral athlete' approved by James Walker, Francis Wayland, and other nineteenth-century textbook writers. Some of these earnest men convey a picture of the world as an arena in which people are engaged in the testing of virtue, like athletes striving for the greatest distance or the fastest time. Another sort of spiritual egotist is the perfectionist who regards detachment from political affairs as a necessary condition of the attainment of his ideal. . . .

The charge of 'spiritual egotism', if well founded, converts an apparent advantage of the Thesis into a disadvantage. An apparent advantage of the Thesis over other conceptions of what it is to justify a moral conclusion is that it bridges the supposed gap between the description of an act or policy and the conclusion that it ought to be done or adopted. It performs this feat, supposedly, by describing the feat in such a way—for example, as dishonest—that if I do it, I am to that extent dishonest. But since I ought not do what is dishonest, I ought not do this act. It also bridges a supposed gap between 'cognition' and motivation, since in coming to know that the act would be dishonest, I come to know that it is something I do not want to do, given that I do not want to be a person of bad character, that is, a person who is not worthy of preference by others. But this double gap-bridging feat can be looked at in another way, the way in which the Deweyan critic might look at it. For he can say that the gaps may be bridged only because my whole moral orientation is askew. In thinking about whether what I am doing is truly honest or kind, I could be concerned just with the perfecting of my own image. I could be a narcissistic moral preener whose motivation is thus morally questionable. The virtue considerations bridge the gap, if they do, because they supposedly look both ways at once. They apply both to me and to the act that I propose to do. If the act has a certain characteristic, then, thus far, I have that characteristic if I do it: if it is kind, I am thus far kind. What, then, is my motivation? Is it to have that characteristic, or is it to do an act that has that characteristic? If it is to have that characteristic—kindness, say—then what is the source of that motive, the motive to do what is kind? Is it a morally defensible motive, or is it pride in the portrait of perfection that I am thereby touching up?

Another way to pose the issue is by drawing a contrast between 'self-regarding' and 'other-regarding' considerations. Is the point that what I propose to do is dishonest a remark about what I would be if I were to do it or about the effect that it would have on other people if I did it? To whatever extent it is self-regarding, Dewey could hold, it presents a morally suspect, because possibly 'spiritually egotistic', reason for doing the act.

What defense of the Thesis can be offered, then, against the charge that it is a form of 'spiritual egotism'? The answer is reasonably clear, once the charge is understood. For the charge amounts to this: that whoever holds that the virtue considerations govern moral acceptability of what we ought to do runs a certain *danger*. He can come to make the virtue considerations the accomplices of a morally repugnant way of thinking. Instead of thinking simply what is the honest or kind or just thing to do, he can think whether by doing the proposed act, he will embellish his character in this or that way. He is concerned to polish up his attainments of justice, honesty, or kindness so that he can be satisfied with the image of self that he then sees. He will *do* what is honest, and so forth, but his motives will be narcissistic ones.

The answer is that the seen danger is a real danger, that we should be on our guard against it, that we should be continually aware of it. It is, however, far from a necessary consequence of accepting the Thesis that one must fall victim to 'spiritual egotism'. Even though the virtue considerations may *seem* to be inherently self-regarding, even though arguing that if I did this or that, I would be being cruel may *seem* to be taking too much interest in my own moral image, there is no necessary narcissistic self-regarding interpretation, no necessity for image burnishing. A more straighforward interpretation is that what is wrong is not that the act would put blotches and smears on the escutcheon of my character, thus ruining the picture of perfection, but that what I propose to do is wrong because it would be cruel to someone. The reflection that a given act would be cruel is no more inherently self-regarding than it is other-regarding. The interesting thing about the virtue considerations is that it is both.

Have I, in this sketch of possible objections to the Thesis as a form of perfectionism, overlooked some underlying source of uncomfortableness with the Thesis's perfectionistic tendency? Perhaps I have. But I think that the chief source of uncomfortableness with perfectionism as an ethical theory is with the amorphousness of the theory, the sense that it can take shapes that we would do well to shy away from. And I have tried to show that Thesis perfectionism does not necessarily have the most repugnant of those shapes. Yet it is a perfectionistic theory. It insists that the moral acceptability of actions or policies turns entirely on the extent to which they approximate the requirements of a set of standards: the closer the approximation, the more preferable the act or policy. The standards set by a perfectionistic theory need not be impossible of attainment, arbitrarily imposed, or made use of in morally questionable ways. These are simply dangers that must be avoided by those who believe, as I suspect, that the virtue considerations constitute the set of standards that govern moral acceptability.

Note

1.   John Dewey, *Human Nature and Conduct* (George Allen & Unwin, 1922), p. 7.

ON SOME VICES OF VIRTUE ETHICS
Robert B. Louden

Robert B. Louden is professor of philosophy at the University of Southern Maine. In the following excerpt, he raises a number of objections to virtue-based moral theories. For example, in emphasizing character over

From Robert B. Louden, "On Some Vices of Virtue Ethics," *American Philosophical Quarterly* 21(3) (1984): pp. 227–236. Reprinted by permission of American Philosophical Quarterly.

conduct, Louden notes, virtue-based views have difficulty dealing with moral quandaries in which what we need is some clear guidance in deciding what to do.

I t is common knowledge by now that recent philosophical and theological writing about ethics reveals a marked revival of interest in the virtues. But what exactly are the distinctive features of a so-called virtue ethics? Does it have a special contribution to make to our understanding of moral experience? Is there a price to be paid for its different perspective, and if so, is the price worth paying?

Contemporary textbook typologies of ethics still tend to divide the terrain of normative ethical theory into the teleological and deontological. Both types of theory, despite their well-defined differences, have a common focus on acts as opposed to qualities of agents. The fundamental question that both types of theory are designed to answer is: What ought I to do? What is the correct analysis and resolution of morally problematic situations? A second feature shared by teleological and deontological theories is conceptual reductionism. Both types of theory start with a primary irreducible element and then proceed to introduce secondary derivative concepts which are defined in terms of their relations to the beginning element. Modern teleologists (the majority of whom are utilitarians) begin with a concept of the good—here defined with reference to states of affairs rather than persons. After this criterion of the good is established, the remaining ethical categories are defined in terms of this starting point. Thus, according to the classic maxim, one ought always to promote the greatest good for the greatest number. Duty, in other words, is defined in terms of the element of ends—one ought always to maximize utility. The concepts of virtue and rights are also treated as derivative categories of secondary importance, definable in terms of utility. For the classic utilitarian, a right is upheld "so long as it is upon the whole advantageous to the society that it should be maintained," while virtue is construed as a "tendency to give a net increase to the aggregate quantity of happiness in all its shapes taken together."[1]

For the deontologist, on the other hand, the concept of duty is the irreducible starting point, and any attempt to define this root notion of being morally bound to do something in terms of the good to be achieved is rejected from the start. The deontologist is committed to the notion that certain acts are simply inherently right. Here the notion of the good is only a derivative category, definable in terms of the right. The good that we are to promote is right action for its own sake—duty for duty's sake. Similarly, the virtues tend to be defined in terms of pro-attitudes toward one's duties. Virtue is important, but only because it helps us do our duty.

But what about virtue ethics? What are the hallmarks of this approach to normative ethics? One problem confronting anyone who sets out to analyze the new virtue ethics in any detail is that we presently lack fully developed examples of it in the contemporary literature. Most of the work done in this genre has a negative rather than positive thrust—its primary aim is more to criticize the traditions and research programs to which it is opposed rather than to state positively and precisely what its own alternative is. A second hindrance is that the literature often has a somewhat misty antiquarian air. It is frequently said, for instance, that the Greeks advocated a virtue ethics, though what precisely it is that they were advocating is not always spelled out. In describing contemporary virtue ethics, it is therefore necessary, in my opinion, to do some detective work concerning its conceptual shape, making inferences based on the unfortunately small number of remarks that are available.

For purposes of illustration, I propose to briefly examine and expand on some key remarks made by two contemporary philosophers—Elizabeth Anscombe and Philippa Foot—whose names have often been associated with the revival of virtue movement. Anscombe, in her frequently cited article, "Modern Moral Philosophy," writes: "you can do ethics without it [viz., the notion of 'obligation' or 'morally ought'], as is shown by the example of Aristotle. It would be a great improvement if, instead of 'morally wrong,' one always named a genus such as 'untruthful,' 'unchaste,' 'unjust'."[2] Here we find an early rallying cry for an ethics of virtue program, to be based on contemporary efforts in philosophical psychology and action theory. On the Anscombe model, strong, irreducible duty and obligation notions drop out of the picture, and are to be replaced by vices such as unchasteness and untruthfulness. But are we to take the assertion literally, and actually attempt to do moral theory without any concept of duty whatsoever? On my reading, Anscombe is not really proposing that we entirely dispose of moral oughts. Suppose one follows her advice, and replaces "morally wrong" with "untruthful," "unchaste", etc. Isn't this merely shorthand for saying that agents *ought* to be truthful and chaste, and that untruthful and unchaste acts are *morally wrong* because good agents don't perform such acts? The concept of the moral ought, in other words, seems now to be explicated in terms of what the good person would do.[3]

A similar strategy is at work in some of Foot's articles. In the Introduction to her recent collection of essays, *Virtues and Vices and Other Essays in Moral Philosophy*, she announces that one of the two major themes

running throughout her work is "the thought that a sound moral philosophy should start from a theory of virtues and vices."[4] When this thought is
considered in conjunction with the central argument in her article,
"Morality as a System of Hypothetical Imperatives," the indication is that
another virtue-based moral theory is in the making. For in this essay Foot
envisions a moral community composed of an "army of volunteers,"
composed, that is, of agents who voluntarily commit themselves to such
moral ideals as truth, justice, generosity, and kindness.[5] In a moral
community of this sort, all moral imperatives become hypothetical rather
than categorical: there are things an agent morally ought to do if he or she
wants truth, justice, generosity, or kindness, but no things an agent
morally ought to do if he or she isn't first committed to these (or other)
moral ideals. On the Foot model (as presented in "Morality as a System"),
what distinguishes an ethics of virtue from its competitors is that it
construes the ideal moral agent as acting from a direct desire, without first
believing that he or she morally ought to perform that action or have that
desire. However, in a more recent paper, Foot has expressed doubts
about her earlier attempts to articulate the relationship between oughts
and desires. In "William Frankena's Carus Lectures" (1981), she states
that "*thoughts* [my emphasis] about what is despicable or contemptible,
or low, or again admirable, glorious or honourable may give us the key to
the problem of rational moral action."[6] But regardless of whether she
begins with desires or with thoughts, it seems clear her strategy too is not
to dispense with oughts entirely, but rather to employ softer, derivative
oughts.

In other words, conceptual reductionism is at work in virtue ethics too.
Just as its utilitarian and deontological competitors begin with primitive
concepts of the good state of affairs and the intrinsically right action
respectively and then derive secondary concepts out of their starting
points, so virtue ethics, beginning with a root conception of the morally
good person, proceeds to introduce a different set of secondary concepts
which are defined in terms of their relationship to the primitive element.
Though the ordering of primitive and derivatives differs in each case, the
overall strategy remains the same. Viewed from this perspective, virtue
ethics is not unique at all. It has adopted the traditional mononomic
strategy of normative ethics. What sets it apart from other approaches,
again, is its strong agent orientation.

So for virtue ethics, the primary object of moral evaluation is not the
act or its consequences, but rather the agent. And the respective conceptual starting points of agent and act-centered ethics result in other
basic differences as well, which may be briefly summarized as follows.
First of all, the two camps are likely to employ different models of

practical reasoning. Act theorists, because they focus on discrete acts and moral quandaries, are naturally very interested in formulating decision procedures for making practical choices. The agent, in their conceptual scheme, needs a guide—hopefully a determinate decision procedure—for finding a way out of the quandary. Agent-centered ethics, on the other hand, focuses on long-term characteristic patterns of action, intentionally downplaying atomic acts and particular choice situations in the process. They are not as concerned with portraying practical reason as a rule-governed enterprise which can be applied on a case-by-case basis.

Secondly, their views on moral motivation differ. For the deontological act theorist, the preferred motive for moral action is the concept of duty itself; for the utilitarian act theorist, it is the disposition to seek the happiness of all sentient creatures. But for the virtue theorist, the pre-ferred motivation factor is the virtues themselves (here understood non-reductionistically). The agent who correctly acts from the disposition of charity does so (according to the virtue theorist) not because it maximizes utility or because it is one's duty to do so, but rather out of a commitment to the value of charity for its own sake.

While I am sympathetic to recent efforts to recover virtue from its longstanding neglect, my purpose in this essay is not to contribute further to the campaign for virtue. Instead, I wish to take a more critical look at the phenomenon, and to ask whether there are certain important features of morality which a virtue-based ethics either handles poorly or ignores entirely. In the remainder of this essay, I shall sketch some objections which (I believe) point to genuine shortcomings of the virtue approach to ethics. My object here is not to offer an exhaustive or even thoroughly systematic critique of virtue ethics, but rather to look at certain mundane regions of the moral field and to ask first what an ethics of virtue might say about them, and second whether what it says about them seems satis-factory.

Agents vs. Acts

As noted earlier, it is a commonplace that virtue theorists focus on good and bad agents rather than on right and wrong acts. In focusing on good and bad agents, virtue theorists are thus forced to deemphasize discrete acts in favor of long-term, characteristic patterns of behavior. Several related problems arise for virtue ethics as a result of this particular conceptual commitment.

A. CASUISTRY AND APPLIED ETHICS

It has often been said that for virtue ethics the central question is not "What ought I to *do*?" but rather "What sort of person ought I to *be*?"

However, people have always expected ethical theory to tell them something about what they ought to do, and it seems to me that virtue ethics is structurally unable to say much of anything about this issue. If I'm right, one consequence of this is that a virtue-based ethics will be particularly weak in the areas of casuistry and applied ethics. A recent reviewer of Foot's *Virtues and Vices*, for instance, notes that "one must do some shifting to gather her view on the virtues." "Surprisingly," he adds, "the studies of abortion and euthanasia are not of much use."[7] And this is odd, when one considers Foot's demonstrated interest in applied ethics in conjunction with her earlier cited prefatory remark that a "sound moral theory should start from a theory of virtues and vices." But what can a virtues and vices approach say about specific moral dilemmas? As virtue theorists from Aristotle onward have rightly emphasized, virtues are not simply dispositions to behave in specified ways, for which rules and principles can always be cited. In addition, they involve skills of perception and articulation, situation-specific "know-how," all of which are developed only through recognizing and acting on what is relevant in concrete moral contexts as they arise. These skills of moral perception and practical reason are not completely routinizable, and so cannot be transferred from agent to agent as any sort of decision procedure "package deal." Due to the very nature of the moral virtues, there is thus a very limited amount of advice on moral quandaries that one can reasonably expect from the virtue-oriented approach. We ought, of course, to do what the virtuous person would do, but it is not always easy to fathom what the hypothetical moral exemplar would do were he in our shoes, and sometimes even he will act out of character. Furthermore, if one asks him why he did what he did, or how he knew what to do, the answer—if one is offered—might not be very enlightening. One would not necessarily expect him to appeal to any rules or principles which might be of use to others.

We can say, á la Aristotle, that the virtuous agent acts for the sake of the noble (*tou kalou heneka*), that he will not do what is base or depraved, etc. But it seems to me that we cannot intelligently say things like: "The virtuous person (who acts for the sake of the noble) is also one who recognizes that all mentally deficient eight-month-old fetuses should (or should not) be aborted, that the doctor/patient principle of confidentiality must always (or not always) be respected, etc." The latter simply sound too strange, and their strangeness stems from the fact that motives of virtue and honor cannot be fully routinized.

Virtue theory is not a problem-oriented or quandary approach to ethics: it speaks of rules and principles of action only in a derivative manner. And its derivative oughts are frequently too vague and unhelpful for persons who have not yet acquired the requisite moral insight and sensitivity. Consequently, we cannot expect it to be of great use in applied ethics and casuistry. The increasing importance of these two subfields of ethics in contemporary society is thus a strike against the move to revive virtue ethics.

B. TRAGIC HUMANS

Another reason for making sure that our ethical theory allows us to talk about features of acts and their results in abstraction from the agent and his conception of what he is doing is that sometimes even the best person can make the wrong choices. There are cases in which a man's choice is grounded in the best possible information, his motives honorable and his action not at all out of character. And yet his best laid plans may go sour. Aristotle, in his *Poetics*, suggests that here lies the source of tragedy: we are confronted with an eminent and respected man, "whose misfortune, however, is brought upon him not by vice (*kakia*) and depravity (*mok-theira*) but by some error of judgment (*amartia*)" (1453a8-9). But every human being is morally fallible, for there is a little Oedipus in each of us. So Aristotle's point is that *regardless of character,* anyone can fall into the sort of mistake of which tragedies are made. Virtue ethics, however, since its conceptual scheme is rooted in the notion of the good person, is unable to assess correctly the occasional (inevitable) tragic outcomes of human action. . . .

C. INTOLERABLE ACTIONS

A third reason for insisting that our moral theory enable us to assess acts in abstraction from agents is that we need to be able to identify certain types of action which produce harms of such magnitude that they destroy the bonds of community and render (at least temporarily) the achievement of moral goods impossible. In every traditional moral community one encounters prohibitions or "barriers to action" which mark off clear boundaries in such areas as the taking of innocent life, sexual relations, and the administration of justice according to local laws and customs. Such rules are needed to teach citizens what kinds of actions are to be regarded not simply as bad (a table of vices can handle this) but as intolerable. Theorists must resort to specific lists of offenses to emphasize the fact that there are some acts which are absolutely prohibited. We cannot articulate this sense of absolute prohibition by referring merely to characteristic patterns of behavior.

In rebuttal here, the virtue theorist may reply by saying: "Virtue ethics does not need to articulate these prohibitions—let the law do it, with its list of do's and don't's." But the sense of requirement and prohibition referred to above seems to me to be at bottom inescapably moral rather than legal. Morality can (and frequently does) invoke the aid of law in such cases, but when we ask *why* there is a law against e.g., rape or murder, the proper answer is that it is morally intolerable. To point merely to a legal convention when asked why an act is prohibited or intolerable raises more questions than it answers.

D. CHARACTER CHANGE

A fourth reason for insisting that a moral theory be able to assess acts in abstraction from agents and their conception of what they're doing is that peoples' moral characters may sometimes change. Xenophon, toward the beginning of his *Memorabilia* (I.II.21), cites an unknown poet who says: "Ah, but a good man is at one time noble (*esthlos*), at another wicked (*kakos*)." Xenophon himself agrees with the poet: ". . . many alleged (*phaskonton*) philosophers may say: A just (*dikaios*) man can never become unjust; a self-controlled (*sophron*) man can never become wanton (*hubristes*); in fact no one having learned any kind of knowledge (*mathesis*) can become ignorant of it. I do not hold this view. . . . For I see that, just as poetry is forgotten unless it is often repeated, so instruction, when no longer heeded, fades from the mind."

Xenophon was a practical man who was not often given to speculation, but he arrived at his position on character change in the course of his defense of Socrates. One of the reasons Socrates got into trouble, Xenophon believed, was due to his contact with Critias and Alcibiades during their youth. For of all Athenians, "none wrought so many evils to the *polis*." However, Xenophon reached the conclusion that Socrates should not be blamed for the disappearance of his good influence once these two had ceased their close contact with him.

If skills can become rusty, it seems to me that virtues can too. Unless we stay in practice we run the risk of losing relative proficiency. We probably can't forget them completely (in part because the opportunities for exercising virtues are so pervasive in everyday life), but we can lose a certain sensitivity. People do become morally insensitive, relatively speaking—missing opportunities they once would have noticed, although perhaps when confronted with a failure they might recognize that they had failed, showing at least that they hadn't literally "forgotten the difference between right and wrong." If the moral virtues are acquired habits rather than innate gifts, it is always possible that one can lose relative proficiency in these habits. Also, just as one's interests and skills sometimes change over the course of a life as new perceptions and influences take hold, it seems too that aspects of our moral characters can likewise alter. (Consider religious conversion experiences.) Once we grant the possibility of such changes in moral character, the need for a more "character free" way of assessing action becomes evident. Character is not a permanent fixture, but rather plastic. A more reliable yardstick is sometimes needed.

E. MORAL BACKSLIDING

Finally, the focus on good and bad agents rather than on right and wrong actions may lead to a peculiar sort of moral backsliding. Because the emphasis in agent ethics is on long-term, characteristic patterns of behavior, its advocates run the risk of overlooking occasional lies or acts of selfishness on the ground that such performances are mere temporary aberrations—acts out of character. Even the just man may on occasion act unjustly, so why haggle over specifics? It is unbecoming to a virtue theorist to engage in such pharisaic calculations. But once he commits himself to the view that assessments of moral worth are not simply a matter of whether we have done the right thing, backsliding may result.

I have argued that there is a common source behind each of these vices. The virtue theorist is committed to the claim that the primary object of moral evaluation is not the act or its consequences but rather the agent—specifically, those character traits of the agent which are judged morally relevant. This is not to say that virtue ethics does not ever address the issue of right and wrong actions, but rather that it can only do so in a derivative manner. Sometimes, however, it is clearly acts rather than agents which ought to be the primary focus of moral evaluation. . . .

Notes

1. The rights definition is from Bentham's "Anarchical Fallacies," reprinted in A. I. Melden, (ed.), *Human Rights* (Belmont, CA: Wadsworth, 1970), p. 32. The virtue definition is from Bentham's "The Nature of Virtue," reprinted in Bhiku Parekh, (ed.), *Bentham's Political Thought* (New York: Barnes and Noble, 1973), p. 89.

2. G. E. M. Anscombe, "Modern Moral Philosophy," *Philosophy*, Vol. 33 (1958), pp. 1–19; reprinted in J. J. Thomson and G. Dworkin, (eds.), *Ethics* (New York: Harper & Row, 1968), p. 196.

3. Anscombe appears to believe also that moral oughts and obligations only make sense in a divine law context, which would mean that only divine command theories of ethics employ valid concepts of obligation. I see no reason to accept such a narrow definition of duty. See pp. 192, 202 of "Modern Moral Philosophy." For one argument against her restrictive divine law approach to moral obligation, see Alan Donagan, *The Theory of Morality* (Chicago: University of Chicago Press, 1977), p. 3.

4. Philippa Foot, *Virtues and Vices and Other Essays in Moral Philosophy* (Berkeley and Los Angeles: University of California Press, 1978), p. xi.

5. Foot, "Morality as a System of Hypothetical Imperatives," *The Philosophical Review*, Vol. 81 (1972), pp. 305–16; reprinted in *Virtues and Vices*, pp. 157–73. See especially the long concluding footnote, added in 1977.
6. Foot, "William Frankena's Carus Lectures," *The Monist*, Vol. 64 (1981), p. 31.
7. Arthur Flemming, "Reviving the Virtues." Review of Foot's *Virtues and Vices* and James Wallace's *Virtues and Vices, Ethics*, Vol. 90 (1980), p. 588.